graphis annual 86|87

86|87 graphis annual

The International Annual of Advertising and
Editorial Graphics

Das internationale Jahrbuch der Werbe-
graphik und der redaktionellen Graphik

Le répertoire international de l'art graphique
publicitaire et rédactionnel

Edited by / Herausgegeben von / Réalisé par:

Walter Herdeg

Graphis Press Corp., Zurich (Switzerland)

GRAPHIS PUBLICATIONS

GRAPHIS, International bi-monthly journal of graphic art and applied art
PHOTOGRAPHIS, The international annual of advertising and editorial photography
GRAPHIS POSTERS, The international annual of poster art
GRAPHIS PACKAGING VOL. 4, An international survey of package design
CHILDREN'S BOOK ILLUSTRATION VOL. 4, An international survey of children's book illustration
GRAPHIS DIAGRAMS, The graphic visualization of abstract data
FILM + TV GRAPHICS 2, An international survey of the art of film animation
ARCHIGRAPHIA, Architectural and environmental graphics
GRAPHIS EPHEMERA, Artists' Self-Promotion

GRAPHIS-PUBLIKATIONEN

GRAPHIS, Die internationale Zweimonatsschrift für Graphik und angewandte Kunst
PHOTOGRAPHIS, Das internationale Jahrbuch der Werbephotographie und der redaktionellen Photographie
GRAPHIS POSTERS, Das internationale Jahrbuch der Plakatkunst
GRAPHIS PACKUNGEN BAND 4, Internationales Handbuch der Packungsgestaltung
KINDERBUCH-ILLUSTRATION BAND 4, Eine internationale Übersicht über die Kinderbuch-Illustration
GRAPHIS DIAGRAMS, Die graphische Visualisierung abstrakter Gegebenheiten
FILM + TV GRAPHICS 2, Ein internationaler Überblick über die Kunst des Animationsfilms
ARCHIGRAPHIA, Architektur- und Umweltgraphik
GRAPHIS EPHEMERA, Künstler-Eigenwerbung

PUBLICATIONS GRAPHIS

GRAPHIS, La revue bimestrielle internationale d'arts graphiques et d'arts appliqués
PHOTOGRAPHIS, Le répertoire international de la photographie publicitaire et rédactionnelle
GRAPHIS POSTERS, Le répertoire international de l'art de l'affiche
GRAPHIS EMBALLAGES VOL. 4, Répertoire international des formes de l'emballage
ILLUSTRATIONS DE LIVRES D'ENFANTS VOL. 4, Un aperçu international des illustrations de livres d'enfants
GRAPHIS DIAGRAMS, La visualisation graphique de données abstraites
FILM + TV GRAPHICS 2, Un panorama international de l'art du film d'animation
ARCHIGRAPHIA, La création graphique appliquée à l'architecture et à l'environnement
GRAPHIS EPHEMERA, Autopromotion des artistes

Distributors / Auslieferung / Distribution:

USA: WATSON-GUPTILL PUBLICATIONS, INC., 1515 Broadway, New York, N.Y. 10036 – (ISBN: 0-8230-2130-0)
CANADA: HURTIG PUBLISHERS, 10560-105 Street, Edmonton, Alberta T5H 2W7, tel. (403) 426-2469
ITALIA: INTER-ORBIS, Via Lorenteggio, 31/1, I-20146 Milano, tel. 422 57 46

All other countries / Alle anderen Länder / Tout autres pays:

GRAPHIS PRESS CORP., 107 Dufourstrasse, CH-8008 Zurich (Switzerland)

PUBLICATION No. 183 (ISBN 3-85709-186-X)

Contents   Inhalt   Sommaire

Abbreviations   Abkürzungen   Abréviations

Argentina	ARG	Argentinien	ARG	Afrique du Sud	SAF
Australia	AUS	Australien	AUS	Allemagne occidentale	GER
Austria	AUT	Belgien	BEL	Argentine	ARG
Belgium	BEL	Brasilien	BRA	Australie	AUS
Brazil	BRA	Bulgarien	BUL	Autriche	AUT
Bulgaria	BUL	Dänemark	DEN	Belgique	BEL
Canada	CAN	Deutschland (BRD)	GER	Brésil	BRA
Czechoslovakia	CSR	Finnland	FIN	Bulgarie	BUL
Denmark	DEN	Frankreich	FRA	Canada	CAN
Finland	FIN	Griechenland	GRE	Danemark	DEN
France	FRA	Grossbritannien	GBR	Espagne	SPA
Germany (West)	GER	Hongkong	HKG	Etats-Unis	USA
Great Britain	GBR	Indien	IND	Finlande	FIN
Greece	GRE	Iran	IRN	France	FRA
Hong Kong	HKG	Irland	IRL	Grande-Bretagne	GBR
Hungary	HUN	Italien	ITA	Grèce	GRE
India	IND	Japan	JPN	Hongkong	HKG
Iran	IRN	Jugoslawien	YUG	Hongrie	HUN
Ireland	IRL	Kanada	CAN	Inde	IND
Italy	ITA	Luxemburg	LUX	Iran	IRN
Japan	JPN	Niederlande	NLD	Irlande	IRL
Luxemburg	LUX	Österreich	AUT	Italie	ITA
Netherlands	NLD	Philippinen	PHI	Japon	JPN
Philippines	PHI	Schweden	SWE	Luxembourg	LUX
Singapore	SIN	Schweiz	SWI	Pays-Bas	NLD
South Africa	SAF	Singapur	SIN	Philippines	PHI
Spain	SPA	Spanien	SPA	Singapour	SIN
Sweden	SWE	Südafrika	SAF	Suède	SWE
Switzerland	SWI	Tschechoslowakei	CSR	Suisse	SWI
USA	USA	Ungarn	HUN	Tchécoslovaquie	CSR
Yugoslavia	YUG	USA	USA	Yougoslavie	YUG

Cover/Umschlag: Arnold Saks/Peggy Barnett

Thousands of entries sent in from all over the world form the basis of this volume. The great diversity and the overall high quality of the works did not make the final selection easy. Our heartiest thanks, therefore, go to everyone who contributed – direct or indirect – to this annual.

Den Grundstock für diesen Band bildeten Tausende von Einsendungen aus aller Welt. Die Vielfalt und das allgemein hohe Qualitätsniveau der Arbeiten machten die endgültige Auswahl nicht einfach. Unser herzlicher Dank gilt deshalb allen Einsendern, die direkt oder indirekt zu diesem Jahrbuch beigetragen haben.

Ce livre n'aurait pas vu le jour sans les milliers d'envois reçus du monde entier. Leur variété, leur qualité généralement exceptionnelle n'ont pas facilité la tâche de sélection. Nos remerciements chaleureux vont ainsi à tous ceux et celles qui ont apporté leur contribution directe ou indirecte au présent annuel.

ARNOLD SAKS, born in New York in 1931, has designed the cover of this book. He heads Arnold Saks Associates, New York, and has worked with them on numerous major design projects for industry, government and private institutions. His work encompasses all areas of graphic design: annual reports, booklets, trademarks, corporate identity and publications. Arnold Saks has been a visiting lecturer at various design schools and he is a member of the AGI.
PEGGY BARNETT, the photographer of this cover, studied fine art at Cooper Union and has been running a photo-studio in New York for the past seventeen years. She works primarily for graphic designers, doing mainly annual reports, calendars, posters etc.

ARNOLD SAKS, 1931 in New York geboren, gestaltete den Umschlag für dieses Buch. Zusammen mit seiner Gruppe, Arnold Saks Associates in New York, befasst er sich vor allem mit Jahresberichten, Broschüren, Markenzeichen, Firmendarstellungen und -publikationen für bedeutende Unternehmen. Hinzu kommen grosse Design-Projekte für die Industrie, die Regierung und private Institutionen. Arnold Saks ist Mitglied der AGI, und er hält Gastvorlesungen.
PEGGY BARNETT, die Photographin des Umschlags, studierte Kunst an der Cooper Union. Seit 17 Jahren hat sie ein Photostudio in New York. Hauptsächlich arbeitet sie mit Graphik-Designern zusammen, vor allem für Jahresberichte, Kalender, Plakate etc.

ARNOLD SAKS, né à New York en 1931, est l'auteur de notre couverture. Assisté de ses partenaires au sein d'Arnold Saks Associates, il réalise à New York avant tout des rapports annuels, des brochures, des marques, des présentations d'entreprises et des publications pour les grandes sociétés. S'y ajoutent d'importants projets de design pour l'industrie, le gouvernement et des institutions privées. Ce membre de l'AGI est un conférencier recherché par les Académies d'art.
PEGGY BARNETT, qui a photographié notre couverture, est une ancienne élève de Cooper Union, qui a installé son studio de photo à New York il y a 17 ans. Elle ?oopère surtout avec des graphistes pour la réalisation de rapports annuels, de calendriers, d'affiches, etc.

Rose DeNeve

Responsible Design

For many years, ROSE DeNEVE served on the editorial staff of *Print* magazine. In 1980 she left her position there as managing editor to pursue a freelance writing career. Since then she has written numerous articles about graphic design and designers for *Print* and for the *Journal of the American Institute of Graphic Arts*, of which she was the editor for two years. She has written six *Casebooks* published by *Print* magazine and co-authored, with Nigel Holmes, the book *Designing Pictorial Symbols*.

For those interested in trends and historical analyses, graphic design annuals say a lot about which visual mode is popular at any given time or within a particular segment of the international design community; from a larger view, they describe how graphic design itself has developed as an art and as a profession during the past twenty or thirty years. They provide us with a physical record of a great many works, long after the works themselves may be gone, thus memorializing both good designers and good design.

But most designers have little use for such high-flown contexts in annuals. They look to such collections for inspiration and ideas in solving a problem at hand, with little acknowledgement of larger trends. Indeed, a designer's interest is likely to be far more limited than the scope of an international annual might suggest, for designers primarily seek to create not a solution that will stand out among world class winners, but one that can be sold easily to the client and will keep the client coming back to them. They are looking for design that works in its own arena; they want to both solve the client's problem successfully and maintain a favourable profile among their immediate peers. If the final design also happens to receive national or international acclaim, so much the better. But it is more important that it help the designer stay in business, wherever that business might be.

"Good design" must be at once appropriate and functional, eye-catching and elegant, sensuous and restrained. Its acceptance in juried competitions is as much due to budget as anything else: more money means being able to buy better design talent as well as more luxuriant production. Our notions about what is "good" in graphic design are, like the medium itself, bound up in Western ideas and ideals, and in the values of vast societies deeply rooted in commerce. To be sure, production values have become an integral part of our idea of what constitutes good design, and for us graphic communications cannot exist apart from their presentation: a magnificent idea poorly produced is not likely to win an award on its own merits.

It comes as no surprise, then, that emerging nations will not find works from many of their native designers in international compendiums. True, perhaps many good works are not submitted for consideration. But while "good graphics" are beginning to be seen in these countries, few of their designers have mastered the international style or blended it with the imagery of their own cultures in a manner acceptable to an international audience. And it's not just a matter of education. Businesses in developing countries simply do not have the wherewithal to produce graphics of an international quality; local production facilities are often substandard, and an unfavourable exchange rate, local import regulations, and impoverished economies often prevent them from buying better production outside their own borders.

Still, as the economies of these nations continue to grow, so does their need for and understanding of effective graphic communications. Graphic designers themselves take on an enhanced status and in turn become more aware of the work being done by their counterparts in the rest of the world. They take their place in the international design community, and look to the work being done by that community for inspiration and guidance.

Inherent in graphic media are not only the marketing and communications goals of a specific client but a cultural context in which those goals are to be achieved. If a magazine advertisement features free-spirited youths clad in jeans and T-shirts sporting personal stereos, or an elegantly dressed couple pouring twelve-year-old Scotch into cut-crystal glasses, the reader is apt to be more impressed by these accoutrements of lifestyle than by the name of the product for which the ad appeared. Nor is this proffering of lifestyle and cultural values exclusive to advertising—it is a part of every visual communication, from magazine and newspaper layouts to corporate letterheads and annual reports. It is a message about success and the "good life" to which we all aspire, and to which the peoples of developing nations have begun to lay claim.

Not long ago I was asked to write an article for the annual of Mitra Parishad, a Calcutta-based organization dedicated to bringing harmony among India's various religious, social and economic communities. The suggested topic was the social benefits of advertising, and try as I might, I found it difficult to reconcile this Western phenomenon with that country's rich cultural heritage. (Indeed, Western concepts of marketing and consumerism would seem diametrically opposed to India's traditional attitudes of detachment and the transitoriness of material things.) What I found was that the ads that were most successful from a Western, or international, standpoint also imitated many of the West's less desirable attitudes, often relying on a false set of values to motivate sales. One advertisement in particular sticks in my mind: A young man leans against a non-Indian luxury sedan. His left arm is twined around an attractive woman whose skirt is slit thigh-high; his right is sending a punch to the jaw of what one presumes is a rival. In the midst of the action, our hero's robe falls open to reveal the product—designer briefs. The photography is first-rate; the layout is impeccable; the type is a recent photo-typositor issue. But the imagery is a strictly Western sex-and-violence idiom.

This ad, and others like it, pose significant questions about just what it is that a graphic designer wants—or should want—to communicate. That graphic designers have a social responsibility for the work they do and the images they choose was a notion popular in the sixties. Certainly, as professionals, most designers like to think that what they do is meaningful and worthwhile, if not beyond reproach. But while their concerns for professional practices and personal success have gained momentum in recent years, social consciousness has been eroded by the need to capture the attention of a media-saturated audience. Separated from work-related issues, it now too often finds expression merely in events such as by-invitation-only exhibitions of anti-war posters.

It is not that today's design is without wit or humour or other inventive means of successfully achieving a client's goals; indeed, this book is about such commendable possibilities. But for every image presented here, many thousands more are flooding the marketplace with not just banality but vulgarity, proselytizing lifestyles whose values may not only be irrelevant but questionable. Perhaps graphic designers need to broaden their perspective about the work they do and begin to see it, not only in parochial terms, but with a global consciousness.

Rose DeNeve

Verantwortungsbewusstes Design

ROSE DeNEVE gehörte für viele Jahre zur Redaktion des *Print* Magazins. 1980 verliess sie ihren Posten als Chefredakteurin, um fortan freiberuflich zu arbeiten. Sie hat seitdem u. a. für *Print* und das *Journal of the American Institute of Graphic Arts*, dessen Herausgeberin sie zwei Jahre lang war, zahlreiche Artikel über Graphik Design und Designer geschrieben. Für sechs Bände der von *Print* herausgegebenen *Casebooks* schrieb sie den Text, und zusammen mit Nigel Holmes verfasste sie das Buch *Designing Pictorial Symbols* («Die Gestaltung von Bildsymbolen»).

Wer sich für Trends und historische Analysen interessiert, erfährt durch Graphik-Design-Jahrbücher eine Menge darüber, welche visuelle Ausdrucksform zu einer bestimmten Zeit oder bei einer bestimmten Gruppe der internationalen Gemeinde der Graphik-Designer populär war; über längere Zeit gesehen zeigen Jahrbücher auf, wie sich das Graphik-Design an sich, als Kunst und als Beruf, während der vergangenen 20 oder 30 Jahre entwickelt hat. Eine grosse Anzahl von Arbeiten, deren Lebensdauer eigentlich auf kurze Zeit beschränkt war, wird hier für uns festgehalten, und somit wird sowohl guten Designern als auch gutem Design ein Denkmal gesetzt.

Diese hohen Ansprüche interessieren die meisten Graphik-Designer im Zusammenhang mit den Jahrbüchern allerdings nicht so sehr. Sie suchen hier vor allem Inspiration und Ideen, um eine bestimmte Aufgabe lösen zu können – grosse Trends sind dabei nicht so wichtig. Das direkte Interesse des Graphik-Designers ist wahrscheinlich viel begrenzter, als der Umfang eines internationalen Jahrbuchs vermuten lässt, denn natürlich denkt der Graphik-Designer bei seiner Arbeit nicht an einen Wettbewerb mit den Besten der Welt; er weiss, dass er in erster Linie seinen Auftraggeber zufriedenstellen muss, damit er ihn als Kunden behält. Er sieht seine Arbeit also zunächst im engeren Umfeld; sie muss da akzeptiert werden, wo sie gebraucht wird; eine bestimmte Aufgabe muss erfolgreich gelöst werden, und man muss neben den direkten Konkurrenten bestehen können. Wenn das Ergebnis dann sogar auf nationaler oder internationaler Ebene Anklang findet, um so besser. Aber es ist für den Graphik-Designer wichtiger, im Geschäft zu bleiben, wo immer das auch sein mag.

«Gutes Design» muss zugleich zweckmässig und funktionell, augenfällig und elegant, sinnlich und massvoll sein. Die Akzeptanz bei jurierten Wettbewerben ist wie so oft auch eine Frage des Budgets, denn mehr Geld bedeutet, dass man sich besseres Design-Talent und eine üppigere Ausführung leisten kann. Unsere Vorstellungen von Qualität sind, wie das Medium selbst, eng mit westlichen Ideen und Idealen und den Werten der tief im Kommerz verwurzelten Gesellschaften verbunden. Die Ausführung ist Teil unserer Vorstellung von gutem Design, und für uns kann graphische Kommunikation nicht von der Präsentation getrennt werden: eine hervorragende Idee, schlecht produziert, wird kaum als Idee allein ausgezeichnet werden.

Es ist deshalb nicht verwunderlich, dass nur wenige Arbeiten von Graphik-Designern aus Entwicklungsländern in internationalen Jahrbüchern zu finden sind. Zugegeben, viele gute Arbeiten werden vielleicht nicht eingereicht. Aber obwohl hin und wieder gutes Graphik-Design in diesen Ländern zu finden ist, beherrschen doch nur wenige den internationalen Stil oder haben ihn mit der Symbolik ihrer eigenen Kulturen auf eine Weise verbinden können, die international akzeptabel wäre. Das ist nicht nur eine Frage der Ausbildung. Die Studios in Entwicklungsländern haben einfach nicht das nötige Kleingeld, um Graphik von internationalem Niveau zu machen; lokale Produktionsmöglichkeiten sind oft unbefriedigend, und ein schlechter Wechselkurs, lokale Einfuhrbestimmungen und eine verarmte Wirtschaft machen es unmöglich, im Ausland zu produzieren.

Da jedoch die Wirtschaft dieser Länder ständig wächst, steigt auch das Bedürfnis nach und das Verständnis für wirkungsvolle graphische Kommunikation. Das Ansehen der Graphik-Designer gewinnt dort also an Bedeutung, und damit wächst auch ihr Interesse für die Arbeit der Kollegen in der übrigen Welt. Sie gehören zur internationalen Gemeinde der Graphik-Designer, und innerhalb dieser Gemeinde suchen sie Inspiration und Führung.

Das graphische Medium ist nicht nur eng mit den Marketing- und Kommunikationszielen des Kunden verbunden, sondern auch mit dem kulturellen Umfeld, in dem diese Ziele erreicht werden sollen. Wenn eine Zeitschriftenanzeige gutgelaunte junge Leute in Jeans und T-Shirts zeigt, die der Musik aus ihren Stereo-Geräten lauschen, oder ein elegant gekleidetes Paar, das sich gerade einen 12 Jahre alten Scotch in Kristallgläser einschenkt, so wird der Betrachter mehr von diesen, den Lebensstil kennzeichnenden Ausstaffierungen als vom Namen des beworbenen Produkts beeindruckt. Dieses Anbieten eines Lebensstils und kultureller Werte findet man nicht nur in der Werbung – es ist Teil jeder visuellen Kommunikation, angefangen beim Zeitungs- und Magazin-Layout bis hin zu Briefköpfen und Geschäftsberichten. Es ist eine Botschaft über Erfolg und das «gute Leben», das wir alle anstreben, und auf das auch die Menschen in den Entwicklungsländern einen Anspruch erheben.

Im Zusammenhang mit einem Text über den «positiven sozialen Aspekt der Werbung», den ich für ein indisches Jahrbuch schreiben sollte, stellte ich fest, dass Anzeigen, die aus westlicher oder internationaler Sicht am erfolgreichsten waren, auch viele der wenig wünschenswerten Eigenschaften des Westens imitierten und dass sie oft auf falsche Werte setzten, um den Verkauf zu fördern. Ich erinnere mich besonders an ein Inserat: Ein junger Mann lehnt gegen eine ausländische Luxus-Limousine. Sein linker Arm ist um eine attraktive Frau geschlungen, deren Rock hüfthoch geschlitzt ist; seine Rechte landet unterdes einen Schlag im Gesicht eines – wie man annehmen muss – Rivalen. Bei dieser Aktion hat sich das Gewand des Helden geöffnet, um einen Blick auf das Produkt freizugeben: Marken-Unterhosen. Die Aufnahme ist erstklassig, das Layout einwandfrei, die Typographie dem neusten Stand entsprechend. Aber die Bildsymbolik entspricht völlig dem westlichen «Sex-und-Gewalt»-Idiom.

Diese und ähnliche Anzeigen werfen die Frage auf, was ein Graphik-Designer mitteilen möchte – oder sollte. In den sechziger Jahren war man sich allgemein einig, dass Graphik-Designer eine soziale Verantwortung für ihre Arbeit tragen. Als Professionelle denken die meisten Graphik-Designer natürlich gern, dass das, was sie machen, sinnvoll und der Mühe wert, wenn nicht tadellos ist. Aber während in den vergangenen Jahren berufliches Fortkommen und persönlicher Erfolg immer wichtiger wurden, verdrängte der Zwang, die Aufmerksamkeit der übersättigten Zuschauer zu erregen, das soziale Bewusstsein. Allzuoft wird der soziale Aspekt jetzt getrennt von der Arbeit in Form von Anti-Kriegsplakaten ausgelebt, die in privaten Ausstellungen gezeigt werden.

Das soll nicht heissen, dass im heutigen Graphik-Design nicht Witz und Humor oder gute Einfälle zu finden wären, die erfolgreich für die Ziele der Kunden eingesetzt werden – dieses Buch ist solchen Lösungen gewidmet. Aber für jede Abbildung, die hier gezeigt wird, lassen sich Tausende finden, die nicht nur banal, sondern auch vulgär sind, indem sie einen Lebensstil anpreisen, dessen Werte ebenso irrelevant wie fragwürdig sind. Vielleicht müssen Graphik-Designer ihren Horizont im Hinblick auf ihre Arbeit erweitern und sie nicht nur im Zusammenhang mit dem näheren Umfeld, sondern im Bewusstsein einer globalen Verantwortlichkeit betrachten.

Rose DeNeve

Le design face à ses responsabilités

ROSE DeNEVE a longtemps fait partie de la rédaction du magazine *Print*. Rédactrice en chef, elle quitte *Print* en 1980 pour s'établir à son compte. Depuis elle a écrit de nombreux articles d'art graphique, entre autres pour *Print* et le *Journal of the American Institute of Graphic Arts*, qu'elle a publié pendant deux ans. Elle est l'auteur du texte de six volumes de *Casebooks* publiés par *Print*. En collaboration avec Nigel Holmes, elle a écrit l'ouvrage intitulé *Designing Pictorial Symbols* («La Conception de symbols imagés»).

Pour qui s'intéresse aux grandes tendances de l'histoire du design et à leur analyse, les annuels d'art publicitaire constituent une mine de renseignements sur la mode visuelle du jour en un point donné de la scène internationale. Dans une optique élargie, ils nous informent du cours que suit depuis 20 ou 30 ans le développement de cet art et de la profession qui l'exerce. Préservant la mémoire de nombreux travaux éphémères, ils font passer à la postérité le nom des grands artistes de la branche en même temps que le meilleur de leur œuvre.

Il n'en reste pas moins que la grande majorité des designers n'ont que faire de ce genre de considérations historico-critiques. Ils se servent de ce genre d'annuels pour trouver ou vérifier de l'inspiration et des idées propres à solutionner un problème donné, sans se soucier outre mesure des tendances à l'œuvre. L'intérêt utilitaire d'un designer risque de rester bien en deçà de l'envergure reconnue à un annuel international du design. C'est que les designers ne cherchent pas tant à réaliser une solution visuelle qui leur vaudra les feux de la rampe qu'à résoudre le problème d'une manière acceptée par le client; or, un client satisfait a toutes chances de revenir. Ils recherchent donc un design approprié à l'arène locale ou internationale où il est appelé à évoluer, un design qui leur vale le succès commercial et l'estime de leurs collègues et concurrents immédiats. Tant mieux si, par la suite, leur création leur vaut des applaudissements au plan national ou international. L'essentiel, c'est de bien défendre sa place dans la profession.

Le design de qualité doit être à la fois adéquat au problème posé, fonctionnel, accrocheur, élégant, en appeler aux sens tout en observant une juste mesure. Son acceptation par un jury de concours tient autant au budget disponible qu'à d'autres raisons: un budget plus important permet d'engager de meilleurs designers et de doter la production d'amples moyens matériels. Les notions qui ont cours chez nous sur la qualité du design sont, tout comme le média lui-même, enracinées dans un système de valeurs occidental à forte composante commerciale. Il est hors de doute que la qualité de la production fait aujourd'hui partie intégrante de l'idée que nous nous faisons d'un design de qualité; la communication d'ordre graphique ne peut être dissociée de sa présentation. En effet, une idée sensationnelle mise en œuvre avec des moyens inadéquats n'a aucune chance de remporter un prix sur la foi de ses seuls mérites intrinsèques.

C'est pourquoi on ne s'étonnera guère de la faible représentativité des designers des pays en voie de développement dans les annuels internationaux. On peut admettre que nombre de bons travaux ne trouvent pas le chemin du jury. Or, si le design de qualité existe dans ces pays, il faut tout de même reconnaître que rares sont ceux des designers autochtones qui maîtrisent le style international ou son amalgame avec l'imagerie de leur culture nationale de manière à satisfaire un public international. Ce n'est pas seulement affaire d'éducation. Les entreprises des pays en voie de développement n'ont tout simplement pas les moyens d'une production graphique de niveau international. Les installations de production locales ne disposent souvent pas des équipements nécessaires. Qui plus est, un taux de change peu favorable, les restrictions à l'importation et une économie appauvrie constituent un frein puissant à l'acquisition d'une meilleure production hors des frontières nationales.

Pourtant, la croissance économique continue de ces nations renforce le besoin et la compréhension de communications graphiques efficaces. Le statut des graphistes s'améliorant, ils prennent mieux conscience des réalités transnationales de leur profession. S'intégrant dans la communauté de design internationale, ils se tournent vers les créations de cette communauté comme source d'inspiration.

Le média graphique n'implique pas seulement les objectifs de marketing et de communication d'un client déterminé, mais aussi le contexte culturel au sein duquel ces objectifs doivent être atteints. Lorsqu'une annonce de magazine met en scène des jeunes gens vêtus de jeans et de tee-shirts s'abreuvant de musique à leur chaîne stéréo ou un couple élégant dégustant un scotch de douze ans dans des verres en cristal, le lecteur risque d'être impressionné par ces accessoires d'un style de vie déterminé plus que par le nom du produit mis en valeur par l'annonce. Or, cette présentation d'un style de vie et de valeurs culturelles déterminés n'est pas limitée à la seule publicité, mais fait bien partie de toute communication visuelle quel qu'en soit le support – le magazine, le quotidien, l'en-tête d'une société ou son rapport annuel. C'est un message prônant le succès et le standing de vie auquel nous aspirons tous, et auquel les nations en voie de développement ont commencé à prétendre à leur tour.

C'est en Inde que j'ai alors découvert que les annonces les plus réussies d'un point de vue occidental ou international singeaient bon nombre d'attitudes occidentales peu recommandables et s'inspiraient souvent d'un système de valeurs faussé en fonction du succès commercial à atteindre. Une annonce s'est particulièrement imposée à mon esprit: un jeune Indien adossé à une berline de grand luxe de marque étrangère entoure d'un bras gauche protecteur une femme séduisante dont la robe est fendue haut. Du poing droit, il repousse un rival. Dans le feu de l'action, on voit son caleçon – le produit à annoncer. La photo est de toute première qualité, le layout impeccable, la composition est d'un récent type phototypositor – mais l'image est puisée à un arsenal iconographique purement occidental combinant sexe et violence.

Ce genre d'annonces soulève des questions importantes quant au but recherché par le graphiste. Les années 60 nous ont familiarisés avec le concept de responsabilité sociale en ce qui concerne l'œuvre publicitaire et l'imagerie qu'elle utilise. Comme tout professionnel, le designer tend à considérer son travail comme significatif et utile sinon incontestable. On note ces dernières années une prise de conscience croissante des problèmes liés à la pratique professionnelle et au succès personnel, au détriment de la conscience sociale, tant il devient ardu de capter l'attention d'un public saturé au plan visuel. Cette conscience sociale s'investit alors dans des domaines non commerciaux, ainsi lorsqu'il s'agit de participier sur invitation à des expositions d'affiches antimilitaristes.

Le design d'aujourd'hui n'est pas dépourvu d'esprit, d'humor ni d'autres moyens inventifs permettant de transformer en succès le vœu du client – le présent ouvrage fourmille d'exemples à ce sujet. Ne perdons toutefois pas de vue que pour chaque image que l'on trouvera dans ces pages, des milliers d'autres inondent le marché en assénant des messages en coup de poing pas même simplement banals, mais résolument vulgaires. Quant aux styles de vie qu'ils incarnent et qu'ils aident à propager, ils ne sont trop souvent pas seulement hors de propos, mais franchement contestables. Peut-être les graphistes seraient-ils bien conseillés d'élargir leur horizon et de repenser la merveilleuse tâche qui leur est confiée dans une perspective globale.

Index to Artists
Verzeichnis der Künstler
Index des Artistes

Index to Designers
Verzeichnis der Gestalter
Index des Maquettistes

Index to Art Directors
Verzeichnis der künstlerischen Leiter
Index des Directeurs Artistiques

Index to Publishers
Verzeichnis der Verleger
Index des Editeurs

Index to Agencies and Studios
Verzeichnis der Agenturen und Studios
Index des Agences et Studios

Index to Advertisers
Verzeichnis der Auftraggeber
Index des Clients

■ Entry instructions may be requested by anyone interested in submitting samples of exceptional graphics or photography for possible inclusion in our annuals.
Closing dates for entries:
GRAPHIS ANNUAL (advertising and editorial art and design): 31 January
PHOTOGRAPHIS (advertising and editorial photography): 30 June
GRAPHIS POSTERS (an annual of poster art): 30 June
Write to: Graphis Press Corp., Dufourstrasse 107, 8008 Zurich, Switzerland

■ Einsendebedingungen können von jedermann angefordert werden, der uns Beispiele hervorragender Photographie oder Graphik zur Auswahl für unsere Jahrbücher unterbreiten möchte.
Einsendetermine:
GRAPHIS ANNUAL (Werbe- und redaktionelle Graphik): 31. Januar
PHOTOGRAPHIS (Werbe- und redaktionelle Photographie): 30. Juni
GRAPHIS POSTERS (ein Jahrbuch der Plakatkunst): 30. Juni
Adresse: Graphis Verlag AG, Dufourstrasse 107, 8008 Zürich, Schweiz

■ Tout intéressé à la soumission de travaux photographiques et graphiques recevra les informations nécessaires sur demande.
Dates limites:
GRAPHIS ANNUAL (art graphique publicitaire et rédactionnel): 31 janvier
PHOTOGRAPHIS (photographie publicitaire et rédactionnelle): 30 juin
GRAPHIS POSTERS (annuaire sur l'art de l'affiche): 30 juin
S'adresser à: Editions Graphis SA, Dufourstrasse 107, 8008 Zurich, Suisse

Editor and Art Director: Walter Herdeg
Assistant Editor: Joan Lüssi
Project Managers: Romy Herzog, Heinke Jenssen
Designers: Marino Bianchera, Martin Byland, Ulrich Kemmner
Art Assistant: Walter Zuber

1

Magazine Advertisements

Newspaper Advertisements

Zeitschriften-Inserate

Zeitungs-Inserate

Annonces de revues

Annonces de presse

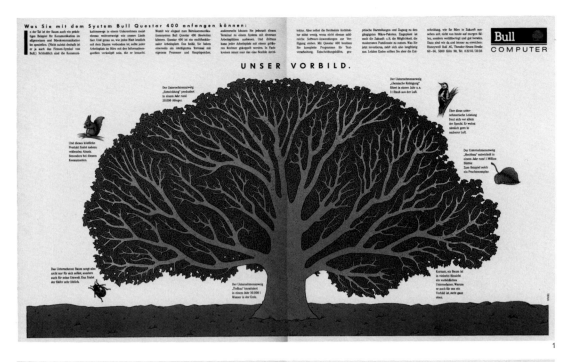

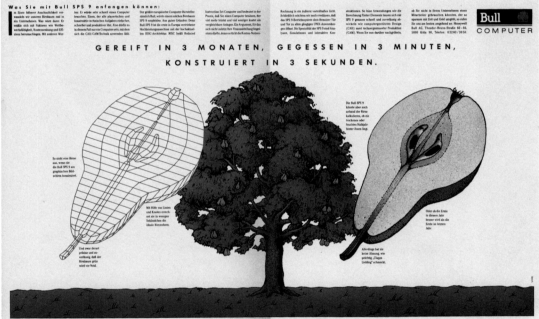

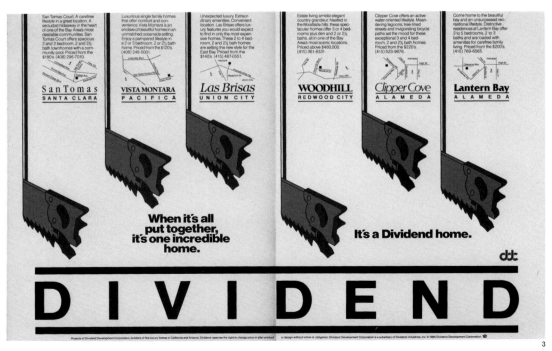

1, 2 Examples of double-spread advertisements from a magazine campaign for *Bull* computers. The firm's symbol is a tree and here the tree also symbolizes communication. The title of Fig. 2 reads: "Ripe in 3 months, eaten in 3 minutes, designed in 3 seconds". Both ads mainly in green and brown tones. (GER)
3 Double-spread magazine ad for Dividend Development Corporation, builders of luxury homes in California and Arizona. Saws in grey, blue, brown and yellow, with black text. (USA)
4, 5 Illustration and complete double-spread magazine advertisement for IBM computers. (SPA)

1, 2 Beispiele der doppelseitigen Anzeigen aus einer Zeitschriften-Kampagne für *Bull*-Computer. Der Baum (auch Firmensymbol von *Bull*) dient hier als Symbol für ein Unternehmen. Beide Anzeigen vorwiegend in Grün- und Brauntönen. (GER)
3 Doppelseitiges Zeitschrifteninserat für Dividend Development Corporation, ein Unternehmen, das hier Häuser in Kalifornien und Arizona anbietet. Sägen grau, blau, braun und gelb, Schrift schwarz. (USA)
4, 5 Illustration und vollständiges, doppelseitiges Zeitschrifteninserat für IBM-Computer. (SPA)

1, 2 Exemples d'annonces double page dans une campagne de magazines pour les ordinateurs *Bull*. L'arbre (emblème du groupe *Bull*) représente ici une entreprise. Tons verts et bruns prédominants. Fig. 1: «Notre modèle.» Fig. 2: «Mûre en 3 mois, mangée en 3 minutes, dessinée en 3 seconds.» (GER)
3 Annonce de magazine double page pour la Dividend Development Corporation, un constructeur de maisons luxueuses en Californie et en Arizona. Scies gris, bleu, marron, jaune «pour réaliser une maison invraisemblable.» Texte noir. (USA)
4, 5 Illustration et annonce de magazine double page complète pour la gamme des ordinateurs IBM. (SPA)

4

5

R E G E N B O G E N

Dem Regenbogen der Druckkunst gewidmet sind die Arbeiten, die Siegwerk bei namhaften Künstlern in Auftrag gegeben hat.
Was Tomi Ungerer, den berühmten Zeichner, zu seiner eigenwilligen Regenbogen-Darstellung veranlaßt hat, können wir wie folgt nachvollziehen:
Jedem Drucker sein Stück vom Regenbogen. Jedem die Qualität und den zuverlässigen Service von Siegwerk, dem Druckfarbenhersteller am Ende des Regenbogens.

Dem Künstler im Drucker gewidmet sind Siegwerks Regenbogenfarben:
Ihre Qualität gewährleistet eine Druckwiedergabe, die der Qualität des Originals entspricht.
Der Siegwerk-Service rund um die Regenbogenfarben tut ein übriges, damit Sie sich voll auf die Kunst des Druckens konzentrieren können.

SIEGWERK DRUCKFARBEN

D E R   D R U C K K U N S T

6

6, 7 From a series of double-spread advertisements for *Siegwerk* printing inks. Renowned artists were commissioned to portray the rainbow (*Siegwerk's* symbol). (GER)
8 Double-spread magazine advertisement for AT&T personal computers. In gouache and coloured pencil technique. (USA)
9 Example of the promotion to sell advertising space in the *Kurier* newspaper, referring to the readership—the wise, the informed and the established. (AUT)

6, 7 Aus einer Serie von doppelseitigen Anzeigen für *Siegwerk*-Druckfarben. Namhafte Künstler erhielten den Auftrag, den Regenbogen (*Siegwerks* Symbol) darzustellen. (GER)
8 Doppelseitige Zeitschriftenanzeige für Personal Computer von AT&T. Gouache und Farbstift. (USA)
9 Beispiel der Inserentenwerbung für die Zeitung *Kurier*, die hier die Studierten, die Informierten und die Etablierten als typische Leserschaft darstellt. (AUT)

6, 7 Annonces double page figurant dans une série réalisée pour les encres d'imprimerie *Siegwerk* par des artistes réputés sur le thème de l'arc-en-ciel, symbole de *Siegwerk*. (GER)
8 Annonce de magazine double page pour les ordinateurs personnels AT&T. Gouache et crayon couleur. (USA)
9 Exemple de la publicité-annonceurs du journal *Kurier*: les lecteurs typés en universitaires (hibou), gens bien informés (éléphant) et membres de l'establishment (renard). (AUT)

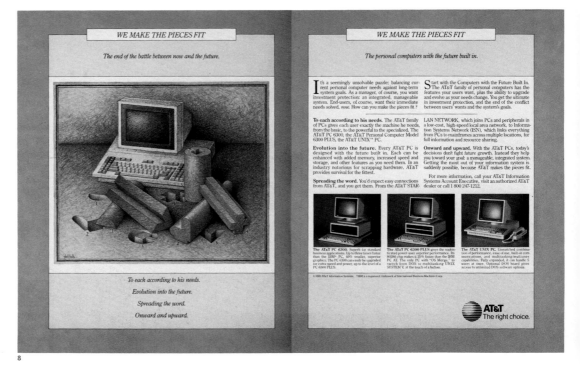

Advertisements / Inserate / Annonces

R E G E N B O G E N

Dem Regenbogen der
Druckkunst gewidmet sind
die Arbeiten, die Siegwerk
bei namhaften Künstlern
in Auftrag gegeben hat.
   Was Ralph Steadman,
den berühmten englischen
Zeichner, zu seiner eigenwilligen Regenbogen-
Darstellung veranlaßt hat,
können wir für uns viel-
leicht wie folgt nachvollziehen:
   Siegwerks Regenbogen-
farben sind der Hahn im
Korb der Drucker, die sich
auf ihre Weise als Künstler
verstehen.

Dem Künstler im Drucker
gewidmet sind Siegwerks
Regenbogenfarben:
   Ihre Qualität gewähr-
leistet eine Druckwieder-
gabe, die der Qualität des
Originals entspricht.
   Der Siegwerk-Service
rund um die Regenbogen-
farben tut ein übriges,
damit Sie sich voll auf die
Kunst des Druckens
konzentrieren können.

SIEGWERK
DRUCKFARBEN

D E R   D R U C K K U N S T

7

ARTIST / KÜNSTLER / ARTISTE:

6 Tomi Ungerer
7 Ralph Steadman
8 Braldt Bralds
9 Bruce Meek

DESIGNER / GESTALTER / MAQUETTISTE:

8 Roy Carruther
9 Franz Merlicek

ART DIRECTOR / DIRECTEUR ARTISTIQUE:

6, 7 Heinz Edelmann
8 Roy Carruther
9 Claus Erwarth

AGENCY / AGENTUR / AGENCE – STUDIO:

6, 7 Robert Pütz GmbH
8 Ogilvy & Mather
9 Demner & Merlicek

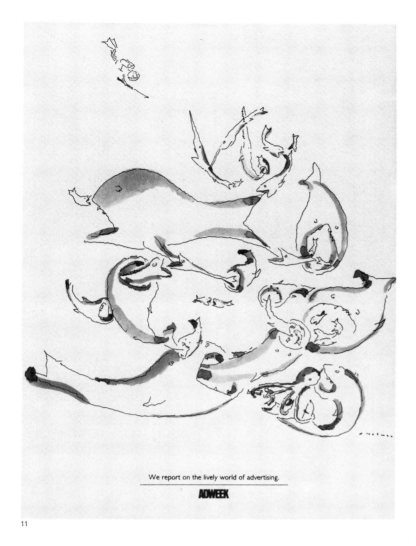

11

12

Advertisements / Inserate / Annonces

ARTIST / KÜNSTLER / ARTISTE:

10 Wayne Anderson
11, 12 R. O. Blechman
13 Lonni Sue Johnson

DESIGNER / GESTALTER / MAQUETTISTE:

10 Gary Betts
11, 12 R. O. Blechman
13 Greg Crossley

ART DIRECTOR / DIRECTEUR ARTISTIQUE:

10 Gary Betts
11, 12 Wally Lawrence
13 Greg Crossley

AGENCY / AGENTUR / AGENCE – STUDIO:

10 S. P. A.
11, 12 R. O. Blechman, Inc.
13 Schroeder Advertising, Inc.

10 Full-page illustration for the announcement by *British Airways* (cargo) of seven new destinations. The accompanying text is in the form of a fable. (GBR)
11, 12 Full-page advertisements for the trade magazine *Adweek*. Fig. 11 is in pale green tones, Fig. 12 is in violet, blue, brown and orange. (USA)
13 Full-page advertisement for a hotel in Atlanta, Georgia. The emphasis is on the amenities and services this hotel is able to offer its business guests. Pastel shades. (USA)

10 Ganzseitige Illustration für die Bekanntgabe sieben neuer Verbindungen der *British-Airways*-Luftfrachtabteilung. Der Text der Anzeige ist in Form eines Märchens verfasst. (GBR)
11, 12 «Wir berichten über die lebendige Welt der Werbung.» Ganzseitige Anzeigen für die Fachzeitschrift *Adweek*. Abb. 11: Grüntöne; Abb. 12: violett, blau, braun, orange. (USA)
13 Ganzseitiges Inserat für ein Hotel, das sich hier an Geschäftsreisende wendet und seine Vorzüge in verschiedenen Bereichen darstellt. Illustration in sanften Farben. (USA)

10 Illustration pleine page annonçant sept nouvelles liaisons aériennes établies par le département frêt de *British Airways*. Le texte adopte le style du conte de fées. (GBR)
11, 12 «Nous rapportons ce qui se passe dans l'univers vivant de la pub.» Annonces pleine page. Revue spécialisée *Adweek*. Fig. 11: tons verts; 12: violet, bleu, brun, orange. (USA)
13 «Comment évaluer l'intérêt d'un hôtel pour les hommes d'affaires.» Publicité d'un hôtel désirant se spécialiser dans ce genre de clientèle. Illustration aux tons adoucis. (USA)

13

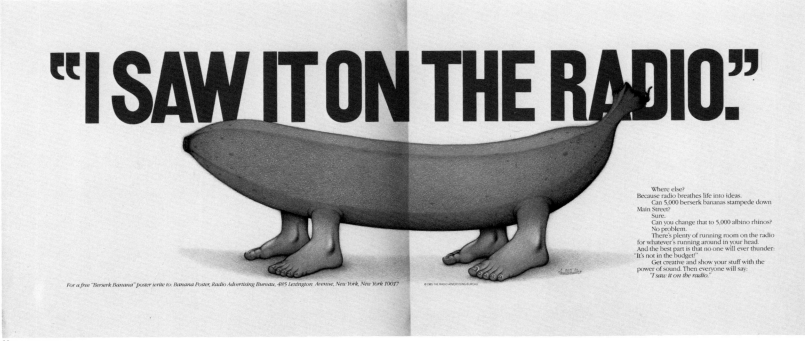

For a free "Berserk Banana" poster write to: Banana Poster, Radio Advertising Bureau, 485 Lexington Avenue, New York, New York 10017

Where else?
Because radio breathes life into ideas.
Can 5,000 berserk bananas stampede down Main Street?
Sure.
Can you change that to 5,000 albino rhinos?
No problem.
There's plenty of running room on the radio for whatever's running around in your head.
And the best part is that no one will ever thunder: "It's not in the budget!"
Get creative and show your stuff with the power of sound. Then everyone will say: "I saw it on the radio."

14

ART DIRECTOR / DIRECTEUR ARTISTIQUE:

14, 15 Roy Carruther/Dick Thomas
16, 17 Steve Stone

ARTIST / KÜNSTLER / ARTISTE:

14–17 Braldt Bralds

AGENCY / AGENTUR / AGENCE – STUDIO:

14, 15 Lord, Geller, Federico, Einstein, Inc.
16, 17 Ketchum Advertising

1 0 0 % C O T T O N

That's what it's all about. And that's exactly what you can expect from Cotoran. Clean cotton with no tough weeds or grasses. No cocklebur.

No teaweed. No morningglory. And no barnyardgrass or crabgrass. Nothing but clean cotton right through harvest. In fact, Cotoran gives

you cleaner fields than any other cotton herbicide. And now Cotoran is available in liquid formulation. Which means you get cleaner cotton

than ever, *easier* than ever. That's what Cotoran is all about. Cotoran from Ciba-Geigy. **COTORAN**

© 1985 Ciba-Geigy Corporation. Ciba-Geigy, Ag Division, Box 18300, Greensboro, NC 27419

16

Where else?
On the radio you can show practically any idea you've got swimming around.
From a pipe-puffing pike to a bevy of be-bopping barracudas. And no one's ever going to scream "Holy Mackerel!" when they see the cost.
Get creative and show your stuff with the power of sound. Then everyone will say: *"I saw it on the radio."*

"I SAW IT ON THE RADIO."

15

How to stop soil disease from tieing down your profits.

Until recently, Phytophthora and Pythium fungi have been reducing tomato growers' yields by causing damping off, root rot and foot rot. These diseases can put the squeeze on tomato production from the moment planting begins.

But now there's Ridomil 2E.® Only Ridomil provides the dual action you need to control and prevent Phytophthora and Pythium-caused diseases.

First, Ridomil is applied where the disease begins—directly to the soil where it kills Phytophthora and Pythium on contact.

Once absorbed into the roots, Ridomil then works systemically, providing a long lasting defense against disease from within.

Apply Ridomil at planting to prevent seed rot and damping off. Apply Ridomil at lay-by to prevent root rot. And 4-8 weeks prior to harvest for fruit rot protection.

Don't let soil disease get you into a bind. This season protect your tomatoes inside and out with Ridomil.

CIBA-GEIGY **RIDOMIL 2E**

17

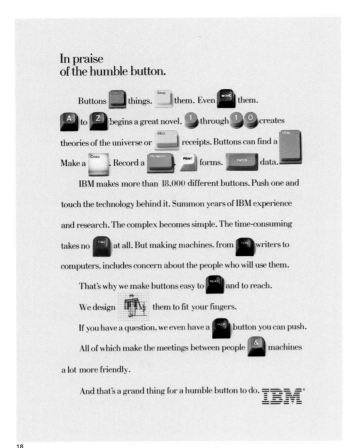

18

19

BEVORZUGEN SIE EINE SOLIDE RUNDE ODER TRÄUMEN SIE LIEBER VON EINEM HOLE IN ONE?

*0041120122060

WIR MACHEN DAS BESTE AUS IHREM VERMÖGEN,
DAMIT SIE DAS BESTE AUS IHREM GOLF MACHEN KÖNNEN.

BHF-BANK (Schweiz) AG
GRÜNDUNG DER BERLINER HANDELS- UND FRANKFURTER BANK
CH-8027 Zürich, Seestraße 135

20

MANCHMAL LOHNT ES SICH, DIE KIRSCHEN IN NACHBARS GARTEN DOCH ETWAS GENAUER ANZUSEHEN.

*0041120122060

WIR MACHEN DAS BESTE AUS IHREM VERMÖGEN,
DAMIT SIE DAS BESTE AUS IHREM GOLF MACHEN KÖNNEN.

BHF-BANK (Schweiz) AG
GRÜNDUNG DER BERLINER HANDELS- UND FRANKFURTER BANK
CH-8027 Zürich, Seestraße 135

21

18, 19 Full-page advertisements for IBM Corporation. (USA)
20, 21 Examples from an advertising campaign for the BHF Bank (Berlin Trade & Frankfurt Bank) in Zurich. Both ads relate to the fair play immanent in golf. Fig. 20: "Do you prefer a clear round or dream of a hole in one?" Fig. 21: "Sometimes it pays to look closely at the cherries in your neighbour's garden." (GER)
22, 23 Full-page advertisements for a telephone company. Fig. 22 relates to the amenities for telephone conferences that the firm offers. Fig. 23 is to promote the company's "Telemarketing" programme. (USA)
24 Full-page ad as self-promotional piece for the printers Stephenson. (USA)

18, 19 Ganzseitige Anzeigen für IBM. Abb.18: «Zum Lob der bescheidenen Taste»; Abb.19: «Es gab eine Zeit, da alle Computer gross waren.» (USA)
20, 21 Beispiele aus einer Inseratenkampagne für die Berliner Handels- und Frankfurter Bank in Zürich. Beide Illustrationen sind mehrfarbig. (GER)
22, 23 Ganzseitige Anzeigen für eine Telephongesellschaft. Abb. 22 wirbt für Telephonkonferenzen: «Wie man alle Gesprächspartner (das ganze Bündel) zusammenbekommt, ohne auf die Palme (going bananas) gebracht zu werden.» Abb. 23: Die hohen Kosten «des Fusses in der Tür» gegenüber dem Telephon-Marketing. (USA)
24 Ganzseitiges Inserat als Eigenwerbung der Druckerei Stephenson. (USA)

BETTER WAYS TO DO BUSINESS

The toughest part of a business meeting can be getting a bunch of people in one room around one table at one time. So instead of going bananas next time you plan a meeting, think: "The time is ripe for a phone conference."

Research shows that up to 40% of all business meetings can be held effectively as phone conferences. More and more Connecticut businesses are finding that phone conferences not only cut out a lot of hassle, they save time and money — particularly when the participants are spread all over.

And there's something about phone conferences that encourages people to cut down on monkey business and get down to *business* business. So phone conferences can be very productive.

Do you need elaborate equipment? Not at all. You may be able to set up a three-person phone conference yourself using ordinary telephones.

If not, or for larger conferences,

a Southern New England Telephone conference operator can assist you. Just call 1-800-544-2333 and arrange a time for the meeting. The conference operator assigns you a special phone number and participants simply call that number at the appointed time from wherever they are — and the meeting begins. It's that easy.

So next time you want to get the whole bunch together, think of a phone conference. It's an idea worthy of a top banana. Call toll-free: **1-800-544-2333.**

HOW TO GET THE WHOLE BUNCH TOGETHER WITHOUT GOING BANANAS.

Southern New England Telephone

22

BETTER WAYS TO DO BUSINESS

Here's a compelling reason why you can't overlook Telemarketing:

The cost of an in-person, business-to-business sales call is now estimated at $205*.

That's up 14 percent over two years ago, 34 percent over just four years ago — and climbing. Telemarketing is a powerful weapon against this costly escalation.

With a well-structured Telemarketing program working for you, you can generate and qualify leads more quickly. You can explain customer benefits. You can announce new products and features. You can answer customer questions. You can, in fact, do many of the things that it costs so much to do with a face-to-face sales call.

But Telemarketing goes beyond selling — it can be an important part of your total marketing approach.

For example, you can use Telemarketing to gather demographic information to help you target

new markets and tap new prospects.

Or you can use it as a customer relations tool, following up *after* a sale to continue to demonstrate your personal interest to your customers.

However you use Telemarketing, you'll find it one of the most controllable and cost-effective marketing aids you've ever used. You'll always know just how well it's working. Just how many responses you're getting, leads you're generating, orders you're filling.

Telemarketing. It's a Better Way To Do Business. And one you ought to find out more about before your salespeople put an expensive foot in too many more doors.

A Southern New England Telephone account representative can show you how Telemarketing can work for your business, whether it's small or large or in-between.

Call us and ask for information about Telemarketing: **1-800-272-SNET.**

*Source: McGraw Hill Research

THE PRICE OF A FOOT IN THE DOOR JUST CROSSED THE $200 THRESHOLD.

Southern New England Telephone

23

"When my husband suggested
a color printer other than Stephenson,
I took the appropriate action."

Lucrezia Borgia

Stephenson incorporated

Printers, Color Separators & Binders   5731 General Washington Drive   Alexandria Virginia 22312   703 642-9000

Illustrated by Michael David Brown   Represented by Gerald & Cullen Rapp, Inc.   212 889-3337

24

*Our international
insurance starts with an
uncommon understanding.*

Chubb understands the potential problems
facing anyone doing business overseas.
The international insurer you choose can
make a world of difference in helping you
handle complex risks.
To understand our difference, consult
with your agent or broker.

CHUBB

Insurance from Chubb.
Understanding is the difference.

25

*Our insurance begins with an
uncommon understanding of
the nature of your business.*

At Chubb, we make it our business to know
your business from the ground up. This
know-how permits us to design insurance
that responds to your particular needs.
Quality coverage through in-depth
knowledge of the industries we serve—it's a
commitment that has defined Chubb and has
set us apart in the insurance marketplace for
over 100 years.
To understand our difference, consult with
your agent or broker.

CHUBB

Insurance from Chubb.
Understanding is the difference.

26

Advertisements
Inserate
Annonces

ARTIST / KÜNSTLER / ARTISTE:

25, 26 Guy Billout
27 James McMullan
28–30 Eduardo A. Cánovas
31 Giovanni Mulazzani

DESIGNER / GESTALTER / MAQUETTISTE:

27 Kenny Garrison
28–30 Eduardo A. Cánovas

ART DIRECTOR / DIRECTEUR ARTISTIQUE:

25, 26 Alan Chin/Paula Herman
27 Woody Pirtle
31 Fritz Tschirren

AGENCY / AGENTUR / AGENCE – STUDIO:

25, 26 Herman Associates
27 Pirtle Design
28–30 Eduardo A. Cánovas
31 STZ Srl

Protocol.

Correct papers for communicating . . .
intelligently.

Protocol. New cotton fiber bond and writing papers from Simpson.

S I M P S O N

Simpson Paper Company One Post Street San Francisco, California 94104

27

La microcirculación: una nueva frontera terapéutica.

Flebotropín (Diosmina) restaura o preserva esencial de la microcirculación. Aumenta la resistencia capilar y asegura un mejor control de la permeabilidad capilar.
Flebotropín (Diosmina) es anti-edema y evita el riesgo hemorrágico de cualquier etiología.
Moviliza la estasis microcirculatoria, nudo de la insuficiencia venosa crónica.
Flebotropín (Diosmina) ejerce una acción tónica directa sobre la pared venosa. Inhibe la

degradación de la noradrenalina estimulante de los receptores alfa de la pared venosa.
Flebotropín (Diosmina) posee una actividad flebotónica superior, de 6 a 25 veces más que la de los productos corrientes.
Flebotropín (Diosmina) es antiálgico, antiedematoso, anti-hemorrágico y descongestivo hemorroidal.
Flebotropín (Diosmina) moviliza la estasis venosa.

Flebotropín.
Comprimidos recubiertos.

28

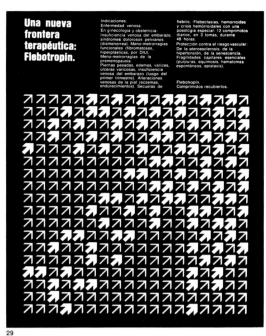

Una nueva frontera terapéutica: Flebotropín.

Indicaciones:
Enfermedad venosa.
En ginecología y obstetricia:
Insuficiencia venosa del embarazo, síndromes dolorosos pelvianos (dismenorrea). Meno-metrorragias funcionales (fibromatosas, hiperplásticas, por DIU). Meno-metrorragias de la premenopausia.
Piernas pesadas, edemas, várices, úlceras varicosas, insuficiencia venosa del embarazo (luego del primer trimestre). Alteraciones venosas de la piel (eczemas, endurecimientos). Secuelas de

flebitis.- Flebectasias, hemorroides y crisis hemorroidales con una posología especial: 12 comprimidos diarios, en 3 tomas, durante 48 horas.
Protección contra el riesgo vascular:
De la aterosclerosis, de la hipertensión, de la senescencia. Fragilidades capilares esenciales (purpuras, equimosis, hematomas espontáneos, epistaxis).

Flebotropín.
Comprimidos recubiertos.

29

Flebotropín, comprimidos recubiertos.

Fórmula:
Cada comprimido contiene:
Flavonoides extraídos de las rutáceas (equivalente a 150 mg. de Diosmina), 375 mg.
Posología:
La dosis habitual es de 4 comprimidos diarios, administrados en dos tomas.
La dosis mínima, de 2 comprimidos diarios, suele ser suficiente en casos leves o como dosis de mantenimiento. La dosis máxima es de entre 8 y 12 comprimidos diarios.

Presentación:
Envases por 20 comprimidos.
Comprimidos recubiertos.
Terapéutica de la insuficiencia venosa con resultados a corto plazo.

Laboratorios Bagó S.A.
Investigación y Tecnología.
Argentina.

30

25, 26 Full-page magazine advertisements for an insurance company. The illustrations relate, respectively, to the help afforded clients doing overseas business and to the company's knowledge "from the ground up" of the industries it serves. (USA)
27 Full-page advertisement in watercolour (mainly green and brown) for *Protocol*—a new paper from *Simpson*. (USA)
28–30 A sequence of three black-and-white advertisements for the medicinal drug *Flebotropin*, administered to improve the blood-stream's micro-circulation. (ARG)
31 Double-spread advertisement for a sofa with adjustable arm and back-rest; designed by Paolo Piva in 1980. (ITA)

25, 26 «Der Unterschied liegt im Verstehen.» Ganzseitige Magazin-anzeigen für eine Versicherung, die hier ihr grundlegendes Verständnis der Geschäfte und Bedürfnisse ihrer Kunden darstellen will. In Abb. 25 geht es um Geschäfte in Übersee, Abb. 26 interpretiert den Anspruch der Gründlichkeit. (USA)
27 Ganzseitiges Inserat in Aquarellfarben (vorwiegend grün und braun) für die neue Papierqualität *Protocol* von *Simpson*. (USA)
28–30 Serie von drei Schwarzweiss-Inseraten für das Medikament *Flebotropin* für die Mikro-Zirkulation. (ARG)
31 Doppelseitiges Inserat für ein von Paolo Piva entworfenes Sofa mit verstellbaren Lehnen. (ITA)

25, 26 «La différence réside dans la compréhension.» Annonces de magazines pleine page pour une compagnie d'assurances affichant beaucoup de compréhension pour les affaires et les besoins de sa clientèle. Fig. 25: affaires d'outre-mer; la fig. 26 symbolise la propension d'aller au fond des problèmes. (USA)
27 Annonce pleine page aux teintes d'aquarelle (surtout du vert et du brun) pour le nouveau papier *Protocol* de *Simpson*. (USA)
28–30 Série de trois annonces noir et blanc pour un remède améliorant la microcirculation, la *Flebotropin*. (ARG)
31 Annonce double page pour un canapé aux dossier et accoudoirs réglables créé par Paolo Piva. (ITA)

Divano Alanda, con braccioli e schienali regolabili. Design Paolo Piva, 1980.

B&B ITALIA

31

32

32 Advertisement illustration for *Daewoo*, a South Korean cargo shipping company. (USA)
33 Magazine advertisement for the motor oil *Essolube HDX Plus*, with recommendations by users of the product. (FRA)
34–36 Illustration (about actual size), the corresponding complete page, and a further example of an informative "White Paper" advertising insert in *Fortune* magazine: PC's and their use in various branches. Here: for an ambulance service and for farming. (USA)
37 Double-spread trade magazine ad for the International Design Center in New York. (USA)

32 Anzeigenillustration für die Container-Schiffe der südkoreanischen Reederei *Daewoo*. (USA)
33 Zeitschrifteninserat für Motorenöl der Marke *Essolube HDX Plus* mit befürwortenden Argumenten der Verwender des Produkts. (FRA)
34–36 Illustration (ungefähr in Originalgrösse), die entsprechende vollständige Seite sowie ein weiteres Beispiel aus einer informativ gestalteten Inseratenbeilage im Magazin *Fortune*; PCs und ihr Einsatz in unterschiedlichen Bereichen; hier in der Ambulanz und der Landwirtschaft. (USA)
37 Doppelseitiges Fachzeitschrifteninserat des International Design Center in New York. (USA)

32 Illustration d'une annonce pour les porte-conteneurs de l'armateur sud-coréen *Daewoo*. (USA)
33 Annonce de magazine pour l'huile de moteur *Essolube HDX Plus* avec des témoignages d'utilisateurs satisfaits. (FRA)
34–36 Illustration (approximativement grandeur nature), page complète où elle figure et autre exemple d'une publiscopie sur les ordinateurs personnels, dans le magazine *Fortune*. (USA)
37 Annonce double page de l'International Design Center newyorkais. Revues spécialisées. (USA)

33

34

35   36

37

40

42

Advertisements / Inserate / Annonces

38 Magazine advertisement in about actual size, for a Russian tea room in New York. In red, brown and beige with a red border. (USA)
39–41 Examples from an advertising campaign for mineral water from *Perrier*. Fig. 39, 40: new variations "with a twist" of orange, lemon or lime; Fig. 41: the salt-free water. (USA)
42 Double-spread magazine advertisement in predominantly reddish-brown tones for the traditional *Heinz* Bar-B-Q sauce—now in a newly-designed bottle. (USA)
43 Full-page magazine advertisement for spaghetti sauce marketed under the *Prince* label, available in two sorts—both with the classic Italian taste. (USA)

38 Magazinanzeige, ungefähr in Originalgrösse, für eine russische Teestube in New York. In Rot, Braun und Beige mit rotschwarzem Rahmen. (USA)
39–41 Zeitschrifteninserate für *Perrier*. Abb. 39, 40: Neue Varianten des Mineralwassers mit «einem Schuss» Zitrone, Limone und Orange; Abb. 41: «Salzfrei geboren». (USA)
42 Doppelseitige Magazinanzeige, überwiegend in Rottönen, für Grill-Saucen von *Heinz*: «Heinz Bar-B-Q-Sauce ist so gut, dass wir einzig und allein die Flasche verbessern konnten.» (USA)
43 Ganzseitige Zeitschriftenanzeige für Tomatensauce der Marke *Prince*, erhältlich in zwei klassischen italienischen Geschmacksrichtungen. (USA)

38 Annonce de magazine, approximativement grandeur nature, pour un salon de thé russe à New York. Rouge, brun, beige, cadre rouge et noir. (USA)
39–41 Exemples d'annonces pour *Perrier*. Fig. 39, 40: nouvelles sortes d'eau minérales parfumées aux fruits; fig. 41: une eau purement naturelle, sans sel. (USA)
42 Annonce de magazine double page pour les sauces à griller *Heinz*. Tons rouges prédominantes. «La sauce barbecue de *Heinz* est parfaite: nous n'avons pu améliorer que le flacon.» (USA)
43 Annonce de magazine pleine page pour la sauce tomate *Prince* présentée en deux arômes italiens classiques. (USA)

44–46 Three examples from a series of advertisements for *Kikkoman* sauces. Illustrations in various green tones, the flesh of the radish in violet and white. (JPN)
47–49 The shell, formerly used in Japan as currency, is the subject of this campaign with full-page advertisements for the Taiyo Kobe Bank. The Chinese characters denote the various shells, which are portrayed in full colour. (JPN)
50 Full-page advertisement for *Nynex*, the parent company of two telephone companies and several business communications equipment firms, here offering to ease the consumer's fear and confusion in today's jungle of telecommunications systems. (USA)

44–46 Drei Beispiele aus einer Serie von Anzeigen für Saucen der Marke *Kikkoman*. Illustrationen in verschiedenen Grüntönen, das Innere des Rettichs in Violett und Weiss. (JPN)
47–49 Die Muschel, früher in Japan als Zahlungsmittel verwendet, ist Gegenstand dieser Kampagne mit ganzseitigen Anzeigen für die Taiyo Kobe Bank. Die chinesischen Schriftzeichen bezeichnen die verschiedenen Muscheln, die mehrfarbig dargestellt sind. (JPN)
50 Ganzseitige Anzeige für *Nynex*, Muttergesellschaft zweier Telephon-Gesellschaften, die durch kompetente Beratung ihren Kunden die Angst vor der Hochtechnologie der Telekommunikations-Systeme zu nehmen verspricht. (USA)

44–46 Trois exemples d'une série d'annonces pour les sauces *Kikkoman*. Illustrations exécutées en divers tons verts; l'intérieur du raifort est violet et blanc. (JPN)
47–49 Le coquillage, qui servait autrefois de monnaie aux Japonais, est le sujet de cette campagne d'annonces pleine page de la Banque Taiyo Kobe. Les caractères chinois identifient les différentes espèces illustrées en polychromie. (JPN)
50 Annonce pleine page pour *Nynex*, société coiffant deux compagnies des téléphones qui assurent à leur clientèle potentielle l'aide compétente qui lui permettra de faire usage de moyens de télécommunication même très sophistiqués. (USA)

ARTIST / KÜNSTLER / ARTISTE:

44–49 Tadashi Ohashi
50 Griesbach/Martucci

DESIGNER / GESTALTER / MAQUETTISTE:

44–49 Tadashi Ohashi
50 Matt Basile

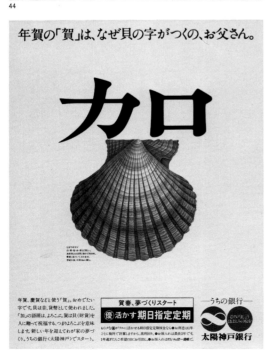

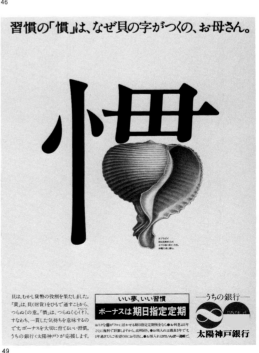

If high technology gives you high anxiety, we cut it down to size.

Stepping into the jungle of confusion surrounding telecommunications is no picnic.

Conflicting advice...demands that you make a decision...it all leads to anxiety. At our NYNEX companies we remove it.

Worried about what equipment to trust? Or who?

Relax. We don't make any of it. So we're free to select the best from different sources.

Can't keep up with new technologies? We can and do.

By the time you've heard about something new, NYNEX technical experts have already investigated its capabilities, located its weaknesses, and determined its effectiveness.

Worrying about obsolescence?

Don't. As new technologies are approved, we automatically integrate them into our network. So you avoid the downtime needed for an update later on.

No matter how high your anxiety, NYNEX has ways to cut it down.

After all, in today's high-tech jungle nobody is more at home than we are.

NYNEX is the parent company of New York Telephone and New England Telephone, plus other companies that offer business communications equipment, cellular services, directory publishing and international telecommunications consulting. For more information, write NYNEX Investor Relations Dept., P.O. Box 2945, NY, NY 10185 USA.

It pays to know us.

© NYNEX Corporation 1985

NYNEX

50

ART DIRECTOR / DIRECTEUR ARTISTIQUE:

44–46 Tadashi Ohashi
47–49 Hiroshi Wakamatsu
50 Matt Basile

AGENCY / AGENTUR / AGENCE – STUDIO:

50 Young & Rubicam

Advertisements / Inserate / Annonces

51

51, 52 Illustration and complete advertisement for the Dutch post-giro savings plan. A prepaid telephone call gives the caller all the necessary information. (NLD)
53 Double-spread magazine advertisement for *Agfa* copiers. White harlequin on yellowish background, balls in various colours. (GBR)
54 Full-page advertisement for the jewellers *J. C. Sipe*, here with the attention on pearls. (USA)
55, 56 From an advertising campaign for *The New York Times*. Birds in various pale colours in Fig. 55; throne in purple and yellow. King with yellow crown, red sash, in Fig. 56. (USA)

51, 52 Illustration und vollständiges Inserat für ein Sparkonto bei der holländischen Post, über das man sich durch einen kostenlosen Anruf informieren kann. (NLD)
53 «Wie talentiert ist Ihr Kopiergerät?» Doppelseitiges Zeitschrifteninserat für *Agfa*-Kopiergeräte. Weisser Harlekin vor gelblichem Hintergrund, mit verschiedenfarbigen Bällen. (GBR)
54 Ganzseitiges Inserat des Juweliers *J. C. Sipe*, hier speziell für Perlen. (USA)
55, 56 Aus einer Inseratenkampagne mit Wortspielen für die *New York Times*, hier mit den Attributen «höchst anregend» (Abb. 55) und «ohne gleichen» (Abb. 56) bezeichnet. (USA)

ARTIST / KÜNSTLER / ARTISTE:

51, 52 Ben Verkaaik
53 Wayne Anderson
54 Jeff Laramore
55, 56 Ronald Searle

AGENCY / AGENTUR / AGENCE – STUDIO:

51, 52 P. M. S. & v. W.
53 Grey Advertising
54 Young & Laramore
55, 56 Bozell Jacobs Kenyon &
       Eckhardt

DESIGNER / GESTALTER / MAQUETTISTE:

53 Alan Docherty
54 Jeff Laramore

ART DIRECTOR / DIRECTEUR ARTISTIQUE:

51, 52 Bela Stamenkovits
53 Alan Docherty
54 Young & Laramore
55, 56 Marce Mayhew

Eén gratis telefoontje en postgiro
helpt je de juiste spaarvorm kiezen.

52

51, 52 Illustration et annonce complète pour les comptes d'épargne de la poste aux Pays-Bas: il suffit d'un coup de fil, gratuit de surcroît, pour obtenir tous les renseignements. (NLD)
53 «De quels talents dispose votre photocopieur?» Annonce de magazine double page pour les photocopieurs *Agfa*. Arlequin blanc sur fond jaunâtre, balles de diverses couleurs. (GBR)
54 Annonce pleine page du joaillier *J. C. Sipe* où il est question de perles. (USA)
55, 56 Campagne d'annonces pour le *New York Times*. Jeux de mots visuels: fig. 55, «très tentant» (supplice de Tantale), fig. 56, «hors pair» (allusion aux pairs du royaume). (USA)

54

55

56

Forbes makes you a force to be reckoned with.

Forbes
Capitalist Tool°

57

ARTIST / KÜNSTLER / ARTISTE:

57, 58 Seymour Chwast
59 René Gruau
60 R. O. Blechman
61 Ray-Mel Cornelius
62 John Collier

DESIGNER / GESTALTER / MAQUETTISTE:

59 René Gruau
60 Thomas E. Williams
61 Carol Carson
62 Brooke Kenney

ART DIRECTOR / DIRECTEUR ARTISTIQUE:

57 Paul Shields
58 John Donaghue
60 Thomas E. Williams
61 Richard Solomon
62 Brooke Kenney

AGENCY / AGENTUR / AGENCE – STUDIO:

57, 58 The Pushpin Group
59 Studio Belekda
60 CBS Print Advertising & Promotion
61 Carol Carson Design
62 Dodge and Kenney, Inc.

57 Example of an advertising campaign for the business magazine *Forbes*. (USA)
58 Full-page ad, polychrome, to promote beef, for the National Live Stock and Meat Board. (USA)
59 Black-and-white magazine advertisement for menswear under the *Pancaldi* label. (ITA)
60 Full-page ad for entertainment on the CBS television channel. With colour accents. (USA)
61 Polychrome ad of the artist's representative Richard Solomon for Rey-Mel Cornelius. (USA)
62 Advertisement for a film-production company who claim that they can offer more unconventional and creative work than just "dog and pony shows". Mainly brown and green tones. (USA)

57 «*Forbes* macht Sie zu einer Kraft, mit der man rechnen muss.» Beispiel aus einer Anzeigenkampagne für das Wirtschaftsmagazin *Forbes*. (USA)
58 Ein Vergleich des Cholesterin-Gehalts ist Gegenstand dieses Inserats für Rindfleisch. (USA)
59 Schwarzweisses Zeitschrifteninserat für Herrenbekleidung der Marke *Pancaldi*. (ITA)
60 Inserat für TV-Unterhaltungssendungen von CBS, anlässlich eines Rosen-Corsos. (USA)
61 Mehrfarbiges Inserat der Künstler-Agentur Richard Solomon für Ray-Mel Cornelius. (USA)
62 Anzeige für eine Filmproduktionsgesellschaft, die behauptet, mehr zu bieten, als das, was man in den USA unter «Hund-und-Pony-Shows» versteht. (USA)

57 «*Forbes* fera de vous une force (de la nature) avec laquelle on devra compter.» Exemple des annonces illustrant une campagne en faveur du magazine économique *Forbes*. (USA)
58 Annonce pour la viande de boeuf, avec un état comparatif du taux de cholestérol. (USA)
59 Annonce de magazine noir et blanc pour les modes masculines *Pancaldi*. (ITA)
60 Annonce pleine page pour les émissions de variété TV CBS à l'occasion d'un corso fleuri. (USA)
61 Annonce polychrome de l'agence artistique Richard Solomon pour Ray-Mel Cornelius. (USA)
62 Annonce pour une société de production cinématographique qui affirme être en mesure d'offrir bien davantage que les sempiternelles «dog and pony shows». (USA)

58

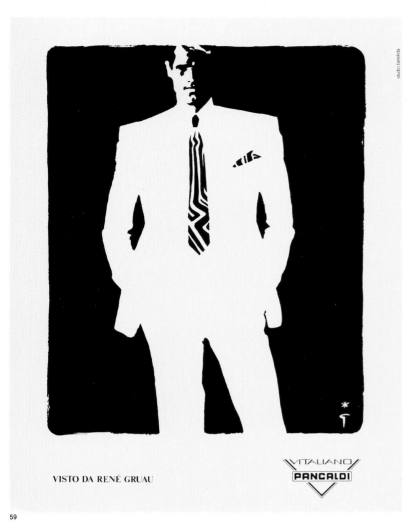

VISTO DA RENÉ GRUAU

VITALIANO
PANCALDI

59

PUTTING MILLIONS OF VIEWERS IN STEP WITH
NEW YEAR'S ROSIEST TRADITION!
CBS ENTERTAINMENT

60

KAY-MEL CORNELIUS

121 MADISON AVE., NEW YORK, NY 10016 · (212) 683-1362

61

A Russell-Manning Show.

It's not your average audio-visual presentation.

We create sounds and images that touch the emotions and linger in the mind. And we bring them to life on film, video, multi-image and combinations thereof. Our work is not conventional. It's intended for people who want to communicate in a way that's uncommonly moving and memorable. Russell-Manning Productions, 612/338-7761.

62

ARTIST / KÜNSTLER / ARTISTE:

63 Seymour Chwast
64 Steven Guarnaccia
65 Takeshi Ohno

DESIGNER / GESTALTER / MAQUETTISTE:

63 Dick Davis
64 Steven Guarnaccia/Bruce Crocker
65 Muneaki Andoh/Masako Ohyama

ART DIRECTOR / DIRECTEUR ARTISTIQUE:

63 Bob Manley/Dick Davis
64 Bruce Crocker
65 Muneaki Andoh

AGENCY / AGENTUR / AGENCE – STUDIO:

63, 64 Altman & Manley, Inc.
65 Dentsu Inc.

63 Advertisement for the Harvest Restaurant, bearing a maxim on the "eat, drink, and be merry" theme. Black and white. (USA)
64 Example from a series of black-and-white newspaper ads introducing a "shared" health service to a new area, whereby the stress is on closer contact with the medical group. (USA)
65 Newspaper advertisement in black and white for Kirin—a Japanese beer. (JPN)

63 Anzeige für das Restaurant Harvest (Ernte) mit einem Zitat von Crimod de la Raynière, in dem es u. a. heisst, man solle versuchen, das Glück in seinem Glas und Teller festzuhalten. (USA)
64 Beispiel aus einer Serie von Zeitungsanzeigen für die Bekanntmachung einer neuen Art der medizinischen Versorgung und Gruppenversicherung, wobei es um das Miteinander geht. (USA)
65 Zeitungsinserat für ein japanisches Bier der Marke Kirin. (JPN)

63 Annonce pour le restaurant Harvest (= récolte), avec une citation de Crimod de la Raynière qui nous invite à saisir le bonheur rencontré dans le verre et dans l'assiette. (USA)
64 Annonce de journal parue dans une série qui met en vedette un nouveau plan d'assistance médicale et d'assurance de groupe basé sur une communauté d'intérêts. (USA)
65 Annonce de journal pour une bière japonaise commercialisée par Kirin. (JPN)

66

Advertisements / Inserate / Annonces

66–68 Illustration and complete examples from a series of newspaper advertisements for *United Technologies* and their subsidiaries. Each advertisement pays tribute to a particular Arab science (Fig. 66 relates to mathematics and the decimal system) and the lead it gave to modern technology. (USA)
69, 70 Small-format, black-and-white newspaper advertisements for *Johnnie Walker* whisky in Holland. Fig. 70: "Papa always wants the little walking man." (NLD)

66–68 Illustration und vollständige Beispiele aus einer Serie von Zeitungsanzeigen für *United Technologies* und deren Tochtergesellschaften. In den Inseraten wird ein Bezug zu der alten arabischen Kultur und den Erzeugnissen der heutigen Computerwelt hergestellt: «Ein Tribut an die arabische Mathematik – Astronomie – Medizin.» (USA)
69, 70 Zeitungsinserate für *Johnnie-Walker*-Whisky. Abb. 70: «Papa will immer das laufende Männchen.» (NLD)

66–68 Illustration et annonces de journaux complètes figurant dans une série réalisée pour *United Technologies* et ses filiales. On s'y réfère à l'antique culture arabe et aux produits de l'informatique moderne: «Un tribut à la mathématique – à l'astronomie – à la médecine arabes.» (USA)
69, 70 Annonces de journal au petit format pour le whisky *Johnnie Walker*. La légende de la fig. 70 se traduit ainsi: «Ce que papa veut, c'est toujours le petit bonhomme qui court.» (NLD)

67

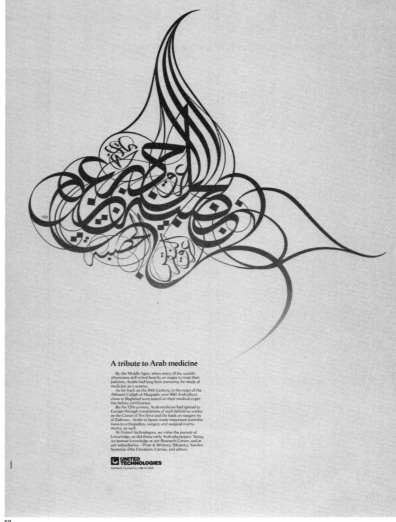

68

ARTIST / KÜNSTLER / ARTISTE:

66–68 M. E. Rouya
69 Marien de Goffau
70 Vincent de Goffau

DESIGNER / GESTALTER / MAQUETTISTE:

66–68 M. E. Rouya
69, 70 Marien de Goffau

ART DIRECTOR / DIRECTEUR ARTISTIQUE:

66–68 M. E. Rouya
69, 70 Marien de Goffau

AGENCY / AGENTUR / AGENCE – STUDIO:

66–68 M. E. Rouya
69, 70 McCann-Erickson

69

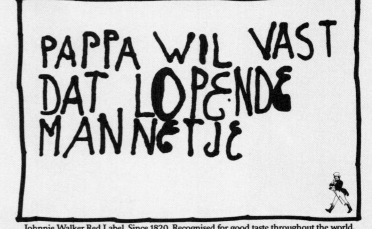

70

71 Double-spread black-and-white newspaper advertisement on behalf of the Madison Financial Corporation. Aimed at banks, the ad offers help in attracting new customers, thus enabling the smaller banks to fight in the "financial battleground" alongside America's greatest banking giants. (USA)

72, 73 Illustration and full-page newspaper ad for the advertising and public relations firm Ervin/Taft. It states that the battle of creative minds is never over. (USA)

71 Doppelseitiges Zeitungsinserat der Madison Financial Corp., die hier kleineren Banken ihre Dienste für die Anwerbung neuer Kunden anbietet. In einem «Überblick über die Finanz-Strategie» werden Informationen zur «Aufnahme des Kampfes» mit den drei grössten Finanzierungsgesellschaften der USA geliefert. (USA)

72, 73 «Tausende sterben im Krieg der Ideen.» Illustration und ganzseitige Zeitungsanzeige des Werbebüros Ervin/Taft, wonach der «Ideenkrieg» nie zu Ende sein wird. (USA)

71 Annonce de journal double page de la Madison Financial Corp. offrant ici aux petites banques ses services pour l'acquisition d'une nouvelle clientèle. Un «aperçu de stratégie financière» renseigne sur les «mesures de combat» à l'égard des trois majeures sociétés financières des Etats-Unis. (USA)

72, 73 «La guerre des idées fait des milliers de morts.» Illustration et annonce de journal pleine page de l'agence publicitaire Ervin/Taft pour qui cette guerre est interminable. (USA)

Advertisements
Inserate
Annonces

72

ARTIST / KÜNSTLER / ARTISTE:
71–73 Brad Holland

DESIGNER / GESTALTER / MAQUETTISTE:
72, 73 Ron Taft

ART DIRECTOR / DIRECTEUR ARTISTIQUE:
71 Tom Wright
72, 73 Ron Taft

73

53

Bear Crossing

KRAFT smooth cremeux PEANUT BUTTER BEURRE D'ARACHIDES

KRAFT Everyone knows there's a secret inside.

74

Monday's dateline. And Saturday's child.

Come the weekend, it's easy to spot the Barron's readers.

They're the ones who fly to the nearest newsstand every weekend to pick up a copy of next week's Barron's.

Smart move. Since we give readers a head start on the rest of the world.

Which may explain why more than one third of our circulation comes from newsstand sales. And why our primary readers—newsstand or subscrip- tion—spend nearly two hours with the typical issue.

The readers we reach?

They're the same sort of readers you reach with The Wall Street Journal. The affluent. The influential. The movers and the shakers.

They run for Barron's for good reason.

We cover what's most important to the most important people.

Money. Markets. Investments. And the value the world puts on the companies they own or manage.

Shouldn't you be reading Barron's? And shouldn't you be advertising to the fast-trackers and highfliers who do? Barron's.

When you just can't wait for the business week to begin.

Barron's. How the smart money gets that way.

75

We Make Sure The Music Never Stops.

Washington's varied and full cultural life is due in part to the efforts of the business community. Whether it means raising money or donating space, local businesses have encouraged both the per- forming and visual arts.

One way to make sure the music never stops is to support young artists. Business helps to fund the D.C. Youth Orchestra and contributed to the drive to send the Roosevelt-Macfarland Marching Band to the Olympics.

So when the Washington area is applauded as a vibrant cultural center, it's music to our ears.

Washington Area Businesses.
Working to make the Washington area better.

Sponsored by The Greater Washington Board of Trade

76

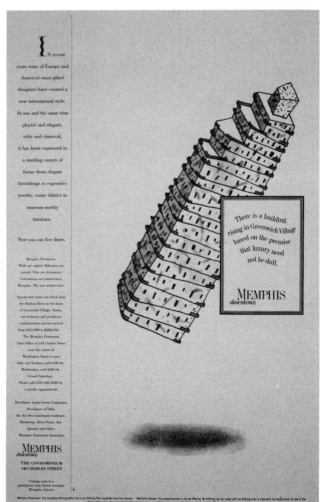

IN recent years some of Europe and America's most gifted designers have created a new international style. At one and the same time playful and elegant, witty and classical, it has been expressed in a startling variety of forms—from elegant furnishings to expensive jewelry, exotic fabrics to museum-worthy furniture.

Now you can live there.

There is a building rising in Greenwich Village based on the premise that luxury need not be dull.

MEMPHIS downtown

MEMPHIS downtown THE CONDOMINIUM 140 CHARLES STREET

77

79

80

81

56

Rabenschwarze Nacht.
Gleich dringt der Waldkauz gezielt durchs finstere Dunkel. In beträchtlicher Entfernung sieht er eine wühlende Feldmaus. Klar, wie am hellen Tag.

82

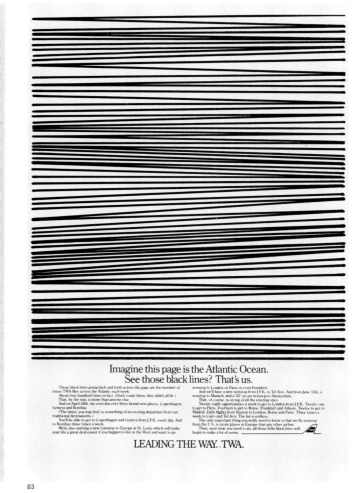

Imagine this page is the Atlantic Ocean.
See those black lines? That's us.

LEADING THE WAY.··TWA.

83

VOTRE OPINION FAIT PLIER LES DICTATURES. DONNEZ-LA!

FEDERATION INTERNATIONALE DES
DROITS DE L'HOMME

27, RUE JEAN-DOLENT, 75014 PARIS, FRANCE. TÉL. (1) 331.94.95.

84

2

Booklets

Folders

Catalogues

Programmes

Broschüren

Faltprospekte

Kataloge

Programme

Brochures

Dépliants

Catalogues

Programmes

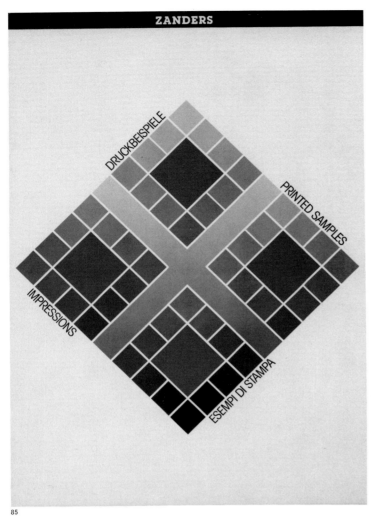

85

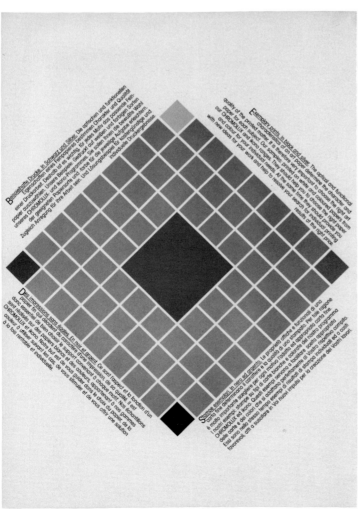

86

26   27

87

89

85, 86 Cover and back flap of a promotional gatefold portfolio, with print samples on *Chromolux* and *Ikono* paper, for *Zanders Feinpapiere;* here for black and silver print on white. (GER)
87, 88 Double spread and cover of a brochure printed on and promoting recycled paper. (GER)
89, 90 Inside double spread and cover of a promotional portfolio with typographical variations by well-known artists on the theme "Up to Date". Issued by *Zanders Feinpapiere.* (GER)
91, 92 Expensively-produced cassette holding a 4"×4" diary with 48 photographs of China and comments on a designer's two-week cultural tour. For *Kromekote* paper by *Champion.* (USA)
93 Promotional concertina folder, featuring Memphis design, for new papers by *Simpson.* (USA)

85, 86 Umschlag und aufklappbare Innenseite einer Mappe für *Zanders Feinpapiere*, mit Druckbeispielen auf *Chromolux-* und *Ikono*-Papier; hier für den Druck mit Schwarz und Silber auf Weiss. (GER)
87, 88 Doppelseite und Umschlag einer ganz auf Umweltschutzpapier gedruckten Broschüre. (GER)
89, 90 Inhaltsdoppelseite und Umschlag einer Werbemappe mit dem Thema «Up to date», die typographische Interpretationen bekannter Künstler enthält. Für *Zanders Feinpapiere.* (GER)
91, 92 Deckel und offen präsentierte, aufwendig konzipierte Kassette, die ein kleinformatiges Tagebuch mit 48 Photos aus China enthält. Für *Kromekote*-Papier von *Champion.* (USA)
93 Prospekt in Leporelloform, mit Memphis-Design, für neue Papiersorten von *Simpson.* (USA)

85, 86 Couverture et page intérieure dépliante d'un portfolio de *Zanders Feinpapiere* imprimées sur *Chromolux* et papier *Ikono;* ici, impression noir et argent sur blanc. (GER)
87, 88 Double page et couverture d'une brochure imprimée sur papier recyclé. (GER)
89, 90 Double page intérieure et couverture d'un portfolio publicitaire pour *Zanders Feinpapiere:* des artistes connus interprètent typographiquement le thème «Up to date». (GER)
91, 92 Couvercle et intérieur d'une cassette luxueuse renfermant un petit livre-journal illustré de 48 photos de la Chine. Pour les papiers *Kromekote* de *Champion.* (USA)
93 Prospectus à pliage accordéon et design Memphis pour de nouveaux papiers *Simpson.* (USA)

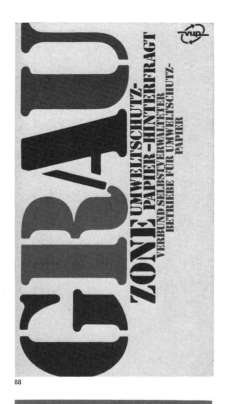

DESIGNER / GESTALTER / MAQUETTISTE:

85, 86 Hoffmeister & Partner GmbH
87, 88 Christof Gassner
89 Wim Crouwel / Henry Steiner
90 Helmut Langer
91, 92 Jim Miho
93 Michael Vanderbyl

ART DIRECTOR / DIRECTEUR ARTISTIQUE:

91, 92 Jim Miho

AGENCY / AGENTUR / AGENCE – STUDIO:

87, 88 Christof Gassner
93 Vanderbyl Design

88

91

90

92

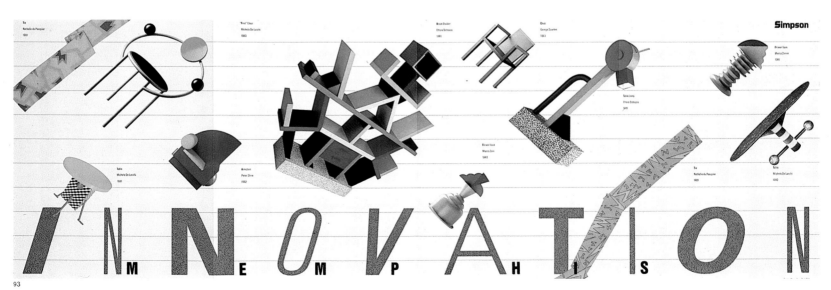

93

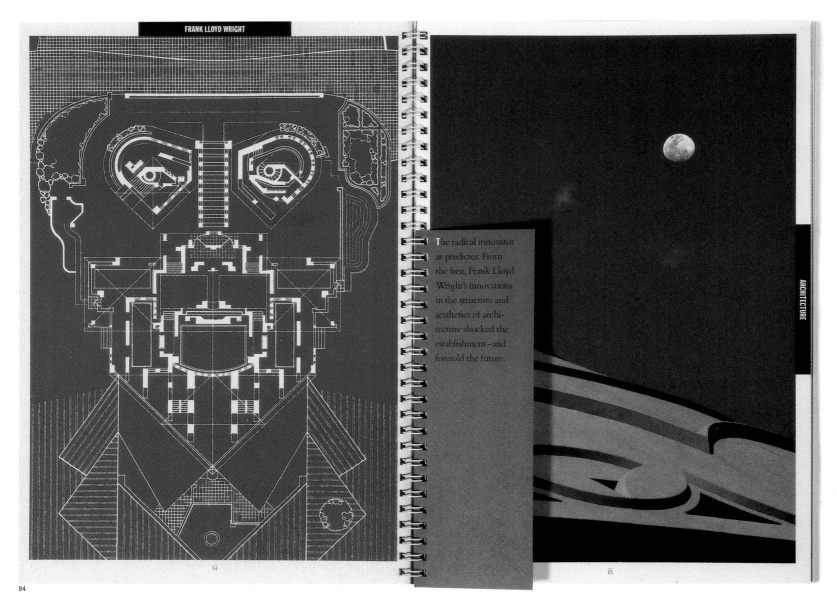

The radical innovator as predictor. From the first, Frank Lloyd Wright's innovations in the structure and aesthetics of architecture shocked the establishment – and foretold the future.

94

ARTIST / KÜNSTLER / ARTISTE:

94, 97 David Stevenson/
     Charly Franklin (Photo)
95 Douglas Smith
96 Ward Schumaker

DESIGNER / GESTALTER / MAQUETTISTE:

94–97 Kit Hinrichs/
     Francesca Bator

ART DIRECTOR / DIRECTEUR ARTISTIQUE:

94–97 Kit Hinrichs

AGENCY / AGENTUR / AGENCE – STUDIO:

94–97 Jonson Pedersen Hinrichs &
     Shakery

94–97 Double spreads and page from a spiral-bound brochure for *Simpson Paper*, entitled *Predictions*. Fig. 97 (about actual size) portrays Charles Richter, whose Richter Scale, for measuring the intensity of earthquakes, now leads to the probability of their prediction. (USA)

94–97 Doppelseiten und Einzelseite aus einer spiralgehefteten Broschüre für *Simpson Paper*, mit dem Titel «Prophezeiungen». Abb. 97 (ungefähr Originalgrösse) zeigt Charles Richter, dank dessen Skala für die Messung der Intensität von Erdbeben jetzt die Möglichkeit einer Voraussage denkbar ist. (USA)

94–97 Doubles pages et page simple d'une brochure à reliure spirale conçue pour *Simpson Paper* et intitulée «Prédictions». La fig. 97 (à peu près grandeur nature) montre un portrait de Charles Richter, qui découvrit l'échelle permettant d'évaluer la force des séismes. (USA)

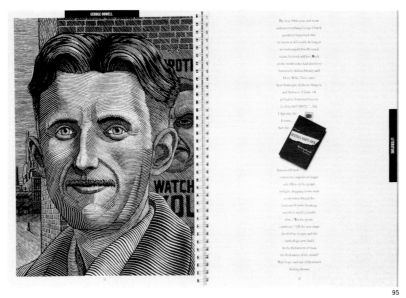

95

96

97

**Booklets
Prospekte
Brochures**

98 Eraser in the form of a red telephone, on a card to announce the new telephone number of the Chemigraphisches Institut. (SWI)
99–101 Examples from a portfolio containing sheets (illustrated in full colour by Pushpin Associates) entitled "The Great American 6-Course Dinner", from a series of portfolios featuring the works of outstanding photographers/illustrators, issued by Sterling-Roman Press, Inc. (USA)
102 Yellow gloss-coated miniature carrier-bag and the folded cards contained inside. Each is die-cut to the shape of a clothing item and the cards were sent out singly, one card a month, over a 6-month period as direct-mail advertising for a shop-display equipment company. (GBR)

98 Radiergummi in Form eines roten Telephons auf einer Karte, als Ankündigung der neuen Telephonnummer des Chemigraphischen Instituts. (SWI)
99–101 In einer Werbemappe der Druckerei Sterling-Roman Press enthaltene Blätter mit Rezepten. Abb. 99: «Alaska»-Dessert; Abb. 100: Die «Atlantic City-Spiel»-Pastete, zu der zwei Fasane gehören; Abb. 101: Ein Hummergericht, das seinen Namen einer Baseball-Mannschaft verdankt. (USA)
102 Gelbe, lackierte Miniatur-Tragtasche und Beispiele der in Form von Kleidungsstücken gestanzten Doppelkarten, die darin einzeln als Direktwerbung für ein Ladeneinrichtungsgeschäft versandt wurden. (GBR)

98 Gomme rouge en forme de téléphone posée sur une carte: annonce du nouveau numéro de téléphone de l'Institut de zincographie. (SWI)
99–101 Fiches de recettes rassemblées dans un portfolio publicitaire de l'imprimerie Sterling-Roman Press. Fig. 99: l'ours polaire annonce un dessert nommé «Alaska». Fig. 100: l'«Atlantic City Game Pie», un pâté composé à base de faisans. Fig. 101: un plat de homard qui doit son nom à une équipe de baseball. (USA)
102 Sac miniature laqué jaune et exemples de doubles cartes découpées en forme de vêtements qui, glissées dedans, ont été envoyées par un commerce d'installations de magasins pour sa promotion. (GBR)

99

98

100

101

ARTIST / KÜNSTLER / ARTISTE:

99 Christoph Blumrich
100 Seymour Chwast
101 Michael Aron
102 Connie Jude

DESIGNER / GESTALTER / MAQUETTISTE:

98 Peter Wirth
99–101 Seymour Chwast
102 Peter Chodel/Judi Barrington

ART DIRECTOR / DIRECTEUR ARTISTIQUE:

98 Peter Wirth
99–101 Dick Lopez
102 Peter Chodel

AGENCY / AGENTUR / AGENCE – STUDIO:

98 Doyle Dane Bernbach
99–101 The Pushpin Group
102 Right Angle Design

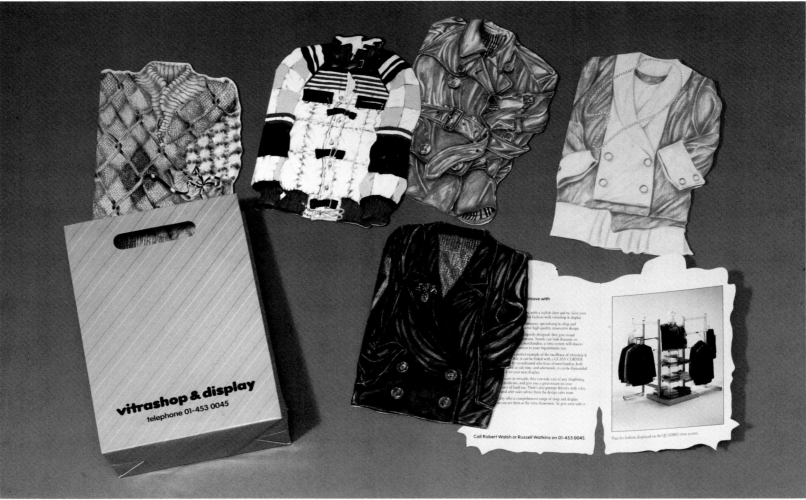

102

103

103 Illustration (pink skin tones on dark ground) from a call for entries to the Advertising Club of Indianapolis contest. (USA)
104–106 Double spreads and cover of a brochure "Fun and Games with 2 Colors"; one item from the contents in a case of promotional material, issued by *Champion* paper manufacturers. (USA)
107 The inside of a large call-for-entries folder to the Functional Graphics competition organized by the AIGA. (USA)

103 Illustration (rosa Hautton zu dunklen Farben) aus einer Wettbewerbseinladung des Werbe-Clubs von Indianapolis. (USA)
104–106 Doppelseiten und Umschlag einer Broschüre mit dem Titel «Spass und Spiele mit zwei Farben» aus dem Inhalt einer Schachtel mit Werbematerial des Papierherstellers *Champion*. (USA)
107 Innenseite einer Faltkarte als Einladung der AIGA zu einem Wettbewerb unter dem Motto «funktionelle Graphik». (USA)

103 Illustration d'une invitation à un concours du club de publicité d'Indianapolis. Visage rose sur tons foncés. (USA)
104–106 Doubles pages et couverture d'une brochure intitulée «De l'amusement et des jeux en deux couleurs» figurant au contenu d'une boîte de matériel publicitaire distribuée par le fabricant de papier *Champion*. (USA)
107 Intérieur d'une carte d'invitation pliante de l'AIGA pour un concours sur «le graphisme fonctionnel». (USA)

104

105

106

ARTIST / KÜNSTLER / ARTISTE:

103 Jeff Laramore

DESIGNER / GESTALTER / MAQUETTISTE:

103 Young & Laramore
104–106 Jim Miho
107 Rudolph de Harak/Frank Benedict

ART DIRECTOR / DIRECTEUR ARTISTIQUE:

103 Young & Laramore
104–106 Jim Miho
107 Rudolph de Harak

AGENCY / AGENTUR / AGENCE – STUDIO:

103 Young & Laramore
107 Rudolph de Harak & Associates

Functional
Graphics

108

109

Booklets / Prospekte / Brochures

THE BURSARY SHOW

A selection of recent work by seven Arts Council Bursary Award winners

110

Cecily Brennan

Born Athenry, County Galway in 1955
Graduated from National College of Art and Design 1979

**One woman
exhibitions**

Project Art Centre, Dublin
1982
Taylor Galleries, Dublin 1985

Group exhibitions

Best Graduate Show, Project Arts Centre, Dublin 1978
NCAD Staff/Student Show, Douglas Hyde Gallery 1978
Limerick Exhibition of Visual Art 1979
Independent Artists, Municipal Gallery, Dublin 1980
Independent Artists, Project Arts Centre, Dublin 1981
Graphic Studio Touring Print Exhibition 1983
Independent Artists, Douglas Hyde Gallery, Dublin 1983
Cibeal Cincise, Kenmare, County Kerry 1983
Figurative Image Exhibition, Bank of Ireland, Dublin 1983
Black Church Print Studio Exhibition, Triskel Arts Centre, Cork 1983
University Collage, Collection of University College, Dublin 1983
Group Shows, Taylor Galleries 1984
Represented Ireland at the International Exhibition of Painting, Cagnes-sur-Mer France 1984

Awards

Arts Council Bursary 1982
Grumbacher Artists Brushes
Award 1984

Commissions

St Patrick's Hospital, James
Street, Dublin 1984
Jury's Hotel Group, Dublin
1984

Collections

The Arts Council of Ireland
University College, Dublin
Bank of Ireland
Allied Irish Banks

Allied Irish Investment Banks
Algemene Bank Nederland
Contemporary Irish Arts
Society
Industrial Development
Authority

Institute of Chartered
Accountants in Ireland
Life Association Ireland
P J Murphy
V A Ferguson
Ronald Tallon
John Meagher

111

ARTIST / KÜNSTLER / ARTISTE:

108, 109 Ken Laidlaw
110, 111 Tony O'Hanlon
112 Andrea Rauch/Stefano Rovai/
Piero Mazzoni

DESIGNER / GESTALTER / MAQUETTISTE:

108, 109 Ken Laidlaw
110, 111 Tony O'Hanlon
112 Andrea Rauch
113 Aage Plener
114 Michael Vanderbyl

ART DIRECTOR / DIRECTEUR ARTISTIQUE:

108, 109 Ken Laidlaw
110, 111 Tony O'Hanlon
112 Andrea Rauch
113 Aage Plener

AGENCY / AGENTUR / AGENCE – STUDIO:

110, 111 Kilkenny Design
112 Graphiti
113 Aage Plener Kommunikation & Design
114 Vanderbyl Design

108, 109 Self-promotion by illustrator Ken Laidlaw. Fig. 108 is from a series "Animals on Holiday" (here, "far-away places"). Fig. 109 is from an "animal clichés" series. (GBR)
110, 111 Cover (black and grey with yellow triangle on white) and page from a catalogue with a selection of works by seven Arts Council (of Ireland) Bursary Award winners. (IRL)
112 Invitation (original size) to a poster exhibition by Graphiti, a Florentine studio. (ITA)
113 "Closer"—the change-of-address-notice motto for a designer. Black and red on grey. (DEN)
114 Cover of a portfolio for *Simpson* to promote the paper quality *Sequoia*. Devoted to designer Massimo Vignelli; the theme (with examples of Vignelli's works) is "uncompromising quality". (USA)

108, 109 Eigenwerbung des Illustrators Ken Laidlaw. Abb. 108 zu einer Serie mit dem Titel «Tiere in Ferien», Abb. 109 zu einer Reihe über Tier-Clichés, hier Krokodilstränen. (GBR)
110, 111 Umschlag (schwarzweiss mit Grau und Gelb) und Seite aus einem Katalog für eine Wander-ausstellung der Preisträger einer irischen Kunstkommission (Arts Council of Ireland). (IRL)
112 Einladung (Originalgrösse) zu einer Plakatausstellung des Graphik-Studios Graphiti. (ITA)
113 «Näher» ist das Motto dieser Umzugsanzeige eines Designers. Schwarz und Rot auf Grau. (DEN)
114 Umschlag einer Werbemappe für den Papierhersteller *Simpson*, die dem Architekten und Designer Massimo Vignelli gewidmet ist – als Beispiel für Beständigkeit hoher Leistung. (USA)

108, 109 Autopromotion de l'illustrateur Ken Laidlaw. La fig. 108 appartient à la série «Animaux en vacances», la fig. 109 à une série de clichés, comme les larmes de crocodile. (GBR)
110, 111 Couverture (en noir et blanc avec gris et jaune) et page du catalogue d'une exposition itinérante consacrée aux lauréats de la commission de l'Arts Council of Ireland. (IRL)
112 Carte autopromotionnelle grandeur nature de l'atelier Graphiti de Florence. (ITA)
113 «Plus près»: annonce de changement d'adresse d'un designer. Noir et rouge, sur gris. (DEN)
114 Couverture d'un portfolio promotionnel du fabricant de papiers *Simpson* consacrée à l'architecte et designer Massimo Vignelli – exemple de constance dans la performance. (USA)

112

113

114

ARTIST / KÜNSTLER / ARTISTE:

115 Randall Enos
116 Paul Peter Piech
117 Georgi Tschauschow
118 Jiří Sliva

DESIGNER / GESTALTER / MAQUETTISTE:

115 Randall Enos
116 Paul Peter Piech
117 Petko Andreew
118 Karel Šejna

ART DIRECTOR / DIRECTEUR ARTISTIQUE:

115 Randall Enos
117 Christo Christow

115 Portrait of the painter Frida Kahlo (wife of Diego Riuera) as self promotion for Randall Enos. Various linocuts were printed on coloured paper and then superimposed. (USA)
116 Linocut card in the cause of peace. In petrol and old rose on white ground. (GBR)
117 Charter of the Gabrovo House of Humour and Satire for the "world to survive through the laughter of the people". Issued by a Bulgarian satirical publishing house. (BUL)
118 For an exhibition of works by Slíva. Black and white and pale rust-red. (CSR)

115 Porträt der Malerin Frida Kahlo als Eigenwerbung für Randall Enos, der hierfür verschiedene Linolschnitte auf farbige Papiere druckte, die er dann zusammenfügte. (USA)
116 Linolschnitt-Karte für die Sache des Friedens. In Petrol und Altrosa auf Weiss. (GBR)
117 Urkunde eines humoristisch-satirischen Verlags in Bulgarien, ausgestellt für die Förderung des Lachens, «dessen Macht selbst das Böse zu besiegen vermag». (BUL)
118 Für eine Ausstellung mit Werken von Slíva. Schwarzweiss und helles Rostrot. (CSR)

115 Portrait de l'artiste Frida Kahlo (femme de Diego Riuera): autopromotion de Randall Enos composée d'un assemblage de plusieurs linogravures imprimées sur papiers colorés. (USA)
116 Carte en linogravure pour la paix. Pétrole et vieux rose sur fond blanc. (GBR)
117 Certificat d'une maison d'éditions bulgare spécialisée dans les publications satiriques, établi pour son action en faveur du rire «qui triomphe même du mal». (BUL)
118 Pour une exposition d'œuvres de Slíva. Noir et blanc, rouille clair. (CSR)

116

117

118

Booklets / Prospekte / Brochures

119

120

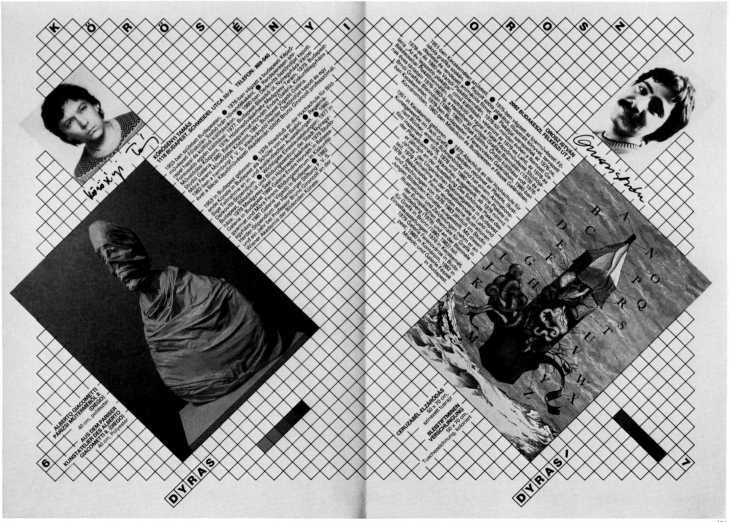

121

Cheers!

VANITY FAIR

122

119, 120 Double spread from a brochure entitled "Music on ZDF" (German TV channel). Fig.119 announces the programme "Biblical Music", here relating to Handel's oratorio "Jephta". Polychrome illuminations on black background. Fig.120: introductory double spread for a chapter, in black and white. (GER)
121 "Art and technique" is the theme of this brochure dedicated to Hungarian artists, from *Dyras,* producers of entertainment electronics. The works are reproduced in full colour. (HUN)
122 Concertina-fold invitation, by *Vanity Fair* magazine. (USA)
123 Cover of a book catalogue for publishers Carroll & Graf. (USA)

119, 120 Doppelseiten aus einer Broschüre mit dem Titel «Musik im ZDF». Abb.119 kündigt das Programm «Musica Biblica» an, das mit einer Aufzeichnung von Händels «Jephta» beginnt. Illuminationen mehrfarbig auf schwarzem Grund. Abb.120: Einleitende Doppelseite für ein Kapitel, in Schwarzweiss. (GER)
121 «Kunst und Technik» ist das Thema dieser Broschüre, die *Dyras,* Hersteller von Produkten der Unterhaltungselektronik, Künstlern aus Ungarn gewidmet hat. Werkabbildungen in Farbe. (HUN)
122 Leporello als Einladung für das Magazin *Vanity Fair.* (USA)
123 Umschlag eines Katalogs für den Verlag Carroll & Graf. (USA)

119, 120 Doubles pages d'une brochure intitulée «Musique sur ZDF». La fig.119 annonce le programme «Musica Biblica» qui commence par un enregistrement de «Jephta» de Händel. Enluminures polychromes sur fond noir. Fig.120: double page initiale d'un chapitre, en noir et blanc. (GER)
121 «Art et technique», tel est le thème de la brochure que *Dyras,* fabricant d'électronique récréative, a consacrée à des artistes hongrois. Reproductions en couleurs. (HUN)
122 Dépliant d'une invitation du magazine *Vanity Fair.* (USA)
123 Couverture d'un catalogue de Carroll & Graf. (USA)

CARROLL & GRAF PUBLISHERS, INC.
FALL/WINTER 1985

123

Rowohlt
VORANKÜNDIGUNG
FRÜHJAHR '85

ARTIST / KÜNSTLER / ARTISTE:

124 Roland Topor
125 Ute Krause
126–128 Hans Hillmann
129 Pierre Le-Tan
130 Philippe Weisbecker

DESIGNER / GESTALTER / MAQUETTISTE:

124, 125 Thomas Brink

ART DIRECTOR / DIRECTEUR ARTISTIQUE:

124, 125 Thomas Brink
129, 130 Louise Fili

129

128

130

124, 125 Recto and verso of a catalogue cover for the children's book publishers Gertraud Middelhauve. Polychrome illustrations, red and yellow lettering on white ground. (GER)
126–128 Covers and an illustration detail, for advance announcements (spring and autumn) for Rowohlt publishers. Fig. 126 in grey, pale green, chamois and pale pink. (GER)
129, 130 Covers of the spring catalogues 1985 and 1986 for Pantheon Books, the New York publishing house. (USA)

124, 125 Vorder- und Rückseite des Umschlags eines Katalogs des Kinderbuchverlags Gertraud Middelhauve. Illustrationen mehrfarbig, Schrift rot und ocker auf weissem Grund. (GER)
126–128 Vollständige Umschlagvorderseiten und Ausschnitt einer Illustration für Vorankündigungen des Rowohlt-Verlags. Abb. 126 in Grautönen, hellem Grün, Chamois und zartem Rosa. (GER)
129, 130 Umschläge für die Frühjahrskataloge 1985 und 1986 des New Yorker Verlags Pantheon Books. (USA)

124, 125 Recto et verso de la couverture d'un catalogue de l'éditeur de livres d'enfants Gertraud Middelhauve. Illustrations polychromes, texte rouge et ocre sur blanc. (GER)
126–128 Pages de couverture complètes et détail d'une illustration pour une brochure de l'édition Rowohlt. Fig. 126: tons gris, vert clair, chamois et rose tendre. (GER)
129, 130 Couvertures des catalogues de printemps 1985 et 1986 de l'édition newyorkaise Pantheon Books. (USA)

131

ARTIST / KÜNSTLER / ARTISTE:

131 Tullio Pericoli
132 Michael Orzech
134, 135 Lanny Sommese

ART DIRECTOR / DIRECTEUR ARTISTIQUE:

132 David Lopes/Cheryl Heller
133 Willi Kunz
134, 135 Lanny Sommese

DESIGNER / GESTALTER / MAQUETTISTE:

131 Bartsch & Chariau
132 David Lopes/Cheryl Heller
133 Willi Kunz
134, 135 Lanny Sommese

AGENCY / AGENTUR / AGENCE – STUDIO:

132 HBM/Creamer Design Group
133 Willi Kunz Associates
134, 135 Lanny Sommese Design

131 Federico Fellini on the cover of an invitation (actual size) to an exhibition at the Bartsch and Chariau gallery, devoted to graphic artist/painter Tullio Pericoli. (GER)
132 White square box, presented open, showing the invitation card (contained inside) to a celebration marking the firm's 100th anniversary. The bow tie at the folded shirt-collar is made from a toy banknote. (USA)
133 Cover of a catalogue of Bodoni typefaces for *Typogram,* a typesetting firm. (USA)
134, 135 Closed and opened-out invitation to a poster exhibition by Lanny Sommese. (The person is "hanging" when the card is opened.) Black on brown paper. (USA)

131 Federico Fellini auf der Vorderseite einer Einladungskarte (Originalgrösse) zu einer dem graphischen Zeichner und Maler Tullio Pericoli gewidmeten Ausstellung in der Münchener Galerie Bartsch und Chariau. (GER)
132 Geöffnete Schachtel und die darin enthaltene Einladung zur 100-Jahr-Feier einer Firma. Als Fliege zum gefalteten Kragen dient eine Spielgeldnote. (USA)
133 Vorderseite eines Katalogs mit Bodoni-Schriften für eine Setzerei. (USA)
134, 135 «Sie sind zum Hängen eingeladen.» Zusammen- und auseinandergefaltete Einladung zu einer Plakatausstellung von Lanny Sommese. Schwarz auf braunem Papier. (USA)

131 Federico Fellini au recto d'une carte d'invitation (grandeur nature) d'une exposition de la galerie Bartsch & Chariau consacrée au dessinateur et peintre Tullio Pericoli. (GER)
132 Boîte ouverte contenant l'invitation au 100e anniversaire d'une firme. Le nœud-papillon qui orne le col plié est fait à l'aide d'un billet de jeu. (USA)
133 Caractères Bodoni au recto du catalogue d'un atelier de composition. (USA)
134, 135 «Vous êtes invités à pendre.» Invitation pliée et dépliée à une exposition d'affiches de Lanny Sommese. Noir sur papier brun. (USA)

132

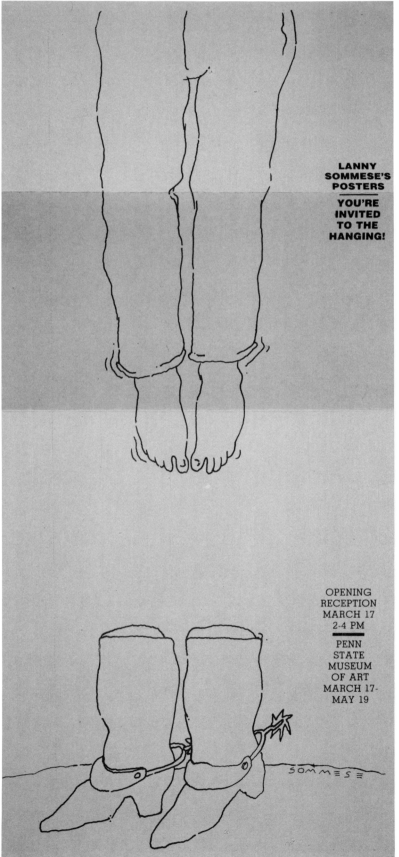

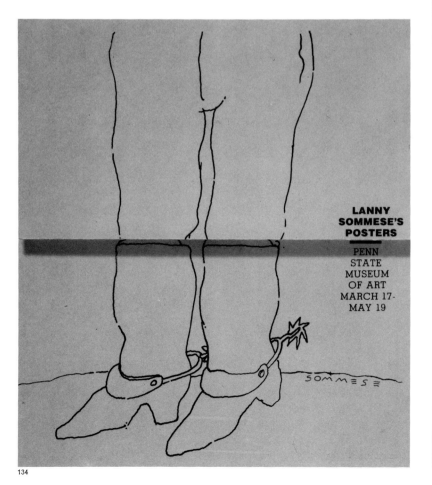

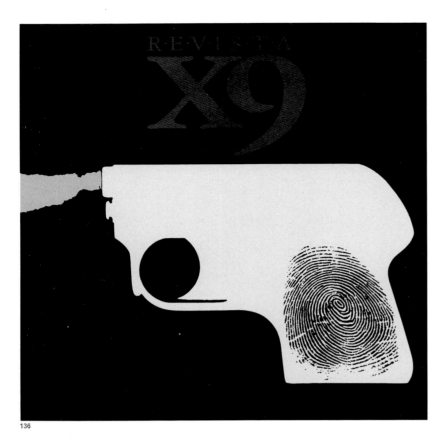

ARTIST / KÜNSTLER / ARTISTE:

136 Oswaldo Miranda (Miran)
138 Filippo Fantoni
139 Braldt Bralds

DESIGNER / GESTALTER / MAQUETTISTE:

136 Oswaldo Miranda
137 Santamarina
138 Fabio Chiantini
139 Braldt Bralds

ART DIRECTOR / DIRECTEUR ARTISTIQUE:

136 Oswaldo Miranda
137 Santamarina
138 Fabio Chiantini
139 Piet van Oss

AGENCY / AGENTUR / AGENCE – STUDIO:

136 Miran Studio
137 Elias/Santamarina
138 Limite

136 Cover of a brochure to promote X9, a political magazine. Black, white, grey and red. (BRA)
137 Card printed in azure blue and black. In text and with semaphore, the firm's annual summer holiday shut-down is announced. (SPA)
138 Cover of a brochure in full colour to publicize educative residential summer holidays at various institutions in the region around Florence. (ITA)
139 For the announcement of a lecture given by Dutch artist Braldt Bralds. (USA)

136 Umschlag einer Werbebroschüre für die politische Zeitschrift X9. In Schwarz, Weiss und Grau, mit rotem «Schuss». (BRA)
137 Azurblau und schwarz bedruckte Karte, mit der eine spanische Druckerei ihre Sommerferien bekanntgibt – auch mit dem in der Seefahrt verwendeten Winkeralphabet. (SPA)
138 Farbige Informationsbroschüre zu schulischen Möglichkeiten in der Region Florenz. (ITA)
139 Für die Ankündigung eines Vortrags des holländischen Künstlers Braldt Bralds. (USA)

136 Couverture d'une brochure publicitaire pour le magazine politique X9. En noir, blanc et gris, le coup de feu est en rouge. (BRA)
137 Sur cette carte imprimée en bleu azur et noir, une imprimerie espagnole annonce ses vacances d'été – avec les signaux à bras utilisés par les navigateurs. (SPA)
138 Brochure d'informations polychrome sur les écoles de la région de Florence. (ITA)
139 Pour l'annonce d'une conférence de l'artiste hollandais Braldt Bralds. (USA)

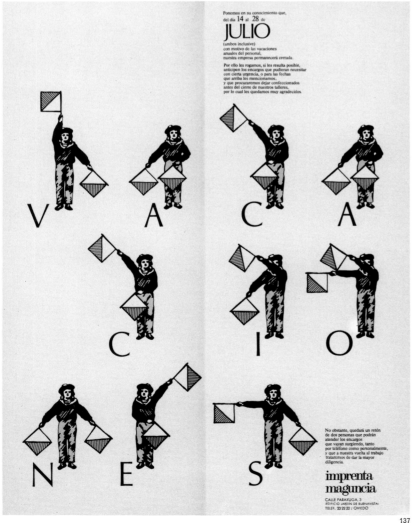

140

141

143

Delacorte Theater/Central Park Summer 1985

142

ARTIST / KÜNSTLER / ARTISTE:

141, 142 Paul Davis
143 Luis Trimano
144, 145 Fritz Dommel

DESIGNER / GESTALTER / MAQUETTISTE:

140 Liza Feraldis
141, 142 Paul Davis/Jose Conde
143 Luis Trimano
144, 145 Fritz Dommel

ART DIRECTOR / DIRECTEUR ARTISTIQUE:

140 Agni Katzourakis
141, 142 Paul Davis
143 Gil López
144, 145 Fritz Dommel

AGENCY / AGENTUR / AGENCE – STUDIO:

140 A & M Katzourakis
141, 142 Paul Davis Studio
143 Showbras

140 Covers of various information brochures for the Museum of Cycladic and Ancient Greek Art/Goulandris Foundation. (GRE)
141, 142 Mailer to announce the 30th Anniversary of Free Shakespeare in Central Park; opened as small-format poster and closed, with detail of the illustration portraying William Shakespeare and Charles Dickens. (USA)
143 Double spread from the 1985 programme for the Free Jazz Festival in São Paulo and Rio de Janeiro. (BRA)
144, 145 Recto and verso of a folded brochure announcing the Munich October Festival which celebrated its 175th anniversary in 1985. In bright colours, with border in blue. (GER)

140 Umschläge diverser Informationsbroschüren des Athener Museums für kykladische und alte griechische Kunst. (GRE)
141, 142 Mit der Post versandte Ankündigung des 30. New York Shakespeare Festival, offen (als Kleinplakat) und gefaltet, mit einem Ausschnitt der Illustration, die William Shakespeare und Charles Dickens zeigt. (USA)
143 Doppelseite aus dem Programmheft 1985 für das Free Jazz Festival in São Paulo und Rio de Janeiro. (BRA)
144, 145 Vorder- und Rückseite einer Falzbroschüre zum Münchner Oktoberfest, das 1985 sein 175jähriges Bestehen feierte. In bunten Farben, mit blauem Rand. (GER)

140 Couvertures de diverses brochures d'informations du Musée d'art cycladique et préhellénique d'Athènes. (GRE)
141, 142 Annonce envoyée par la poste pour le 30e New York Shakespeare Festival. Dépliée, elle forme une affichette; pliée, on ne voit qu'un détail de l'illustration qui représente Shakespeare et Charles Dickens. (USA)
143 Doubles pages du programme 1985 du Free Jazz Festival de São Paulo et Rio de Janeiro. (BRA)
144, 145 Recto et verso d'un dépliant sur la Fête de la bière de Munich dont on fêtait le 175e anniversaire en 1985. Couleurs vives et cadre bleu. (GER)

Oktoberfest München

21.9. – 6.10.1985

144

Überreicht durch:

Herausgegeben vom Fremdenverkehrsamt der Landeshauptstadt München.
Grafik u. Titelseite: Fritz Dommel, Betheln
Satz: SchumacherGebler, München
Druck: Ziele Druck, München
Printed in Fed. Rep. of Germany – Imprimé en Allemagne
5.85 – 280'd-80'DB

D

145

Resorts and Classic Hotels: At the turn of the century, as the 1800s climbed their way into the years before World War I, huge hotels grew at the favorite resorts known to Europe's royalty and wealthy. Many of these hotels have held onto their time-honored traditions, continuing to maintain the elaborate interior design in spite of the fact that many of the craftsmen and their skills are slowly disappearing. Modern plumbing, lighting and heat have been added, but little has been sacrificed with traditional ambiance. Although some classic hotels now accept group tours, many continue to offer the elegant service for which European hotels are famous. Dress code is similar to that for the luxury lodgings, since many of these properties are among Europe's best.

Although blue jeans may be acceptable for sport, they should be designer style. Elegant boutiques set the clothing style.

First Class Hotels include some of the older hotels that exhibit high standards of service, and most of the new ones whose very new-ness precludes a luxury status in the best European terms. Usually located in cities, bigger towns and the popular resorts, first class hotels that have been built in recent years have all the modern comforts that are found in the United States' chain hotels, and many that have yet to appear on American shores.

A private bath is a fact of life, as are a telephone, radio and other services. Since tour groups use these hotels, dress standards vary with the style of the group. Conservative dress is always acceptable.

The Spa Sensation: "Bad" is not bad, but "bod" and good. The word means "bath" in German, with a pronunciation that is akin to "bod" or "pod". It refers to "taking the waters", or a mineral bath, at a spa. With that bit of knowledge, it's safe to assume that all towns with "Bad" in the name – Baden, Badgastein, Bad Kleinkirchheim, Bad Tolz, Bad Ragaz, Bad Reichenhall, and the others – are, or were, popular spas at some time in their history. Most have spa and sports facilities now.

Wise Americans are learning what Europeans have known for centuries: spas are special. The word comes from Belgium, where the town of Spa has been known as a place to take the waters since 1326, but the spa procedure, and the health-giving effects were known to the Romans – and before.

Spas come in several varieties. There are, of course, curative spas for serious illness and diseases, but there are also recreational spas, with focus on diet, exercise and general health. In fact, in many Alpine resorts there's a fine line, if there's any line at all, between curative spas and sport-focused resorts where the pools are filled with water from the springs.

For daily dressing, sport clothes will do. At the social spas, since evenings are elegant dress is also. It's wise to ask for guidelines from each specific spa.

Villas and Apartments: Many of the Alpine resort areas have clusters of apartments for rent, on a self-catering arrangement that gives you basic housekeeping facilities. In some cases, bed linen is supplied as are cooking utensils and tableware, but it's wise to inquire. Although some people bring favorite touchstones from home, I prefer to buy local when needed. There's always some "stock up" place nearby. Always inquire about exactly

146

147

ARTIST / KÜNSTLER / ARTISTE:

149, 150 J. L. Lejeune
151, 152 Mike Schwab/Bill Vuksanovich/Holly Thomas

DESIGNER / GESTALTER / MAQUETTISTE:

146–148 Heinz Looser
151, 152 Robert Qually

ART DIRECTOR / DIRECTEUR ARTISTIQUE:

149, 150 Didier Moens
151, 152 Robert Qually

AGENCY / AGENTUR / AGENCE – STUDIO:

149, 150 Partner SSCW
151, 152 Qually & Co., Inc.

146–148 Complete cover and double spreads from a brochure/guide to hotels, resorts, spas, inns and other lodgings in the alpine regions of five countries. (SWI)
149, 150 "Get ahead of the crowd—win the lottery." Two automobile decals, each with the "winning" animal in strong relief, as direct advertising for the Belgian State Lottery. (BEL)
151, 152 Cover and double spread from a brochure for *Railvest*. A golden stake symbolizes intermodal goods transportation—the unity of rail and road for shipments. Cover in black and ochre, with gold-foil stake, on white stock. (USA)

146–148 Vollständiger Umschlag und Doppelseiten aus einer Broschüre über versteckte Plätzchen und elegante Zufluchtsorte in den Alpen. (SWI)
149, 150 «Setzen Sie sich von der Herde ab, gewinnen Sie im Lotto.» Direktwerbung für die belgische Lotterie, wobei jeweils ein Tier farbig als Relief erscheint. (BEL)
151, 152 Umschlag und Doppelseite aus einer Broschüre für *Railvest*-Bahnfracht. Der Nagel, Goldfolie geprägt, symbolisiert die Verbindung von Strasse und Schiene. (USA)

146–148 Couverture complète et doubles pages tirées d'une brochure sur les petits coins peu fréquentés et les lieux de villégiature élégants des Alpes. (SWI)
149, 150 Publicité directe en faveur de la loterie belge; chacune des illustrations représente l'animal «gagnant» en relief, en jaune et en bleu. (BEL)
151, 152 Couverture et double page d'une brochure pour les transports ferroviaires *Railvest*. Fig. 151: le clou, gaufré or, symbolise la conjonction toujours plus grande entre rail et route; fig. 152: présentation du bilan 1980 et progression escomptée jusqu'en 1990. (USA)

The $7.6 billion stake

151

resort areas, where winter skiing started a growth that now includes a summer hiking and walking season, are Schladming, Zell am See, Altenmarkt, Oberndorf, Mayrhofen, Igls, and Zürs. The older resorts have several classic hotels, often with Tyrolean atmosphere and folk art as well as all the modern comforts.

Some hunting and fishing "lodges" with toney surroundings include the Sporthotel Alpenhof at Techendorf am Weissensee and the Hotel Schlosswirt at Dollach, both near Badgastein for fishing, and the Jagdhof Fuschl near Salzburg and the Jagdschloss Graf Recke in the hills at Wald im Oberpinzgau where hunting is popular sport.

First Class Hotels: In addition to the traditional, chalet-style hotels that can be found in almost every Alpine town and village, there are often other modern hotels that offer every comfort. Rooms may be small, by American standards, but they will be spotlessly clean. Most will have telephone and private bathroom. Some newer hotels seem to have sacrificed the traditional Alpine atmosphere in favor of modern trappings, but food is usually regional – and excellent.

The Spa Sensation: Badgastein is a leader, with a thermal pool at its elegant Elisabethpark; Kaiser Franz Josef's Bad Ischl has its Kurhotel Bad Ischl; and Schruns has its Kurhotel Montafon. All three are complete resorts, in addition to having curative springs and programs. There are several smaller spas, each with its speciality and each with its European following.

Villas and Apartments: Many resorts have self-catering units, sometimes in a block of a modern building and also in free-standing private houses. PEGO-Holiday Homes distributes a booklet with details on almost 500 "Austrian Chalets and Apartments". The tourist office has copies.

Alpine Inns and Small Hotels: Almost every village has its country inn, and most of them have at least one or two rooms for rent. Although inns in and near the resort areas and towns will be used to "foreigners", many of the small village inns cater mostly to their village clientele. That's true, even with some of the villages on side roads near the highspeed *Autobahnen*. *Romantik Hotels und Restaurants*, with head office in Germany, has several member properties in Austria, each of which surrounds you with comfort and history.

Farm Holidays: *Urlaub auf dem Bauernhof* is what the Austrians call their program of farm holidays, which is very popular with European visitors but not well known to most Americans. Many of the regions print detailed booklets, with pictures and facts about the various farms. Since most of the literature is printed *only in German*, it's important to have a working knowledge of the language, even if you are not fluent. Many of your farmer-hosts do not speak fluent English; vacationers should speak German, or be comfortable with no common language.

Alpine Huts and Mountain Hotels: The *Österreichischer Alpenverein*, ÖA, (Austrian Alpine Club) and the *Deutscher* (German) *Alpenverein* each maintain a chain of mountain huts throughout their shared Alpine area. Many of the hut-to-hut walks can be enjoyed by hikers as well as climbers. Members have first priority, members of other associations second, and others third. All persons at the hut will be accommodated, but beds with sheets and pillows are limited; others have mattress, blankets and bunk. In addition to the ÖA, there are five other Alpine clubs, all part of the *Verband alpiner Vereine Österreichs*, with head office at Bäckerstrasse 16, A-1010 Wien (Vienna).

149

148

150

1980		1990	
Intermodal Revenues in $Billions (Annual Rate)	1.0	Intermodal Revenues in $Billions (Annual Rate)	4.5
Intermodal Revenues in $Billions (Cumulative)	1.0	Intermodal Revenues in $Billions (Cumulative)	22.5
45' Roadrailer Fleet in Units	none	45' Roadrailer Fleet in Units	24,000
40' to 45' Unit Changeover	none	40' to 45' Unit Changeover	100,000
Boxcar to Trailer Conversions in Units	none	Boxcar to Trailer Conversions in Units	125,000
40' Trailer Fleet in Units	110,000	40' Trailer Fleet in Units	none
45' Trailer Fleet in Units	none	45'/48' Trailer Fleet in Units	250,000

▶Investment	Facilities	$1.0 billion
in	Tractors	$0.6 billion
$Billions	Trailers	$3.0 billion
by	Computer	$0.1 billion
1990	**Required Capital Outlay**	**$4.7 billion**
for		
Intermodal	Trailer Repair	$1.0 billion
	Lift Services	$0.9 billion
	Pick-up & Delivery Labor	$1.0 billion
	Required Service Outlay	**$2.9 billion**
	Total Investment	**$7.6 billion**

Just desserts for railroad intermodalism: a bigger piece of transportation pie. America's railroads have been losing market share to the trucking industry, for decades. In 1950, according to the Wall Street Journal, trucks hauled less than 23% of all truck and rail inter-city freight. By 1982, they were pulling more than 38% of it. While the growth of intermodal has not yet reversed this trend, it is slowing it dramatically. Intermodal shipments have grown to more than 12% of all railroad carloadings, up from 7% or 8% in the years from 1978 through 1981. In the recession year of 1982, while overall rail traffic was depressed 12%, intermodal actually grew 9.5%. In 1983, it grew an impressive 20%. This trend is expected to continue convincingly into the 90's, as significant increases are reported by one railroad CEO after another. For the two *largest* railroads, intermodal accounts for almost one-third of their total freight business, and is rapidly closing in on a full half of it. Figures this clear almost certainly comprise a leading indicator for other railroads as well. As demand for intermodal equipment and facilities mounts, it seems almost indisputable that a growth opportunity of unprecedented proportions is upon us. It will have a profound effect on every aspect of the freight transportation business: equipment, facilities, real estate, operations, marketing, personnel. Railvest projections for the balance of the decade, seen opposite, are based on careful evaluation of current equipment and financial data, coupled with probable extensions. For instance, all bulk and aggregate commodities are still projected to travel boxcar. Everything else will go intermodal. While no projection ever turns out perfect, it is clear that powerful and sustained growth of intermodalism is a fact of life. Thanks now to the Railvest initiative, corresponding — and also unprecedented — freight revenue opportunities await the railroads.

152

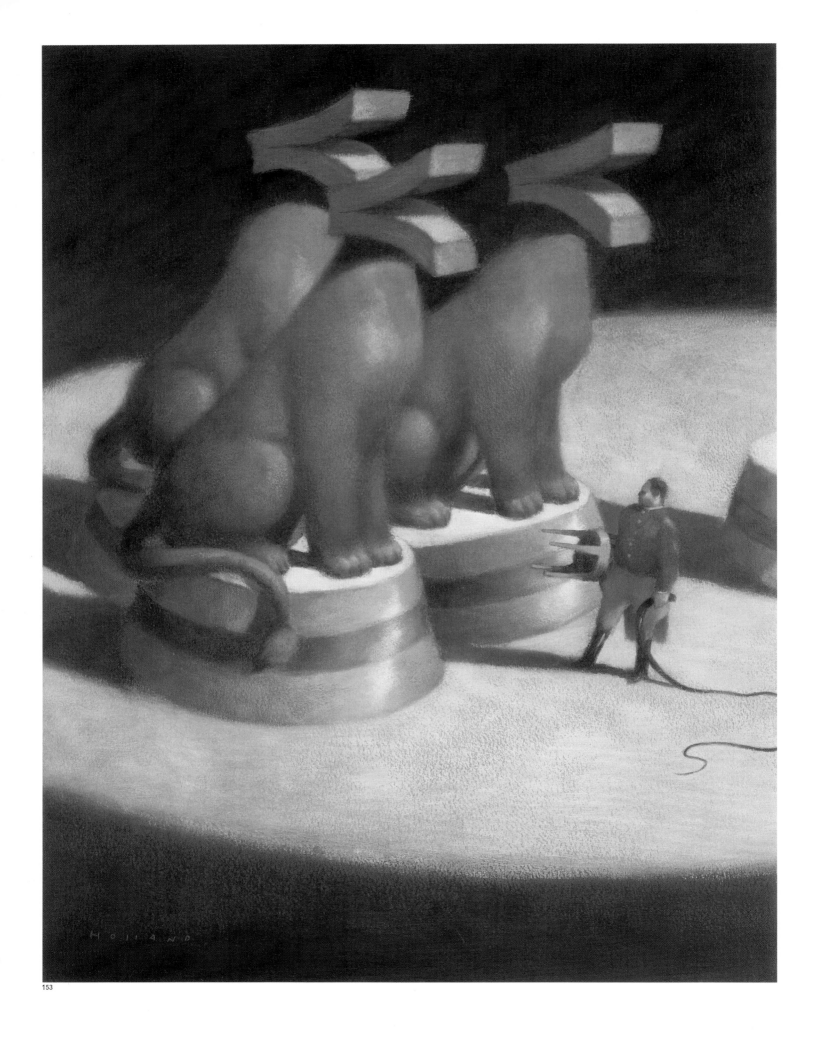

153

Booklets / Prospekte / Brochures

84

154

153, 154 Full-page illustration and double spread from a brochure for *Caddex*. The firm offers a compre-hensive systematic approach to technical documentation procedure. (USA)
155 Sleeve of an illustrated brochure with Longfellow's poem, as promotion for the Revere Press, printers. The cut-away star on the sleeve allows the blue brochure cover to be seen. (USA)
156, 157 Polychrome illustrations from a bank brochure dealing with investment management. (USA)

153, 154 Ganzseitige Illustration und Doppelseite aus einer Broschüre für *Caddex*. Thema sind die Kosten technischen Dokumentationsmaterials, die mit dem *Caddex*-System niedrig gehalten werden. (USA)
155 Karton mit teilweise ausgestanztem Stern, der einen Teil der darin enthaltenen Broschüre (mit blauem Umschlag) sichtbar werden lässt – Werbung für eine Druckerei, die sich nach dem amerikani-schen Patrioten Paul Revere benannt hat und hier seine Geschichte erzählt. (USA)
156, 157 Mehrfarbige Illustrationen aus einer Bank-Broschüre über Investitionen. (USA)

153, 154 Illustration pleine page et double page d'une brochure de *Caddex* traitant des frais de matériel de documentation technique qui, grâce au système *Caddex*, restent modiques. (USA)
155 Carton orné d'une étoile en partie qui laisse apparaître la brochure (à couverture bleue) qu'il renferme. Publicité d'une imprimerie qui porte le nom du patriote américain Paul Revere et dont on raconte ici l'histoire. (USA)
156, 157 Illustrations polychromes d'une brochure de banque sur les investissements. (USA)

155

ARTIST / KÜNSTLER / ARTISTE:

153, 154 Brad Holland
156, 157 Kurt Vargö

DESIGNER / GESTALTER / MAQUETTISTE:

153, 154 Chuck Pennington
155 Bernard Glassman
156, 157 David Broom / Rich Newman

ART DIRECTOR / DIRECTEUR ARTISTIQUE:

153, 154 Chuck Pennington
155 Bernard Glassman
156, 157 David Broom

AGENCY / AGENTUR / AGENCE – STUDIO:

153, 154 Cole & Webber
155 Kramer, Miller, Lomden, Glassman
156, 157 Broom & Broom

156

157

Wenn es die Eltern nicht können, wenn es der Kindergarten nicht vermag, ja, dann muß doch wohl Vater Staat... - wir wollen endlich auch die jüngste Elite schulen... - soll doch nicht schon im Kindesalter die Intelligenz verspielt werden!

158

ARTIST / KÜNSTLER / ARTISTE:

158 Eduard Prüssen
159 Guy Billout
162, 163 Charles Bush / Barry Fahr

DESIGNER / GESTALTER / MAQUETTISTE:

160 Earl Gee
161 Roberto Lanterio
162, 163 Barbara Vick

ART DIRECTOR / DIRECTEUR ARTISTIQUE:

160 Mark Anderson / Antony Milner
161 Roberto Lanterio
162, 163 Jerry Berman

AGENCY / AGENTUR / AGENCE – STUDIO:

160 Mark Anderson Design
162, 163 Sidjakov Berman & Gomez

158 From Eduard Prüssen's satirical house organ *Donkey Post*; the Ministry of Science suggests a project for highly-intelligent infants. (GER)
159 "Deluge." Illustration from *Squid & Spider*, a book written and illustrated by artist Guy Billout. Also used by him as self-promotion. (USA)
160 Three-dimensional-effect accordion folder for the *Pacific Gas and Electric* on the theme of alternative energy resources. (USA)
161 Accordion folder/guide for an IBM exhibition. (GER)
162, 163 Trompe-l'œil as on-site promotion for a new office building: here, complete view of the construction fence and a detail. (USA)

158 Aus Eduard Prüssens Hauszeitschrift *Donkey Post*: Das Modellprojekt des Bundeswissenschaftsministeriums für hochbegabte Kleinkinder. (GER)
159 «Sintflut.» Eigenwerbungskarte in Originalgrösse für Guy Billout. (USA)
160 Für *Pacific Gas and Electric* über alternative Energiequellen. (USA)
161 Leporelloartiger Führer durch eine IBM-Ausstellung. (GER)
162, 163 Trompe-l'œil als Werbung für The New Wilshire, ein neues Bürogebäude; hier die Gesamtansicht des Bauzauns und ein Detail daraus. (USA)

158 Tiré du magazine autopromotionnel d'Eduard Prüssen, *Donkey Post*: le projet pilote du Ministère des Sciences pour enfants surdoués. (GER)
159 «Déluge». Carte autopromotionnelle de Guy Billout. (USA)
160 Dépliant tridimensionnel en accordéon pour *Pacific Gas and Electric* concernant les sources d'énergie alternatives. (USA)
161 Guide d'une exposition IBM, à pliage accordéon. (GER)
162, 163 Publicité en trompe-l'œil pour The New Wilshire, un nouveau bâtiment de bureaux; vue d'ensemble de la palissade et détail. (USA)

159

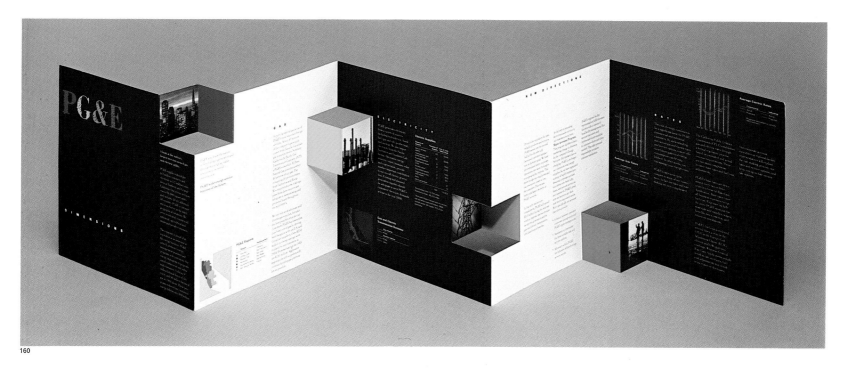

160

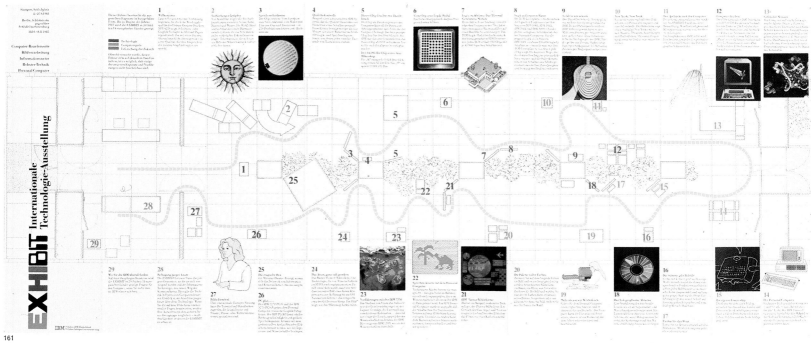

161

162

163

164

ARTIST / KÜNSTLER / ARTISTE:

164–167 Lonni Sue Johnson
168, 169 Susan Hunt Yule
170 Franco Del Rosso

DESIGNER / GESTALTER / MAQUETTISTE:

164–167 Rosemarie Kowalski
170 Claudio Getto

ART DIRECTOR / DIRECTEUR ARTISTIQUE:

164–167 Rosemarie Kowalski
168, 169 Nick Chavin/Lanny Lambert
170 Franco Del Rosso

AGENCY / AGENTUR / AGENCE – STUDIO:

168, 169 Newmark Posner & Mitchell
170 Armando Testa SpA

168

164–167 Three illustrations (Fig. 164 in actual size) and front cover of a graduate programme for the College of Computer Science at Northeastern University. All illustrations are in full colour. (USA)
168, 169 Closed and opened out promotional brochures for the sale of apartments. The polychrome plan shows the surrounding neighbourhood. (USA)
170 Black-and-white cover as example from a series of uniformly designed prospectuses for the holding company of the Banca Nazionale del Lavoro. (ITA)

164–167 Drei Illustrationen (Abb. 164 in Originalgrösse) und Umschlagvorderseite einer Broschüre des College für Computer-Wissenschaft der Northeastern University. Alle Illustrationen sind mehrfarbig. (USA)
168, 169 Zusammen- und auseinandergefaltete Broschüre für den Verkauf von Eigentumswohnungen. Der mehrfarbige Plan zeigt die Umgebung des Gebäudes in Manhattan. (USA)
170 Schwarzweisser Umschlag als Beispiel für eine Reihe von einheitlich gestalteten Prospekten der Holding-Gesellschaft der Banca Nazionale del Lavoro. (ITA)

164–167 Trois illustrations (fig. 164 grandeur nature) et recto de la couverture d'une brochure du collège d'électronique de la Northeastern University. Toutes les illustrations sont polychromes. (USA)
168, 169 Brochure pliée et dépliée pour la vente de logements en copropriété. Le plan en couleurs montre l'environnement du bâtiment. (USA)
170 Couverture en noir et blanc d'un prospectus faisant partie d'une série standard publiée par le holding de la Banca Nazionale del Lavoro. (ITA)

Booklets / Prospekte / Brochures

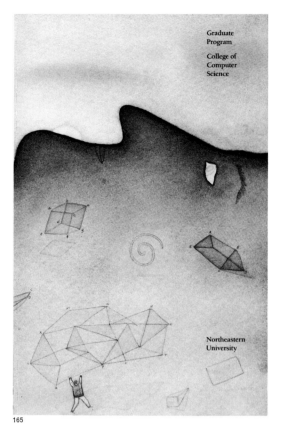

165

Graduate
Program

College
of
Computer
Science

Northeastern
University

166

167

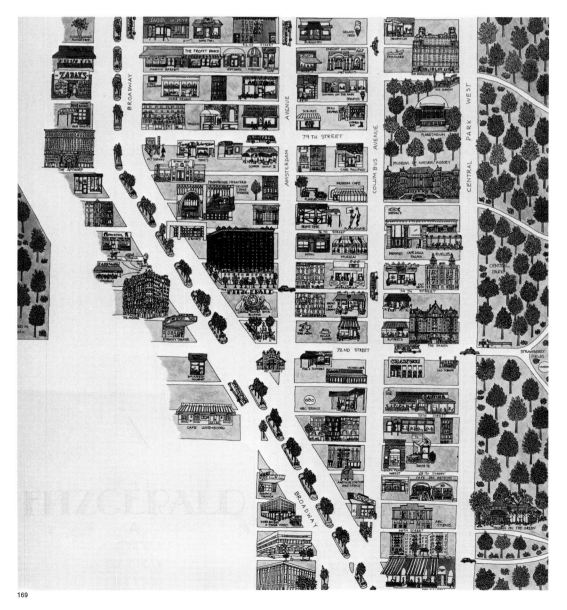

169

170

171

172

173

174

175

176

Booklets / Prospekte / Brochures

171, 172 Three-dimensional invitation card (raised and folded) for the opening of a golf club. Checked blue and green (centre square wine red), text white. (USA)
173, 174 Double spreads from a small manifesto of the Belgian communist party. Linocut illustrations. (BEL)
175, 176 Double spreads, each showing two paper qualities, from a brochure for *Hopper* papers. Fig. 175: Bristol F 2 B fighter planes, in colour; Fig. 176: aviation plaque in colour; black planes on blue stock. (USA)
177 Illustration in actual size from a brochure for a reinsurance company. (USA)
178 Double spread from a brochure issued by *Montefluos* for the grease solvent/cleaner *Delifrene*. (ITA)

171, 172 Geöffnete und zusammengefaltete, dreidimensionale Einladungskarte zur Eröffnung eines Golf-Clubs. Quadrate in Blau, Grün, Rot und Weiss. (USA)
173, 174 Doppelseiten mit Linolschnitten aus einer Broschüre der kommunistischen Partei Belgiens. Schwarzweiss mit Rot. (BEL)
175, 176 Doppelseiten, jeweils in zwei Papierqualitäten, aus einer Broschüre für den Papierhersteller *Hopper*. Abb. 175: Mehrfarbige Kampfflugzeuge; Abb. 176: Plakette mehrfarbig, Modelle schwarz. (USA)
177 Illustration in Originalgrösse aus der Broschüre einer Rückversicherungsgesellschaft. (USA)
178 Doppelseite aus einer Broschüre von *Montefluos* für das Lösungsmittel *Delifrene*. (ITA)

171, 172 Carte tridimensionelle ouverte et pliée invitant à l'ouverture d'un club de golf. Carrés bleus, verts, une fois rouge et blanc. (USA)
173, 174 Doubles pages d'une brochure du Parti communiste belge. Gravures sur linol. (BEL)
175, 176 Doubles pages, d'une qualité de papier différente, d'une brochure du fabricant de papier *Hopper*. Fig. 175: avion de combat polychrome. Fig. 176: plaquette polychrome, modèles noir. (USA)
177 Illustration grandeur nature de la brochure d'une compagnie de réassurance. (USA)
178 Double page d'une brochure de *Montefluos* pour le solvant universel *Delifrene*. (ITA)

177

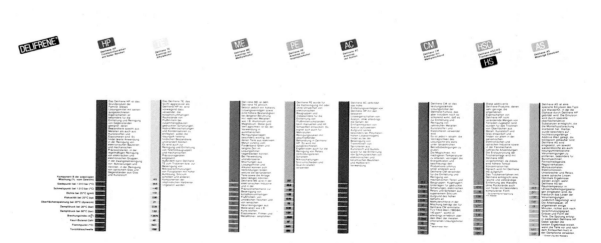

178

ARTIST / KÜNSTLER / ARTISTE:

173, 174 Philippe Deltour
175, 176 John Barchellor
177 Richard Hess

DESIGNER / GESTALTER / MAQUETTISTE:

171, 172 Dave Shelton
173, 174 Philippe Deltour
175, 176 B. Martin Pedersen
178 Christina Gastaldello

ART DIRECTOR / DIRECTEUR ARTISTIQUE:

171, 172 Richard Foy
175, 176 B. Martin Pedersen/Adrian Pulfer
177 Richard Hess
178 Ettore Michele Sguera

AGENCY / AGENTUR / AGENCE – STUDIO:

171, 172 Communication Arts Inc.
173, 174 Bitume S. C.
175, 176 Jonson Pedersen Hinrichs & Shakery
178 BGT

Booklets / Prospekte / Brochures

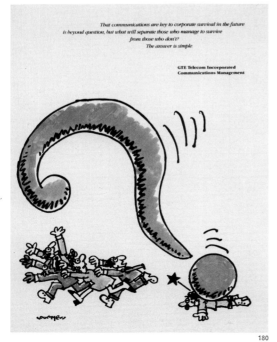

182a

182

ARTIST / KÜNSTLER / ARTISTE:

179 Kazumasa Nagai
180, 181 Lou Myers
182, 182a Brian Bourke
183 Ferenc Pintér

DESIGNER / GESTALTER / MAQUETTISTE:

179 Kazumasa Nagai
180, 181 Diane J. McNamee
182, 182a Tony O'Hanlon

ART DIRECTOR / DIRECTEUR ARTISTIQUE:

179 Kazumasa Nagai
180, 181 Frank C Lionetti
182, 182a Tony O'Hanlon
183 Daniele Baroni

AGENCY / AGENTUR / AGENCE – STUDIO:

179 Nippon Design Center
180, 181 Frank C Lionetti Design Inc.
182, 182a Kilkenny Design

179 Complete brochure cover for the 1986 Store Automation Show in Japan. (JPN)
180, 181 Cover (fuchsia question mark) and double spread from a portfolio in which *GTE Telecom* offers its services in communications management. (USA)
182, 182a James Joyce portrayed by Irish artist Brian Bourke, and cover from his exhibition catalogue. (IRL)
183 Illustration on double spread (mainly in grey, blue and white tones with yellow) from a booklet for the petrochemicals/resins/fibres company *Montedison*. (ITA)

179 Vollständiger Broschürenumschlag für eine Automaten-Ausstellung in Japan. (JPN)
180, 181 Umschlag und Doppelseite einer Werbemappe, mit der *GTE Telecom* ihre Dienste auf dem Gebiet der Telekommunikation anbietet. (USA)
182, 182a Ein Porträt von James Joyce und Umschlag eines Ausstellungskatalogs für Brian Bourke. (IRL)
183 Doppelseitige Illustration (vorwiegend in Grau-, Blau- und Weisstönen mit Gelb) aus einem Prospekt für *Montedison*. Hier für die Bereiche der chemischen Produkte, Reinigungsmittel und Glasherstellung. (ITA)

179 Couverture complète de la brochure d'une exposition d'automatisation au Japon. (JPN)
180, 181 Couverture et double page d'un portfolio dans lequel *GTE Telecom* offre ses services en matière de télécommunications. (USA)
182, 182a Portrait de James Joyce et couverture d'un catalogue d'exposition de l'artiste Brian Bourke. (IRL)
183 Illustration sur double page (tons prédominants: gris, bleu, blanc et jaune) tirée d'un prospectus de l'entreprise *Montedison*. Ici, pour trois domaines. (ITA)

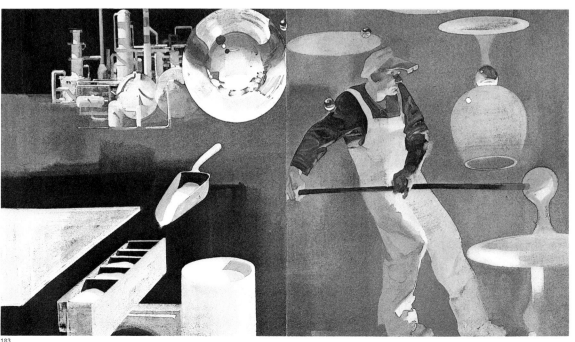

183

184

185

Booklets / Prospekte / Brochures

DESIGNER / GESTALTER / MAQUETTISTE:

184 Paul Rand
185 Takaaki Matsumoto/Chris Mathan
186, 187, 189, 190 Takaaki Matsumoto
188 Carrie Berman

ART DIRECTOR / DIRECTEUR ARTISTIQUE:

184 Paul Rand
185–187, 189, 190 Harold Matossian/
    Takaaki Matsumoto
188 Harold Matossian

AGENCY / AGENTUR / AGENCE – STUDIO:

184 IBM Corporation
185–190 Knoll Graphics

186

184 Cover of an IBM brochure about the graphic use of the IBM logo. (USA)
185 Cover of the *Knoll* textiles catalogue, with price list and specifications. (USA)
186–190 Announcements and invitations in standardized format by *Knoll*. Fig.186: invitation to a "Post Neocon" presentation at the Knoll Design Center. Letters in diverse colours, on white; Fig.187: diskette as invitation to a seminar about office automation; Fig.188: change-of-address card in yellow, green and red on white; Figs.189, 190: envelope containing a cut-out *Venturi* chair poster as invitation—the latter shown in Fig.190 opened out. (USA)

184 Umschlag einer IBM-Broschüre über die graphische Anwendung des IBM-Schriftzugs. (USA)
185 Umschlag eines *Knoll*-Katalogs für Textilien, mit Preislisten und Spezifikationen. (USA)
186–190 In einheitlichem Format gestaltete Einladungen und Ankündigungen von *Knoll*. Abb.186: Einladung zu einer «Post-Neocon»-Präsentation im Knoll Design Center, Text mehrfarbig auf Weiss; Abb.187: Diskette als Einladung zu einem Seminar über Büro-Automatisation; Abb.188: Adressänderungskarte in Gelb, Grün und Rot auf Weiss; Abb.189, 190: Umschlag mit gefalteter Einladung – ein ausgestanztes *Venturi*-Stuhl-Plakat, das in Abb.190 ungefaltet gezeigt ist. (USA)

184 Couverture d'une brochure IBM sur l'utilisation graphique du logo IBM. (USA)
185 Couverture d'un catalogue *Knoll* de textiles, avec liste de prix et spécifications. (USA)
186–190 Invitations et annonces de *Knoll* réalisées dans un format standard. Fig.186: invitation à une présentation «Post-Neocon» au Knoll Design Center, texte polychrome sur fond blanc. Fig.187: disquette d'invitation à un séminaire sur l'automatisation des bureaux. Fig.188: carte de changement d'adresse jaune, vert, rouge sur blanc. Fig.189, 190: enveloppe et invitation pliée – l'affiche découpée du siège *Venturi*, dépliée en fig.190. (USA)

187

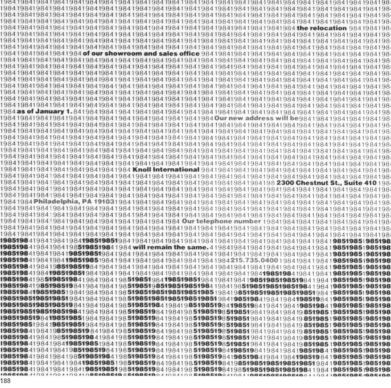

188

189

190

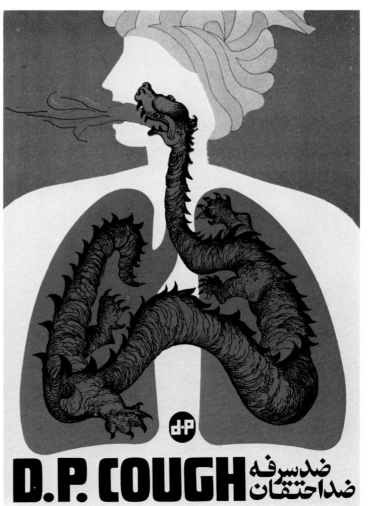

Infecciones respiratorias agudas

191 Cover of a booklet on the therapeutic agent/antibiotic *Eupen* (for treating respiratory infections). Head in pencil, paw in gold-brown with black. (SPA)
192 An educative game on the subject of the alimentary canal as promotion for the packaging producer *Elopak*. Mainly in brown, green and yellow tones. (ITA)
193 Cover of a prospectus for a cough mixture. Red, green and ochre. (IRN)
194, 195 Illustrations for booklets about the anti-depressive drug *Lithobid*. (USA)
196 Cover of a brochure for a medicament used in healing wounds. (IRN)

191 Vorderseite eines Prospektes für das Medikament *Eupen* gegen Infektionen der Atemwege. Tatze in Hellbraun mit Schwarz, sonst schwarzweiss. (SPA)
192 In Form eines Spiels gestaltete Werbung für den Verpackungshersteller *Elopak*. Thema ist die Nahrungsmittelaufnahme des Menschen. Vorwiegend braun, grün und gelb. (ITA)
193 Vorderseite eines Prospektes für ein Hustenmittel. Rot, Grün und Ocker. (IRN)
194, 195 Illustrationen für Prospekte über das Anti-Depressivum *Lithobid*. (USA)
196 Vorderseite eines Prospekts für ein Wundbehandlungsmittel. Braun, Gelb, Weiss. (IRN)

191 Première page d'un prospectus pour *Eupen*, un médicament contre les infections des voies respiratoires. En noir et blanc, patte brun clair et noir. (SPA)
192 Publicité conçue sous forme de jeu pour le fabricant d'emballages *Elopak*. Elle a pour sujet la digestion chez l'homme. Prédominance de brun, vert et jaune. (ITA)
193 Recto d'un prospectus pour un remède contre la toux. Rouge, vert, ocre. (IRN)
194, 195 Illustrations de prospectus sur l'antidépressif *Lithobid*. (USA)
196 Première page d'un prospectus pour un cicatrisant. Brun, jaune, blanc. (IRN)

191

192

193

194

195

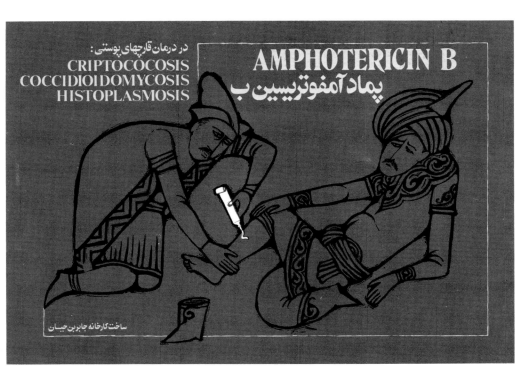

196

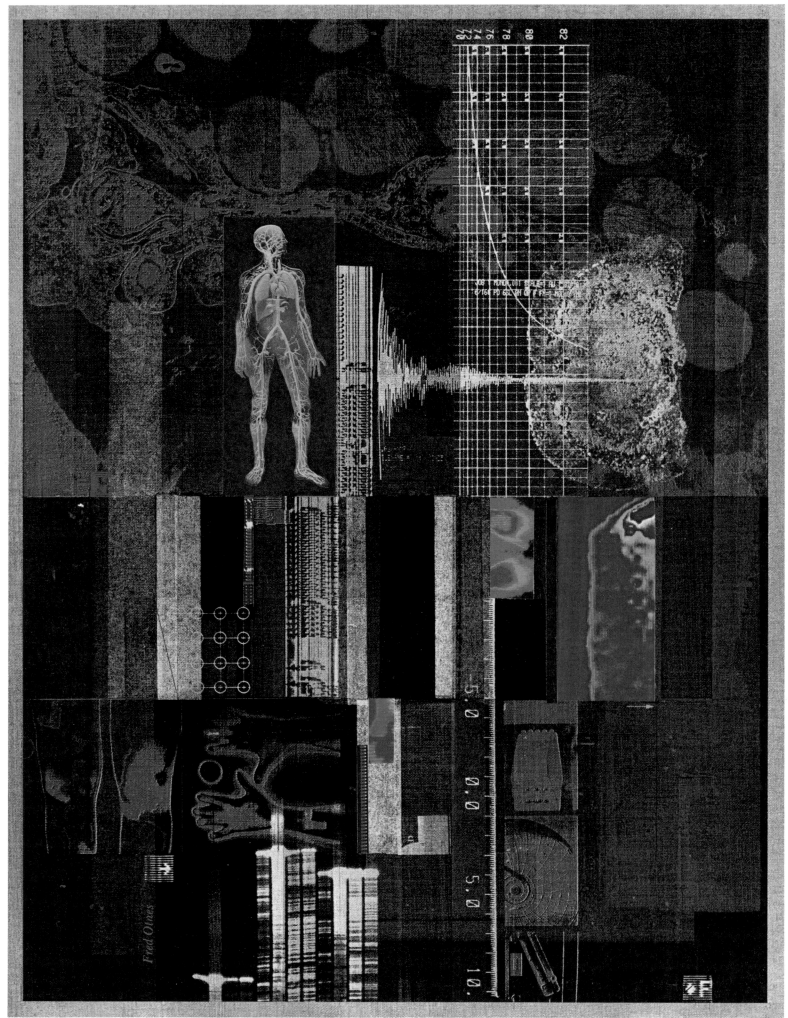

Fred Oines

197 Full-page illustration (in about actual size) from a brochure for a pharmaceutical company. (USA)

198, 199 Pop-up card with "movable" hand, shown in closed and open position, for *Digital*, reminding their customers that the first year's free service is over and encouraging them to take a personal computer service agreement. In predominantly beige-pink tones, with black, green, maroon. (GBR)

200, 201 Complete double spreads from a brochure "Making the News Travel Faster" for the Swiss publishers and printers *Ringier*; here emphasizing international distribution and satellite information transmission. (USA)

197 Ganzseitige Illustration (ungefähr in Originalgrösse) aus der Broschüre eines pharmazeutischen Unternehmens. (USA)

198, 199 Farbiger Pop-up-Steller mit beweglicher Hand, in geschlossener und geöffneter Position, mit dem *Digital* ihre Kunden an die Wiedererneuerung des Service-Abonnements für Personal Computer erinnert, damit sie nicht zur traditionellen Arbeitsmethode zurückkehren müssen. (GBR)

200, 201 Vollständige Doppelseiten aus einer Broschüre des schweizerischen Presse- und Druckhauses *Ringier*, welches hiermit für seine schnelle, weltweite Übermittlung des gedruckten Worts oder Bilds per Satellit wirbt. Titel der Broschüre: «Damit Nachrichten schneller zirkulieren.» (USA)

197 Illustration pleine page (presque grandeur nature) de la brochure d'une entreprise pharmaceutique. (USA)

198, 199 Carte en couleurs avec élément amovible, présentée fermée et ouverte: la maison *Digital* rappelle ainsi à ses clients le renouvellement du service d'abonnements pour ordinateurs personnels, de sorte qu'ils ne reviennent pas à des méthodes de travail traditionnelles. (GBR)

200, 201 Doubles pages complètes figurant dans une brochure publiée par la maison d'éditions suisse *Ringier*: elle y fait de la publicité pour son système de retransmission du mot imprimé ou de l'image par satellite, methode rapide et universelle. Titre de la brochure: «Afin que les nouvelles circulent plus vite.» (USA)

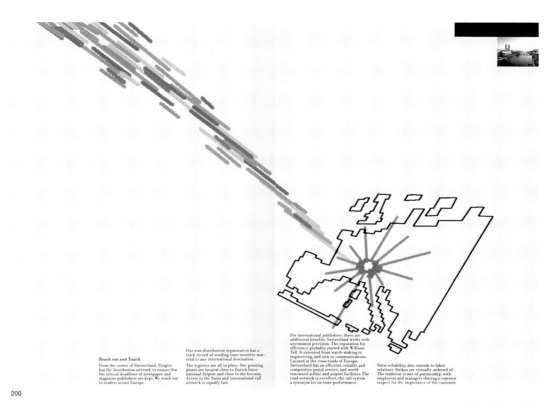

200

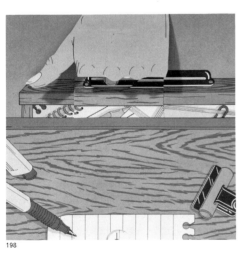

198

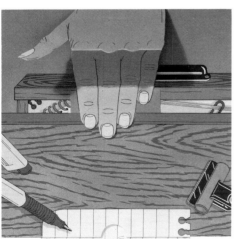

199

ARTIST / KÜNSTLER / ARTISTE:

197 Fred Otnes
198, 199 Debbie Cook

DESIGNER / GESTALTER / MAQUETTISTE:

197 James Hatch
198, 199 Alan Herron
200, 201 F. Gottschalk / F. Burbach

ART DIRECTOR / DIRECTEUR ARTISTIQUE:

198, 199 Jackie Vicary
200, 201 Gottschalk & Ash Int'l

AGENCY / AGENTUR / AGENCE – STUDIO:

197 Corporate Graphics
198, 199 Michael Peters Group PLC
200, 201 Gottschalk & Ash Int'l

Booklets / Prospekte / Brochures

A CELEBRATION OF JAMES BEARD
June 3, 1985

MILTON GLASER

202

ARTIST / KÜNSTLER / ARTISTE:

202 Milton Glaser
203, 204 Sabine Schroer
205, 206 Kurt Wirth

DESIGNER / GESTALTER / MAQUETTISTE:

202 Milton Glaser

ART DIRECTOR / DIRECTEUR ARTISTIQUE:

202 Milton Glaser
203–206 Fritz Girardin

AGENCY / AGENTUR / AGENCE – STUDIO:

202 Milton Glaser, Inc.

100

203

204

Booklets / Prospekte / Brochures

202 Cover of a brochure for Seagram Classic Wine Co. in honour of James Beard, American culinary expert and initiator of Citymeals-on-Wheels for New York's elderly. (USA)
203–206 Illustrations for three different *Swissair* menu series—an integral part of this airline's corporate identity programme. Fig. 205 was used on a title page. (SWI)

202 Umschlag einer Broschüre der Seagram Classic Wine Company zu Ehren von James Beard, dem Initiator des fahrenden Mahlzeiten-Dienstes für alte Menschen in New York. In Farbe. (USA)
203–206 Beispiele von Illustrationen für drei verschiedene *Swissair*-Menu-Serien, die zum Corporate-Identity-Programm dieser Fluglinie gehören. Abb. 205 wurde für ein Titelblatt verwendet. (SWI)

202 Couverture d'une brochure de la Seagram Classic Wine Company en hommage à James Beard, le promoteur du service de repas ambulant pour les pauvres à New York. En couleurs. (USA)
203–206 Exemples d'illustrations de trois séries de menus pour la *Swissair* qui contribuent à l'image de marque de cette compagnie aérienne. La fig. 205 a servi de page de titre. (SWI)

205

206

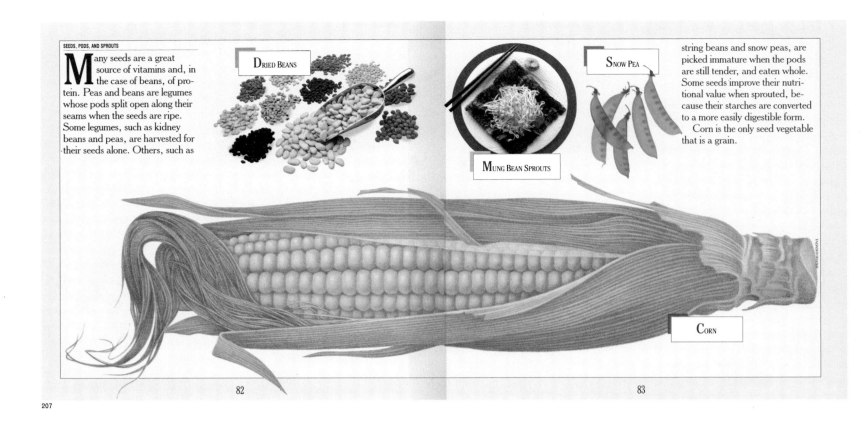

Many seeds are a great source of vitamins and, in the case of beans, of protein. Peas and beans are legumes whose pods split open along their seams when the seeds are ripe. Some legumes, such as kidney beans and peas, are harvested for their seeds alone. Others, such as

string beans and snow peas, are picked immature when the pods are still tender, and eaten whole. Some seeds improve their nutritional value when sprouted, because their starches are converted to a more easily digestible form.

Corn is the only seed vegetable that is a grain.

DRIED BEANS

SNOW PEA

MUNG BEAN SPROUTS

CORN

82   83

207

Booklets / Prospekte / Brochures

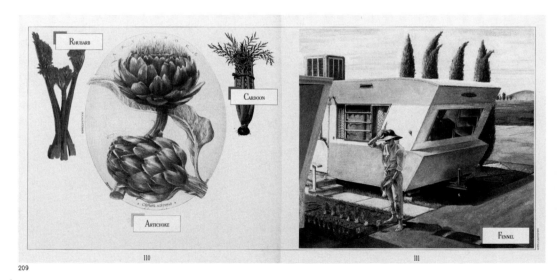

RHUBARB

CARDOON

ARTICHOKE

FENNEL

110   111

209

207–212 Double spreads from a lively "encyclopaedia" entitled *Vegetables*. Figs. 207–209 belong to the colourful section with the title "Visual Vegetables", which combines illustrations and photographs of the various vegetables. Figs. 210 and 211 are from an informative chapter: "Vegetables A to Z", which gives the origin, characteristics and nutritional value, as well as many hints and comments. Illustrations in violet on cream ground, text brown-grey and red, border and spots in pale sage-green. Fig. 212 is from the last chapter, on recipes, here for soups and salads. The title spots are red, the small spots are pale sage-green, the text is violet and brown-grey, the background is écru and the border is cream. (USA)

207–212 Doppelseiten aus einer Publikation mit dem Titel «Gemüse». Abb. 207–209 gehören zum farbenfrohen Bildteil, der aus graphischen und photographischen Illustrationen besteht und den verschiedenen Gemüsearten gewidmet ist. Abb. 210 und 211 stammen aus einem Kapitel mit Informationen über die Herkunft, Geschichte, Eigenschaften, Nährwerte und Erntezeiten verschiedener Gemüse, die in alphabetischer Reihenfolge aufgeführt werden. Illustrationen in Blaugrau auf cremefarbenem Grund, Schrift braungrau und rot, Umrandung in hellem Grün. Abb. 212 gehört zu einem Kapitel mit Rezepten, hier für Suppen und Salate. Die Illustrationen sind rot, die Schrift ist blaugrau und braungrau, der Hintergrund écru, die Umrandung in hellem Gelb. (USA)

207–212 Doubles pages d'une publication intitulée «Légumes». Les fig. 207–209 font partie de la section consacrée aux diverses sortes de légumes et illustrée de dessins et de photographies aux couleurs vives. Les fig. 210 et 211 proviennent d'un chapitre où sont rassemblées des informations sur la provenance, l'histoire, les particularités, les valeurs nutritives et les saisons de récoltes des divers légumes, énumérés par ordre alphabétique. Illustrations gris-bleu sur fond crème, texte gris-brun et rouge, cadre vert clair. La fig. 212 fait partie d'un chapitre sur les recettes, ici des soupes et des salades. Illustrations rouges, texte gris-bleu et gris-brun, fond écru, cadre jaune clair. (USA)

44   45

210

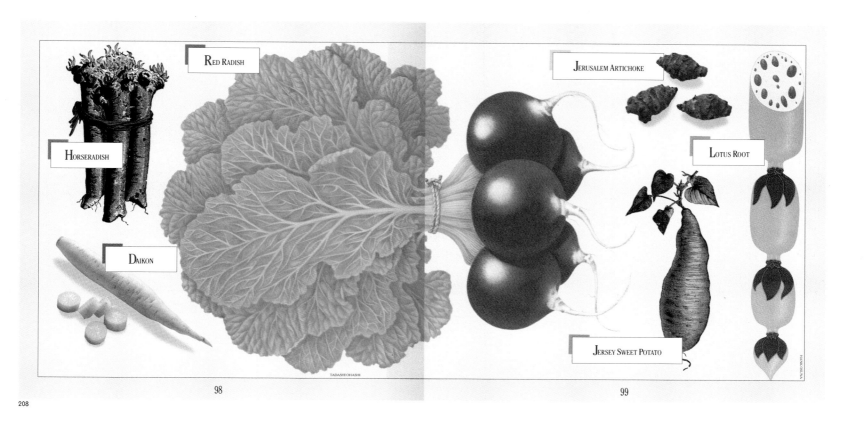

208

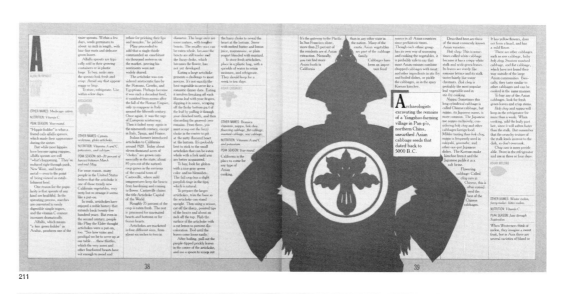

211

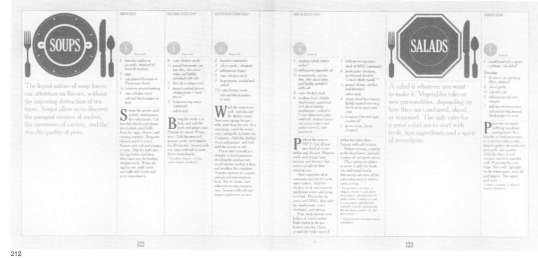

212

ARTIST / KÜNSTLER / ARTISTE:

207 Tadashi Ohashi
208 Tadashi Ohashi/Hank Osuna
209 Dugald Stermer/David Stevenson

DESIGNER / GESTALTER / MAQUETTISTE:

207–212 Kit Hinrichs/Lenore Bartz/D.J. Hyde

ART DIRECTOR / DIRECTEUR ARTISTIQUE:

207–212 Kit Hinrichs

AGENCY / AGENTUR / AGENCE – STUDIO:

207–212 Jonson Pedersen Hinrichs & Shakery

213

214

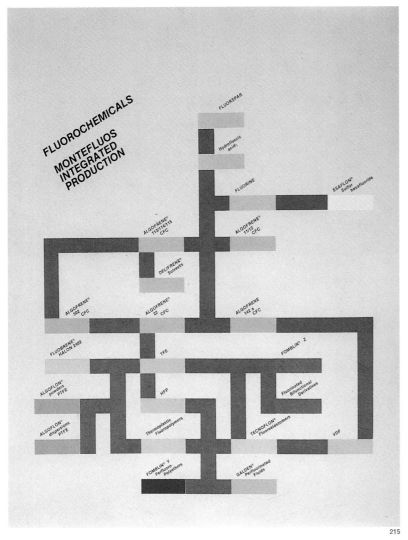

215

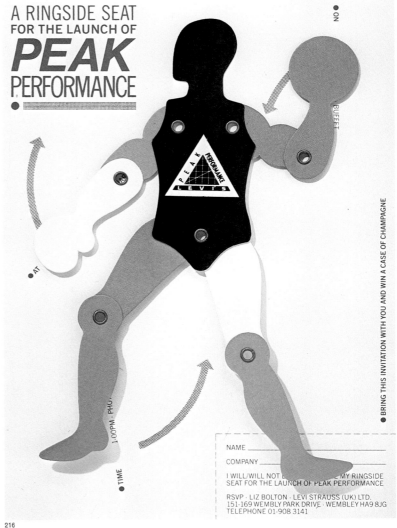

216

Booklets / Prospekte / Brochures

ARTIST / KÜNSTLER / ARTISTE:

213, 214 Paul Wollman/Al Fisher (Photo)
217 Maurizio Tacqui

DESIGNER / GESTALTER / MAQUETTISTE:

213, 214 Mark Kent
215 Christina Gastaldello
216 Roger Bannister

ART DIRECTOR / DIRECTEUR ARTISTIQUE:

213, 214 Mark Kent
215 Ettore Michele Sguera
216 Rod Springett
217 Roberto Borioli

AGENCY / AGENTUR / AGENCE – STUDIO:

213, 214 Cipriani Advertising, Inc.
215 BGT
216 Springett Associates
217 Borioli & C.

213, 214 Cover illustration in actual size and spread from a catalogue for the spring collection of men's footwear by *Cole-Haan*. The illustration, "La Playa", also serves as backdrop, sectionwise (as Fig. 214) for the presentation pages and the theme of "casual elegance". (USA)
215 Page from a brochure about chemicals from *Montefluos*. (ITA)
216 Invitation to a presentation of sportswear by *Levi Strauss* at a boxing club. (GBR)
217 Detail of the illustration on a brochure cover for an NCR training programme. "Fertile ground on which to raise your ambitions." NCR as green oasis (blue water) in the desert. (ITA)

213, 214 Umschlagillustration in Originalgrösse und Doppelseite aus einem Katalog für die Herren-schuh-Frühjahrskollektion von *Cole-Haan*. Wie in Abb. 214 ersichtlich, dienen Ausschnitte des auf dem Umschlag gezeigten Bildes «La Playa» als Illustrationen für die Inhaltsseiten. (USA)
215 Seite aus einer Broschüre über Chemikalien von *Montefluos*. (ITA)
216 Einladung zur Vorführung von Sportbekleidung der Marke *Levi Strauss* im Boxring. (GBR)
217 Ausschnitt der Umschlagillustration einer Broschüre für ein NCR-Ausbildungsprogramm: «Frucht-barer Boden für Ihre Ambitionen.» NCR als grüne Oase (blaues Wasser) in der Wüste. (ITA)

213, 214 Illustration de couverture grandeur nature et double page tirée d'un catalogue présentant la collection de printemps des chaussures *Cole-Haan*. Ainsi qu'on peut le voir sur la fig. 214, des fragments de l'image de couverture illustrent les pages intérieures. (USA)
215 Page d'une brochure sur les produits chimiques *Montefluos*. (ITA)
216 Invitation à une présentation des vêtements de sports *Levi Strauss* sur un ring. (GBR)
217 Détail de l'illustration de couverture d'une brochure pour un programme de formation NCR: «Un terrain fertile pour vos ambitions.» NCR (eau bleue) est une oasis. (ITA)

217

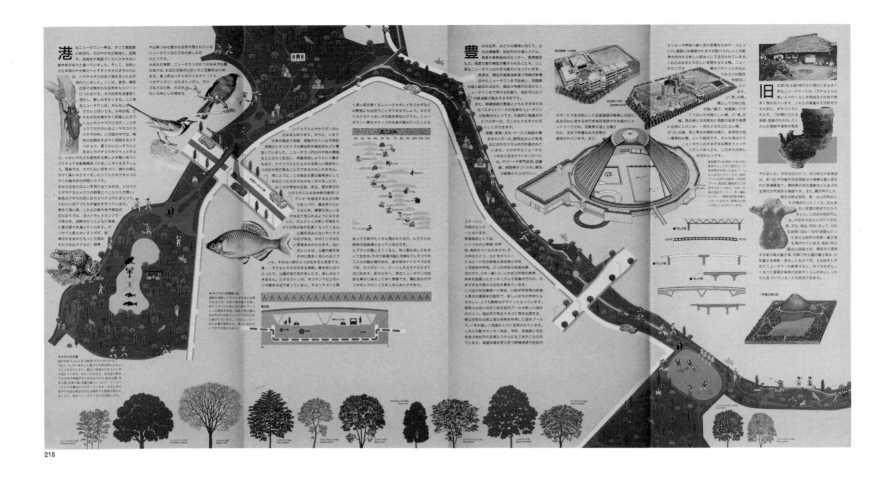

218

ARTIST / KÜNSTLER / ARTISTE:

218, 219 Isao Kusumi/Kenzo Nakagawa/Tokihiro Okuda
222–225 McRay Magleby

DESIGNER / GESTALTER / MAQUETTISTE:

218, 219 Isao Kusumi/Kenzo Nakagawa/Tokihiro Okuda
220, 221 Keizo Matsui/Eiji Shimizu
222–225 McRay Magleby

ART DIRECTOR / DIRECTEUR ARTISTIQUE:

218, 219 Isao Kusumi/Kenzo Nakagawa/Tokihiro Okuda
220, 221 Keizo Matsui
222–225 McRay Magleby

AGENCY / AGENTUR / AGENCE – STUDIO:

218, 219 Bolt & Nuts Studio
220, 221 Keizo Matsui Associates
222–225 BYU Graphics

218, 219 Accordion folder opened out and the title section of it. The aim is to publicize new community leisure facilities and public recreation parks. (JPN)
220, 221 Invitation card to a Paris fashion show, presented opened and half opened to show the crumpled tissue-paper "balloon" affixed inside. In marine blue and white. (JPN)
222–225 A scarab and a harlequin beetle—two of the insects illustrated in colour (the corresponding spreads also shown) from an entomology brochure for Brigham Young University. (USA)

218, 219 Leporello-Prospekt und Vorderseite davon. Hier werden neue städtische Freizeiteinrichtungen und Erholungsgebiete vorgestellt. (JPN)
220, 221 Vollständig und halb geöffnete Einladungskarte zu einer Pariser Modenschau. In Violettblau und Weiss, mit aufgeklebtem Seidenpapier. (JPN)
222–225 Der grüne Skarabäus und der Harlekin-Käfer (Acrocinus Longimanus) sowie die dazugehörigen Doppelseiten aus einer Broschüre über Insektenforschung der Brigham Young University. (USA)

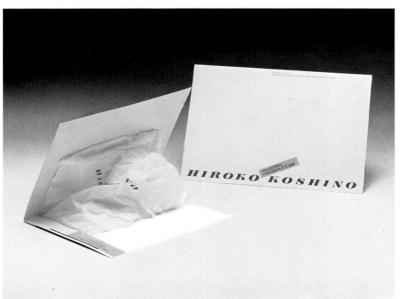

220

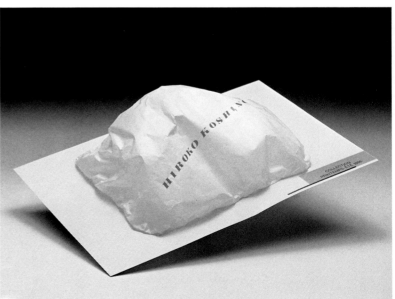

221

219

Booklets / Prospekte / Brochures

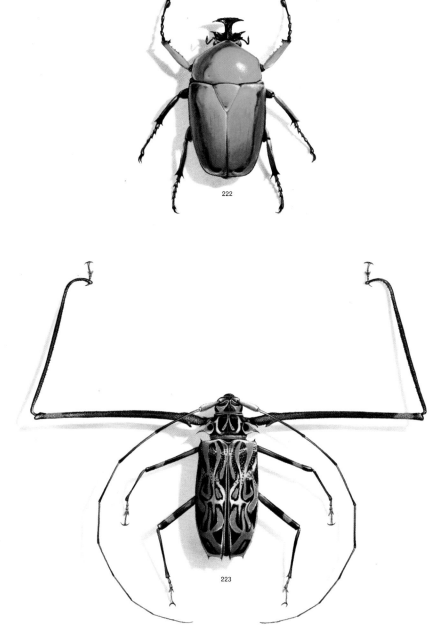

222

223

218, 219 Prospectus à pliage accordéon et recto de ce prospectus. On y présente de nouvelles installations urbaines de loisirs et des aires de repos. (JPN)
220, 221 Carte d'invitation complète et entrouverte, pour une présentation de modes à Paris. En bleu-violet et blanc, papier de soie collé. (JPN)
222–225 Le scarabée vert et l'Arlequin (Acrocinus Longimanus) ainsi que les doubles pages correspondantes d'une brochure de la Brigham Young University sur l'entomologie. (USA)

224

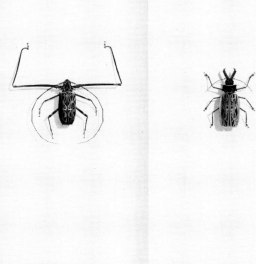

225

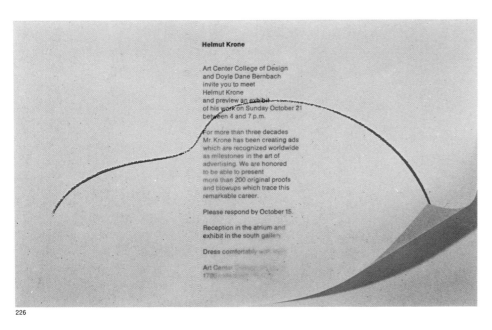

226 Printed card with transparent overlay as invitation to an exhibition organized by the Art Center College of Design and Doyle Dane Bernbach. (USA)
227 Example from a set of reproductions of works by Jean-Michel Folon in a portfolio, to promote the anti-anxiety drug *Ativan*. The symbolic illustrations show various aspects of *Ativan*, here with cardiovascular patients. (USA)
228 Illustration in actual size for an invitation to an international office furniture trade fair in Milan. (ITA)
229, 230 Menu cards issued by the Luxemburg airline *Luxair*. Black and white with red and green vegetables. (LUX)

226 Bedruckte Karte mit durchsichtigem Aufkleber als Einladung zu einer Ausstellung mit Arbeiten von Helmut Krone, die vom Art Center College of Design und der Agentur Doyle Dane Bernbach organisiert wurde. (USA)
227 Beispiel aus einer Mappe mit losen Blättern für das Anti-Depressivum *Ativan*. Die Illustrationen beziehen sich auf Kommentare über die Wirkung des Mittels, hier bei kardio-vaskulären Patienten. (USA)
228 Illustration in Originalgrösse für eine Einladungskarte zu einer internationalen Büromöbel-Messe in Mailand. (ITA)
229, 230 Vorderseiten von Menu-Karten der luxemburgischen Fluglinie *Luxair*. (LUX)

226 Carte imprimée avec autocollant transparent pour l'invitation à une exposition de travaux d'Helmut Krone, organisée par le Art Center College of Design et l'agence Doyle Dane Bernbach. (USA)
227 Un exemple du dossier à feuillets mobiles sur l'antidépressif *Ativan*. Les illustrations se réfèrent aux commentaires sur l'action de ce produit, ici chez des malades présentant des troubles cardio-vasculaires. (USA)
228 Illustration grandeur nature conçue pour une carte d'invitation à une foire internationale de meubles de bureaux à Milan. (ITA)
229, 230 Couvertures de menus de la compagnie aérienne *Luxair*. (LUX)

226

227

228

ARTIST / KÜNSTLER / ARTISTE:

227 Jean Michael Folon
228 Tullio Pericoli
229, 230 Barbara Geissler

DESIGNER / GESTALTER / MAQUETTISTE:

226 Il Chung / Dan Ashcraft
227 Dick Boland
229, 230 Barbara Geissler

ART DIRECTOR / DIRECTEUR ARTISTIQUE:

226 Don Kubly
227 John Geryak
228 Robert Berré

AGENCY / AGENTUR / AGENCE – STUDIO:

226 Doyle Dane Bernbach
227 Kallir, Philips, Ross, Inc.
229, 230 Geissler Design

Booklets / Prospekte / Brochures

229

230

DER ALTE STREIT

„Im Gegensatz zu seiner blauen Periode, aber doch ein bißchen schwach und gar nicht typisch!" „Sie scheinen seine blaue Phase nicht zu kennen, die ganze Kunstwelt stand damals kopf." „Steht sie das nicht noch immer?" „Ach, wissen Sie was, Sie können einem schon richtig leid tun!" „Wie meinen Sie das?" „So, wie ich es sagte." „Daß ich nicht lache. Haha."

16   17

231

232

DER WALD STIRBT. HOLT DIE BÄUME REIN

Dieses ist natürlich keine praktikable Lösung—jedoch gibt es heute schon viele Baumarten, die innen gut leben. Als Zimmerbäume stellen sich vor:

1. Zeder, *Cedrus atl. Glauca* 2. Trompetenbaum, *Datura* 3. Bananenbaum, *Musa Cavinata* 4. Akazie, *Acacia Rosrum* 5. Fingeraralie, *Aralia Elegantissima* 6. Birkenfeige, *Ficus Benjamina* 7. Königswein, *Cissus Rhombifolia* 8. Zimmerlinde, *Sparmannia Africana* 9. Eleganus 10. Zimmertanne, *Araucaria Exelsa* 11. Kletterphilodendron, *Philodendron Scandens* 12. Cissus, *Cissus Antarctica* 13. Rotbuche, *Fagus Sylvatica* 14. Liguster, *Ligutum Jonandum* 15. Gummibaum, *Ficus Elastica Decora* 16. Syngonium, *Syngonium Podophyllum* 17. Birke, *Betula Youngii* 18. Zwergorange, *Citrus Microcarpa* 19. Fichte, *Picea Abies* 20. Heliotrop 21. Lantane 22. Zwergkiefer, *Pinus Mugo* 23. Aralie

18   19

233

Booklets / Prospekte / Brochures

110

ARTIST / KÜNSTLER / ARTISTE:

231 Monica Polasz
233 Dieter Kalenbach
234 Jim Eschinger
236 Dietrich Ebert

DESIGNER / GESTALTER / MAQUETTISTE:

234 Jim Eschinger
235 Juliette Weisbuch
236 Uli Franz

ART DIRECTOR / DIRECTEUR ARTISTIQUE:

234 Nicki Adler
235 Juliette Weisbuch
236 Dietrich Ebert

AGENCY / AGENTUR / AGENCE – STUDIO:

234 Nicki Adler Design
235 Topologies
236 D. & I. Ebert

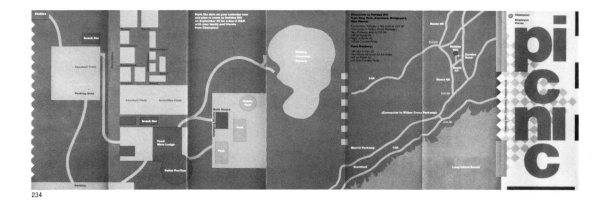

234

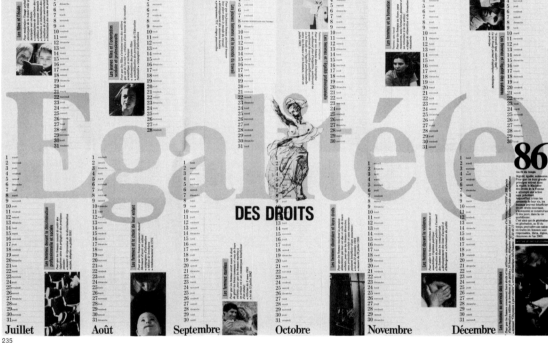

235

231–233 Double spreads and cover of the autumn issue of a large quarterly publication sent by (free) subscription to German customers of the Swedish furniture firm *Ikea*. Fig. 231: "The old argument"—an art discussion; Fig. 232: Spitzweg's "The poor poet"—as computer graphics; Fig. 233: indoor trees—"The woods die, bring the trees inside." (GER)
234 Polychrome accordion folder as invitation to the firm's picnic for employees and their families, for *Champion*. (USA)
235 Folder as calendar for the Ministry of Women's Rights, here about equal rights—equal opportunities. (FRA)
236 Self-promotional card for the graphic studio Irmgard & Dietrich Ebert. In full colour. (GER)

231–233 Doppelseiten und Umschlag einer grossformatigen Publikation des Möbelhauses *Ikea*, die vierteljährlich im Frei-Abonnement an Kunden abgegeben wird. In Abb. 231 geht es um «ein typisches Kunstgespräch» über die blaue Periode Picassos. Abb. 232: Spitzwegs «Der arme Poet» als Computergraphik; Abb. 233: verschiedene Zimmerbäume. (GER)
234 Mehrfarbiges Leporello als Einladung zu einem von der Papierfabrik *Champion* für ihre Angestellten veranstaltetem Familien-Picknick. (USA)
235 Als Kalender gestalteter Prospekt des Ministeriums für Frauenrechte zum Thema «Gleichheit der Frau». (FRA)
236 Eigenwerbungskarte für das Graphik-Studio Irmgard & Dietrich Ebert. In Farbe. (GER)

231–233 Doubles pages et couverture d'une publication grand format du magasin de meubles *Ikea*. La fig. 231 fait allusion à «une conversation artistique typique» sur la période bleue de Picasso. Fig. 232: «Le pauvre poète» de Spitzweg transposé sur ordinateur. Fig. 233: divers arbustes d'appartement. (GER)
234 Dépliant polychrome d'une invitation au pique-nique familial organisé par la fabrique de papier *Champion* à l'intention de ses employés. (USA)
235 Prospectus-calendrier du Ministère des Droits de la femme sur le thème de l'égalité de la femme. (FRA)
236 Carte autopromotionnelle de l'atelier de graphisme Irmgard & Dietrich Ebert. En couleurs. (GER)

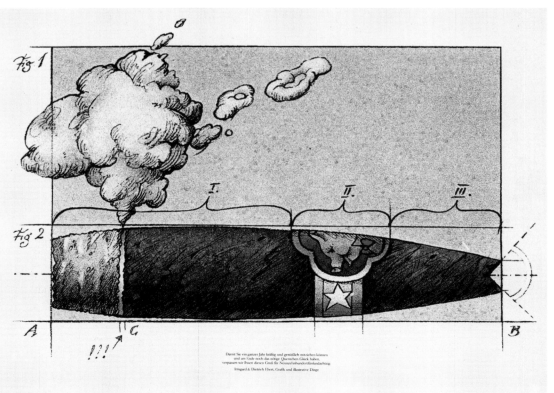

236

3

Newspaper Illustrations

Magazine Covers

Magazine Illustrations

Weekend Supplements

Trade Magazines

House Organs

Annual Reports

Book Covers

Zeitungs-Illustrationen

Zeitschriften-Umschläge

Zeitschriften-Illustrationen

Wochenendbeilagen

Fachzeitschriften

Hauszeitschriften

Jahresberichte

Buchumschläge

Illustrations de journaux

Couvertures de périodiques

Illustrations de périodiques

Suppléments dominicaux

Revues professionnelles

Journaux d'entreprise

Rapports annuels

Couvertures de livres

ARTIST / KÜNSTLER / ARTISTE:

237 Bonnie Timmons
238 Maciek Albrecht
239 Gary Viskupic
240 Eugene Mihaesco
241, 242 Peter Kuper

237

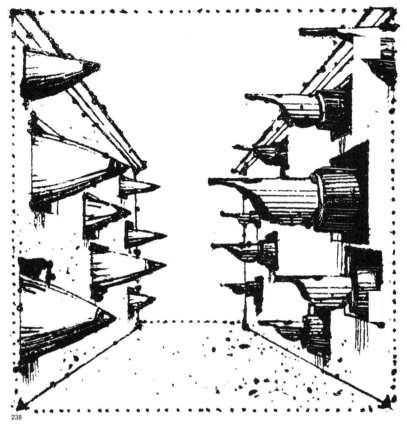

238

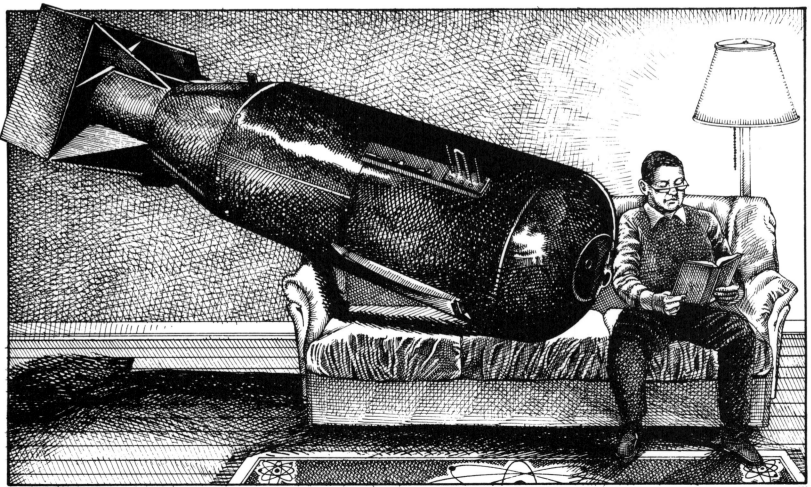

239

Newspaper Illustrations
Zeitungs-Illustrationen
Illustrations de journaux

237 Illustration from a report in *The Denver Post* about attacks on black South African policemen by black activists. (USA)
238 Illustration accompanying a book review about nuclear-arms policy-making in the Reagan administration, from the *New York Times*. (USA)
239 "Living with the Bomb", an illustration for a book review in the newspaper *Newsday*. (USA)
240 Illustration in actual size from the *New York Times* book review for a book about South African apartheid politics. (USA)
241, 242 Illustration (actual size) and complete page with an entertainments guide, from the *Village Voice*. It relates to a "Legs Against Arms" walk to protest against US arms to Central America. (USA)

237 Illustration für einen Beitrag über farbige Südafrikaner, die durch ihren Beruf zwischen den Fronten stehen; aus *The Denver Post*. (USA)
238 Illustration für die Besprechung eines Buches über die atomare Rüstungspolitik der Reagan-Regierung, aus der *New York Times*. (USA)
239 «Mit der Bombe leben» – Illustration für eine Buchbesprechung in der Zeitung *Newsday*. (USA)
240 Illustration in Originalgrösse aus dem Büchersektor der *New York Times* für die Besprechung eines Buches über die Apartheidspolitik. (USA)
241, 242 Illustration (Originalgrösse) und vollständige Seite mit einem Veranstaltungskalender aus der *Village Voice*. Es geht um einen Protest-Marsch gegen US-Waffenlieferungen nach Mittelamerika. (USA)

237 Illustration d'un article du *Denver Post* sur les noirs sud-africains qui, par leur métier, se situent entre les fronts. (USA)
238 Illustration de la critique d'un livre sur la politique reagannienne d'armement nucléaire, parue dans le *New York Times*. (USA)
239 «Vivre avec la bombe» – Illustration d'un compte-rendu de livre publié dans le journal *Newsday*. (USA)
240 Illustration grandeur nature figurant dans la rubrique littéraire du *New York Times*, à propos d'un livre sur l'apartheid. (USA)
241, 242 Illustration (grandeur nature) et page complète d'un calendrier de manifestations contre la livraison d'armes américaines à l'Amérique du Sud, parues dans *Village Voice*. (USA)

240

241

ART DIRECTOR / DIRECTEUR ARTISTIQUE:

237 Randy Miller
238, 240 Steven Heller
241, 242 Dan Zedek

PUBLISHER / VERLEGER / EDITEUR:

237 The Denver Post
238, 240 The New York Times
239 Newsday
241, 242 Village Voice

242

243

244

ARTIST / KÜNSTLER / ARTISTE:

243 Sean Kelly
244, 245 Kent Barton

DESIGNER / GESTALTER / MAQUETTISTE:

243 Sean Kelly
244, 245 Richard Bard

ART DIRECTOR / DIRECTEUR ARTISTIQUE:

243 Randy Stano
244, 245 Kent Barton

PUBLISHER / VERLEGER / ÉDITEUR:

243–245 The Miami Herald

243–245 Examples of illustrations from the newspaper *The Miami Herald*. Fig. 243 refers to an article on the near-paranoiac security measures taken by home owners in South Florida. Fig. 244 illustrates a report about euthanasia; Fig. 245 portrays New Zealand's Prime Minister David Lange for his own article on why he refuses to let US vessels carrying nuclear weapons visit New Zealand ports. (USA)

243–245 Illustrationen aus der Zeitung *The Miami Herald*. Abb. 243 bezieht sich auf einen Artikel über fast paranoid anmutende Sicherheitsvorrichtungen in Haus und Garten. Abb. 244 illustriert einen Beitrag über «Mord aus Erbarmen», verübt an einer geliebten Person, um ihr weiteres Leid zu ersparen. Abb. 245 zeigt den neuseeländischen Premierminister David Lange für eine von ihm verfasste Erklärung zur atomwaffenfreien Politik Neuseelands. (USA)

243–245 Exemples d'illustrations du journal *The Miami Herald*. La fig. 243 se rapporte à un article sur les dispositifs de sécurité des maisons et jardins, quasiment paranoïdes. La fig. 244 illustre un article sur le «meurtre par pitié» d'une personne aimée, pour lui éviter de nouvelles souffrances. La fig. 245 montre le Premier ministre néo-zélandais, David Lange, dans une de ses déclarations sur la politique anti-nucléaire de la Nouvelle-Zélande. (USA)

245

246

247

248

ARTIST / KÜNSTLER / ARTISTE:
246–254 Peter Sis

ART DIRECTOR / DIRECTEUR ARTISTIQUE:
246–254 Steven Heller

PUBLISHER / VERLEGER / EDITEUR:
246–254 The New York Times

249

250

251

246–254 Illustrations by Peter Sis for the *New York Times* book review. Fig. 246: review of the book *The House of the Spirits* by Isabel Allende; Fig. 247 (full page width): for a review of *Fortune's Daughter*; Fig. 248: for a review of a first novel about poverty and a family living in a mobile home; Fig. 249: "Writers and the Nostalgic Fallacy"; Fig. 250 (actual size): for an article by a psycho-analyst on fiction; Fig. 251: for a critique of the book *The Psychology of Self-Deception*. Fig. 252: project for a critique of the book *Solstice* by J. C. Oates. Fig. 253 (actual size): *Amusing Ourselves to Death*; Fig. 254: an art forger as subject of a book. (USA)

246–254 Illustrationen von Peter Sis für den Buchsektor der *New York Times*. Abb. 246: Besprechung von Isabel Allendes *Das Geisterhaus*; Abb. 247: über die ganze Breite der Buchseite reichende Illustration; Abb. 248: für die Besprechung eines Buches über Armut und das Leben in Wohnwagen; Abb. 249: «Schriftsteller und der nostalgische Irrtum»; Abb. 250 (Originalgrösse): für einen Beitrag über Prosa; Abb. 251: für die Rezension eines Buches «über die Psychologie des Selbstbetrugs»; Abb. 252: Entwurf für «Sonnenwende» von J. C. Oates; Abb. 253 (Originalgrösse): *Wir amüsieren uns zu Tode*; Abb. 254: ein Kunstfälscher als Thema eines Buches. (USA)

246–254 Illustrations de Peter Sis pour la rubrique livres du *New York Times*. Fig. 246: critique du livre d'Isabel Allende *La maison aux esprits*. Fig. 247: illustration sur toute la largeur de la page. Fig. 248: critique d'un livre sur la pauvreté. Fig. 249: «les écrivains et l'erreur nostalgique». Fig. 250 (grandeur nature): article sur la prose. Fig. 251: critique d'un livre «sur la psychologie de l'illusion sur soi». Fig. 252: critique du livre «Solstice» de J. C. Oates, (projet). Fig. 253 (grandeur nature): «Nous nous amusons à mourir». Fig. 254: pour un livre sur un faussaire d'art. (USA)

252

253

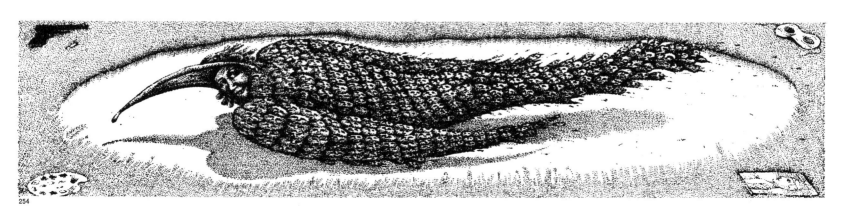

254

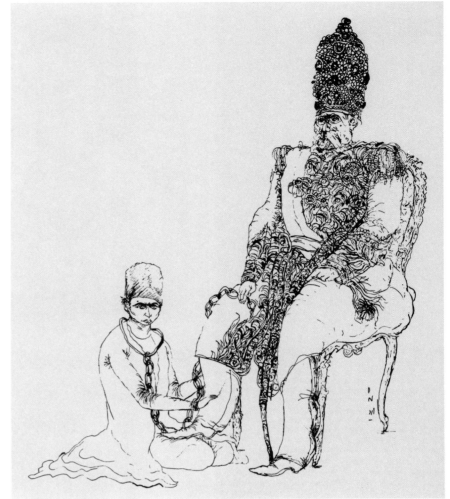

255 Illustration for *Kayhan*, the Iranian newspaper, entitled "The King and I". (GBR)
256 "Riding Tour", for an article in the Iranian newspaper *Morvareed*. (IRN)
257, 258 From the *New York Times*: "Pakistani Critics" and "The Last Blow". (USA)
259 Illustration for a further article in the newspaper *Kayhan*: "Murdered Revolutionaries", in which the torn out thigh skin symbolizes the Central American states. The related article reveals the number of people killed in the insurrection. (GBR)

255 Illustration für die iranische Zeitung *Kayhan*: «Der König und ich.» (GBR)
256 «Ausritt.» Für einen Artikel in der iranischen Zeitung *Morvareed*. (IRN)
257, 258 Aus der *New York Times*: «Pakistanische Kritik» und «Letzter Schlag». (USA)
259 Aus der Zeitung *Kayhan*: «Ermordete Revolutionäre», wobei der Hautfetzen die mittelamerikanischen Staaten symbolisiert und die Zahl der Ermordeten angibt. (GBR)

255 Illustration pour *Kayhan*, un journal publié à Londres: «Le roi et moi.» (GBR)
256 «Promenade à cheval.» Pour un article paru dans le journal iranien *Morvareed*. (IRN)
257, 258 Du *New York Times*: «Critiques pakistanaises» et «Dernier coup». (USA)
259 Du journal *Kayhan*: «Révolutionnaires assassinés». Le morceau de peau arraché symbolise les états d'Amérique centrale et le nombre des assassinés. (GBR)

255

256

257

258

ARTIST / KÜNSTLER / ARTISTE:
255–259 Ardeshir Mohasses

ART DIRECTOR / DIRECTEUR ARTISTIQUE:
257, 258 Jerelle Kraus

PUBLISHER / VERLEGER / EDITEUR:
255, 259 Kayhan
256 Morvareed
257, 258 The New York Times

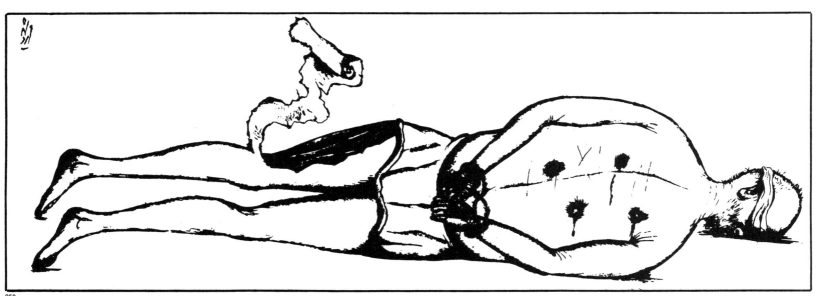

259

260–263 Illustrations from various sections in the *New York Times*. Fig. 260 illustrates an article "Decline of Communism"; Fig. 261 is for an article about conflicts in Atlantic unity during the Achille Lauro affair; Fig. 262 is about new trends in home and foreign politics in the United States; Fig. 263 is from the travel section for the Sunday edition and illustrates an article on travel memories evoked through certain scents and smells. (USA)

260–263 Illustrationen aus verschiedenen Sektoren der *New York Times*. Abb. 260 illustriert einen Beitrag über den «Niedergang des Kommunismus»; Abb. 261 hat die Uneinigkeit innerhalb des atlantischen Bündnisses während der Achille-Lauro-Krise zum Thema; Abb. 262 gehört zu einem Artikel über neue Tendenzen in der Innen- und Aussenpolitik der Vereinigten Staaten; Abb. 263 ist aus dem Reise-Sektor der Sonntagsausgabe und illustriert einen Beitrag über Reiseerinnerungen, die durch bestimmte Gerüche ausgelöst werden. (USA)

260–263 Pour diverses rubriques du *New York Times*. La fig. 260 illustre un article sur le «déclin du communisme». La fig. 261 fait allusion à la désunion au sein de l'alliance atlantique lors de l'affaire de l'Achille Lauro. La fig. 262 se rapporte à un article sur les nouvelles tendances dans la politique intérieure et extérieure des Etats-Unis. La fig. 263 provient de la rubrique voyages de l'édition du dimanche et illustre un article sur les souvenirs de voyage, ravivés par certaines odeurs. (USA)

260

261

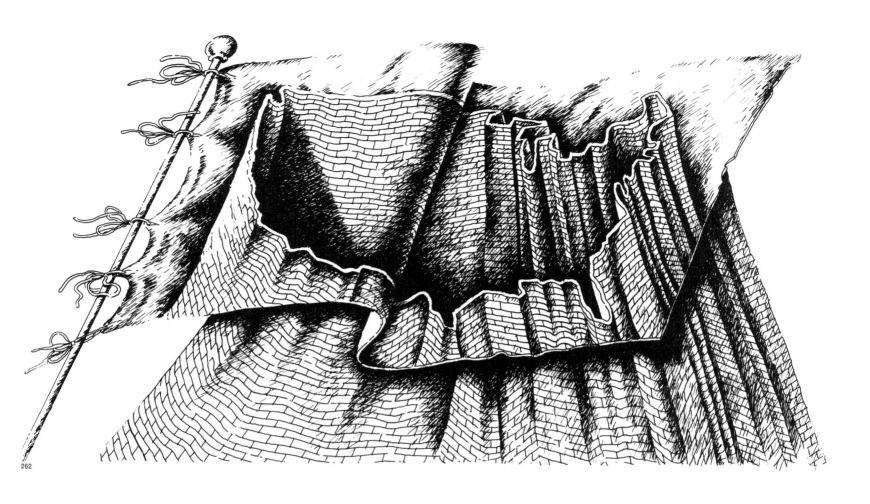

262

ARTIST / KÜNSTLER / ARTISTE:

260, 261 Rafal Olbinski
262 Leszek Wisniewski
263 Roger Roth

ART DIRECTOR / DIRECTEUR ARTISTIQUE:

260–262 Jerelle Kraus
263 Linda Brewer

PUBLISHER / VERLEGER / EDITEUR:

260–263 The New York Times

263

Newspaper Illustrations
Zeitungs-Illustrationen
Illustrations de journaux

ARTIST / KÜNSTLER / ARTISTE:

264 Steven Guarnaccia
265 Patrick Blackwell
266, 267 Randall Enos

DESIGNER / GESTALTER / MAQUETTISTE:

265 Aldona Charlton
266, 267 Richard Baker

ART DIRECTOR / DIRECTEUR ARTISTIQUE:

264 Jim Pavlovitch
265 Aldona Charlton
266, 267 Richard Baker

PUBLISHER / VERLEGER / EDITEUR:

264–267 The Boston Globe

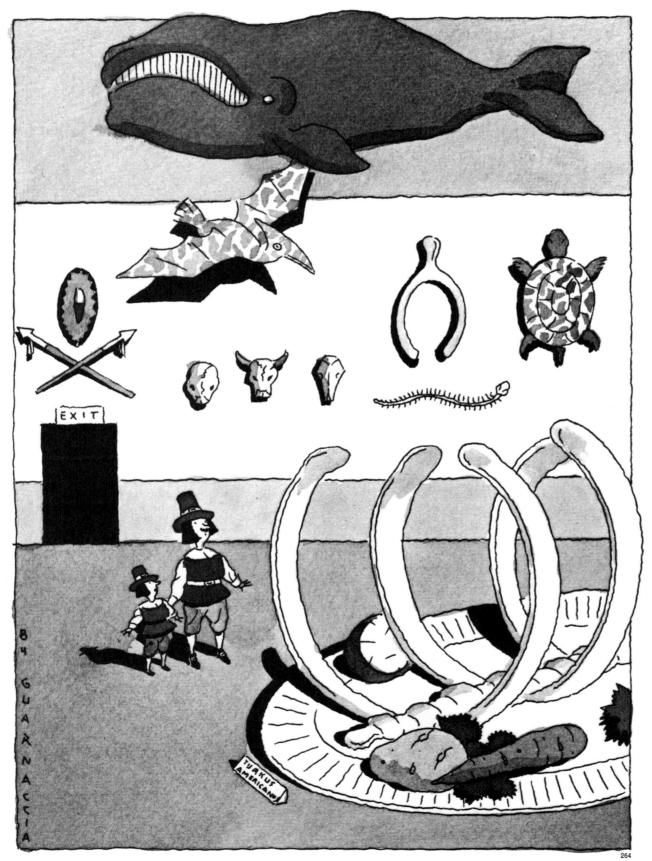

264

264 Cover illustration in full colour for a children's guide to activities, in the *Boston Globe*, for the day following Thanksgiving. (USA)
265 Page from a series of articles in the *Boston Globe* about the influence of Japanese living culture on American home design. Brush-line illustration. (USA)
266, 267 Linocuts in black and white for two articles in the *Boston Globe*. Fig. 266 relates to an article entitled: "Mutual Misunderstandings" and is about the problems (mainly language) facing Americans when on business abroad; Fig. 267: "Is smoking going out of style?"—on the decrease in smoking. (USA)

264 Farbige Umschlagillustration einer für Kinder bestimmten Beilage des *Boston Globe*, mit Anregungen für den freien Tag nach Thanksgiving. (USA)
265 Vollständige Seite aus einer regelmässig im *Boston Globe* erscheinenden Serie über japanische Lebenskultur. Pinselstrichillustration. (USA)
266, 267 Linolschnitte in Schwarzweiss für zwei Beiträge im *Boston Globe*. Abb. 266 gehört zu einem Artikel über gegenseitige Missverständnisse zwischen Menschen verschiedener Kulturen; Abb. 267 illustriert einen Beitrag, der die Frage aufwirft, ob Rauchen unpopulär werden könnte. (USA)

264 Illustration polychrome pour la couverture d'un supplément du *Boston Globe* destiné aux enfants et suggérant des idées d'occupations pour le jour férié suivant le Thanksgiving. (USA)
265 Page complète d'une série sur la culture japonaise paraissant périodiquement dans le *Boston Globe*. Illustrations au pinceau. (USA)
266, 267 Linogravures en noir et blanc illustrant deux articles du *Boston Globe*. La fig. 266 se réfère à un article sur les malentendus réciproques entre des individus de culture différente. La fig. 267 visualise cette question: le fumeur deviendrait-il impopulaire? (USA)

266

265

267

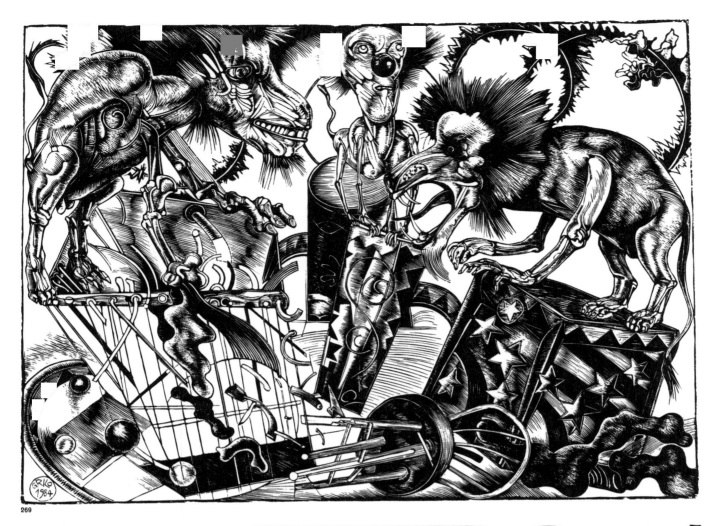

269

268

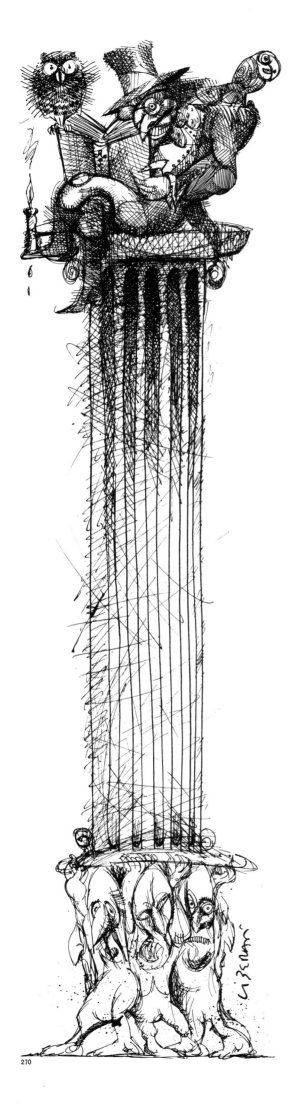

268, 269 Woodcut illustrations (Fig. 269 unpublished) under the titles "Theatre" and "Lions", as political comments. (BRA)
270, 271 Illustration and complete page for the newspaper *Jornal do Brasil* with an article about the education and cultural politics of the country. (BRA)
272 For the book page of the *Jornal do Brasil*—a caricature of Sigmund Freud, to illustrate two newly published books about him. (BRA)

268, 269 Holzschnitt-Illustrationen (Abb. 269 unveröffentlicht) mit den Titeln «Theater» und «Löwen» als politische Kommentare. (BRA)
270, 271 Illustration und vollständige Seite aus der Zeitung *Jornal do Brasil* mit einem Beitrag über die Erziehungs- und Kulturpolitik des Landes. (BRA)
272 Zwei Abhandlungen über Sigmund Freud sind Gegenstand der Buchseite des *Jornal do Brasil*, zu der diese Karikatur gehört. (BRA)

268–269 Illustrations gravées sur bois (fig. 269 inédite) intitulées «Théâtre» et «Lions»; l'image sert de commentaire politique. (BRA)
270, 271 Illustration et page complète d'un article du *Jornal do Brasil* sur la politique éducative et culturelle de ce pays. (BRA)
272 Cette caricature a été publiée dans la rubrique littéraire du *Jornal do Brasil*, à propos de deux études sur Sigmund Freud. (BRA)

Newspaper Illustrations
Zeitungs-Illustrationen
Illustrations de journaux

ARTIST / KÜNSTLER / ARTISTE:

268, 269 Rubem Campos Grilo
270–272 Bruno Liberati

PUBLISHER / VERLEGER / EDITEUR:

268 Retrato do Brasil
270–272 Jornal do Brasil

271

270

272

273

273, 274 Illustrations for the literature pages of the *Frankfurter Allgemeine Zeitung*. Fig. 273: Gerhart Hauptmann, dramatist and Nobel Prize winner: Fig. 274: the Mann family, from left to right: Erika, Julia, Heinrich, Klaus, Thomas, Katja and Golo Mann. (GER)
275 Brazilian politician Magalhães Pinto—for an article in the *Jornal do Brasil*. (BRA)

273, 274 Illustrationen für die Literaturseiten der *Frankfurter Allgemeine Zeitung*. Abb. 273: Gerhart Hauptmann; Abb. 274: die Familie Mann von links nach rechts: Erika, Julia, Heinrich, Klaus, Thomas, Katja und Golo Mann. (GER)
275 Der brasilianische Politiker Magalhães Pinto für einen Artikel im *Jornal do Brasil*. (BRA)

273, 274 Illustrations pour les pages littéraires du *Frankfurter Allgemeine Zeitung*. Fig. 273: Gerhart Hauptmann. fig. 274: la famille Mann; de gauche à droite: Erika, Julia, Heinrich, Klaus, Thomas, Katja et Golo Mann. (GER)
275 Le politicien brésilien Magalhães Pinto pour un article du *Jornal do Brasil*. (BRA)

ARTIST / KÜNSTLER / ARTISTE:

273–275 Loredano Silva

ART DIRECTOR / DIRECTEUR ARTISTIQUE:

273, 274 Konrad Boch
275 Nélio Horta

PUBLISHER / VERLEGER / EDITEUR:

273, 274 Frankfurter Allgemeine Zeitung GmbH
275 Jornal do Brasil

274

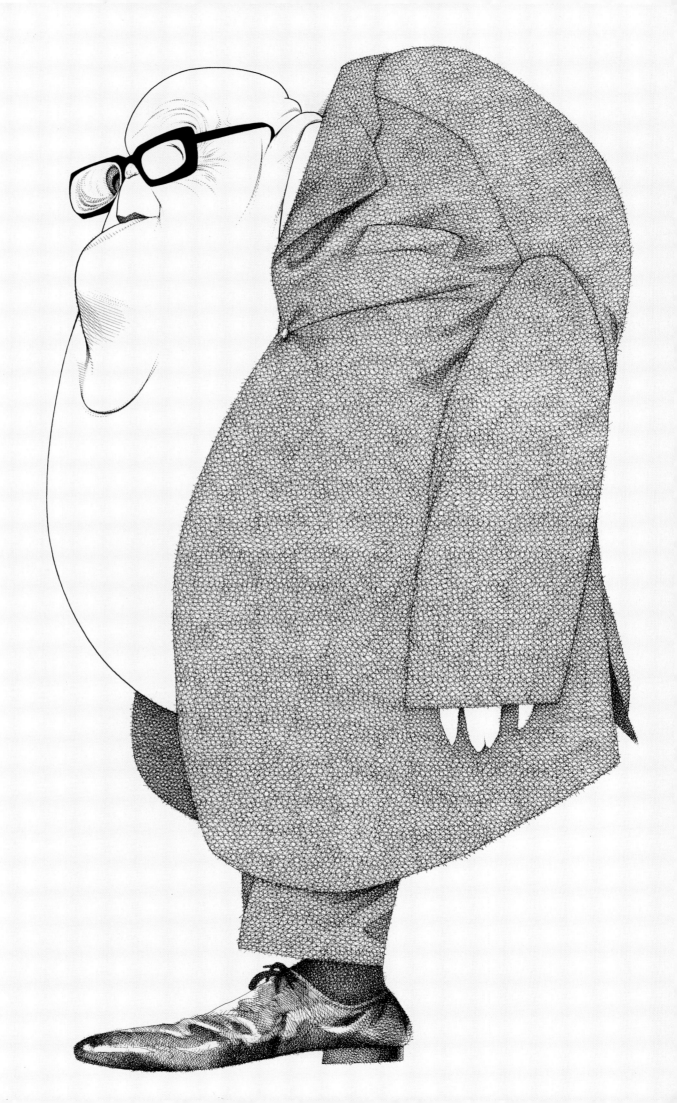

276

277

Newspaper Illustrations
Zeitungs-Illustrationen
Illustrations de journaux

ARTIST / KÜNSTLER / ARTISTE:

276 David Shannon
277, 279 Janis Bryza
278 Roger Roth

ART DIRECTOR / DIRECTEUR ARTISTIQUE:

276 Robert Neubecker
277, 279 Broc Sears
278 Lucy Bartholomay

PUBLISHER / VERLEGER / EDITEUR:

276 Inx Inc.
277, 279 Dallas Times Herald
278 The Boston Globe

276 "Fear of Flying." An illustration for a feature published in various newspapers. (USA)
277 Illustration for an article in the *Dallas Times Herald*: "Surviving the Teen Years." (USA)
278 "Cover Blurbs"—title of an article in the *Boston Globe* to which this illustration belongs. It refers to the necessity of lavish praise on the book cover in order to sell the book. (USA)
279 Complete page from the *Dallas Times Herald* entitled "Style". The corresponding article gives advice and helpful tips on how to best organize one's clothing cupboards. (USA)

276 «Angst vorm Fliegen.» Eine in verschiedenen Zeitungen erschienene Illustration. (USA)
277 Illustration für einen Beitrag in *Dallas Times Herald*: «Wie man die Pubertät überlebt.» (USA)
278 «Klappentexte» ist der Titel des Beitrags im *Boston Globe,* zu dem diese Illustration gehört. Hier geht es um die Werbeanstrengungen für Bücher. (USA)
279 Vollständige Seite aus *Dallas Times Herald* mit dem Titel «Stil». Der dazugehörige Beitrag enthält Ratschläge für die sinnvolle Ausnützung von Kleiderschränken. (USA)

276 «La peur de voler.» Illustration publiée dans différents journaux. (USA)
277 Illustration d'un article du *Dallas Times Herald*: «Survivre à la puberté.» (USA)
278 Cette illustration accompagne un article du *Boston Globe* intitulé «Textes de rabat». Il est question ici de l'effort publicitaire pour la promotion des livres. (USA)
279 Page complète du *Dallas Times Herald* intitulée «Style». Elle concerne un article où l'on donne des conseils quant à l'utilisation rationnelle des armoires à vêtements. (USA)

278

STYLE

Janis Bryza / Dallas Times Herald

SOLVING CLOSET
HANGUPS

BY KIM MARCUM

It's the last thing any-one sees in your house, but the first thing you look into every morn-ing: Your closet.

"Most people's clos-ets are their last bas-tion of privacy," says Bill Brad-ford of Closet Concepts. "Anything they don't want someone else to see ends up there."

With everything from skis to safes hidden behind closet doors, it can be tough to find your clothes. Expensive silk dresses and cost-ly tailored suits turn into unrecognizable masses of wrinkles. That is, when you can find them. The rest of the time, they're lost to

the world — and sometimes to you.

How many times has it happened: You find a wonderful blouse in your favorite color and come home to discover you've got two just like it stashed way in the back of your closet. Or you pull out the skirt you want to wear to

the office that day and can't find the summer blouse to go with it. A week later it turns up crammed between your black leather skirt and gray flannel pants.

The woes of a disorganized closet can be costly, time-consuming and frustrating.

"Before I straightened out my closets," says Kelley Moncrieff of Bloomingdale's, "it would take so long to get ready in the morning because I couldn't find what I was looking for. If you start your morning off looking for something, it messes up the whole day. When you know what you've got and what it goes with, it makes life a lot easier."

Well-organized closets also can increase your actual living space. With homes and closets shrinking as building costs soar, a sys-tem for storing your clothing investments be-comes critical.

Continued on Page 2

281

282

ARTIST / KÜNSTLER / ARTISTE:

280, 281, 283 Bruce Bjerva
282 Jody W. Smith

ART DIRECTOR / DIRECTEUR ARTISTIQUE:

280, 281, 283 Bruce Bjerva
282 Jody W. Smith

PUBLISHER / VERLEGER / EDITEUR:

280–283 Minneapolis Star and Tribune

280–283 Examples of the introductory pages to the food section in the newspaper *Minneapolis Star and Tribune*. Figs. 280 and 281 were published during the pre-Christmas period—Fig. 281: green wreath with red bow, door in brown tones, blue background. Fig. 282: "Posh pizza." Top-hatted gent in black and white, pale yellow pizza background "filled" with red, green and black. Fig. 283: "Cooking with spirits"—mainly in blue tones with white, yellow, red and grey; green and brown bottles. (USA)

280–283 Beispiele der einleitenden Seiten des Essens-Sektors der Zeitung *Minneapolis Star and Tribune*. Abb. 280 und 281 erschienen in der Vorweihnachtszeit – Abb. 281: grüner Kranz mit roter Schleife, Tür in Brauntönen, Hintergrund blau. Abb. 282: «Vornehme Pizza» – Figur in Schwarzweiss, Konfetti grün, rot und schwarz auf Hellgelb. Abb. 283: «Kochen mit Alkohol» – vorwiegend in verschiedenen Blautönen mit Weiss, Gelb, Rot und Grau, Flaschen in Grün und Braun. (USA)

280–283 Exemples des pages de titre de la rubrique cuisine du journal *Minneapolis Star and Tribune*. Les fig. 280 et 281 furent publiées peu avant Noël – fig. 281: couronne verte et ruban rouge, porte marron, fond bleu. Fig. 282: «Pizza chic» – Figure en noir et blanc, confettis verts, rouges et noirs sur fond jaune clair. Fig. 283: «Cuisiner à l'alcool» – prédominance de tons bleus avec blanc, jaune, rouge et gris; bouteilles vert et brun. (USA)

283

ARTIST / KÜNSTLER / ARTISTE:
284–289 Tomi Ungerer

ART DIRECTOR:
284–289 Wolfgang Behnken

PUBLISHER / VERLEGER:
284–289 Gruner & Jahr AG & Co.

284

285

286

287

288

284–289 Examples of the illustrations by Tomi Ungerer and a double spread from the serialized criminal novel by Friedrich Dürrenmatt: "Justice" published in *Stern* magazine. Figs. 288, 289 relate to the point of departure for the story, the murder of the German philologist Dr. Isaak Winter in the Zurich café "Du Théâtre" by county councillor Dr. h. c. Isaak Kohler. (GER)

284–289 Beispiele der Illustrationen von Tomi Ungerer und eine Doppelseite aus dem Magazin *Stern*, das Friedrich Dürrenmatts Kriminalroman *Justiz* in Fortsetzungen veröffentlichte. Abb. 288, 289 beziehen sich auf den Ausgangspunkt der Geschichte, die Ermordung des Germanisten Dr. Isaak Winter im Zürcher Lokal «Du Théâtre» durch den Kantonsrat Dr. h. c. Isaak Kohler. (GER)

284–289 Illustrations de Tomi Ungerer et double page du magazine *Stern* qui publia sous forme de feuilleton le roman policier de Friedrich Dürrenmatt, «Justice». Les fig. 288, 289 illustrent le point de départ de l'histoire: un germaniste, le Dr. Isaak Winter, est assassiné au restaurant zurichois «Du Théâtre» par le conseiller cantonal Dr. h. c. Isaak Kohler. (GER)

289

Magazine Illustrations

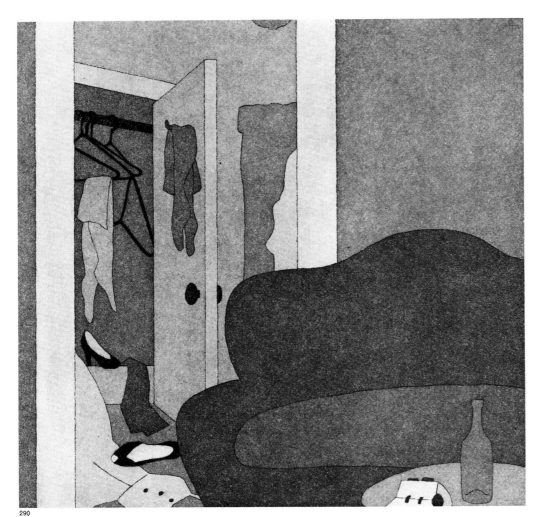

290

290, 291 Black-and-white illustrations for articles in *The Atlantic*. Fig. 290 relates to a short story and Fig. 291 accompanies a non-fiction article entitled "Ideas Move Nations". (USA)
292, 293 Illustrations in original size from the regularly appearing series entitled "First Encounters" in *The Atlantic*. Fig. 292 illustrates the first encounter between Goebbels and Fritz Lang who, on this occasion, was offered the post of Reichsminister of film—which so alarmed Lang that he fled Germany immediately. Fig. 293 portrays criminal story writer Dashiell Hammett encountering gossip columnist and wit Dorothy Parker for the first time. (USA)

290, 291 Schwarzweiss-Illustrationen für Beiträge in *The Atlantic*. Abb. 290: für eine Kurzgeschichte; Abb. 291: für einen Beitrag mit dem Titel «Ideen bewegen Nationen». (USA)
292, 293 Illustrationen in Originalgrösse aus der regelmässig in *The Atlantic* erscheinenden Reihe «Erste Begegnungen». Abb. 292 illustriert die erste Begegnung zwischen Goebbels und Fritz Lang, dem bei dieser Gelegenheit der Posten eines Reichs-Filmministers angeboten wurde, was er zum Anlass seiner sofortigen Flucht nach Paris nahm; Abb. 293 zeigt den Kriminalschriftsteller Dashiell Hammett und Dorothy Parker, eine Dame der New Yorker Gesellschaft, die u. a. Kritiken schrieb. (USA)

290, 291 Illustrations noir et blanc parues dans *The Atlantic*. Fig. 290: pour une nouvelle; fig. 291: pour un article intitulé: «Les idées remuent des nations». (USA)
292, 293 Illustrations grandeur nature extraites d'une série, «Premières rencontres», publiée périodiquement par *The Atlantic*. La fig. 292 relate la première entrevue entre Goebbels et Fritz Lang qui se vit offrir à cette occasion le poste de Ministre du Cinéma du Reich: en conséquence de quoi il s'enfuit pour Paris. La fig. 293 montre l'auteur de romans policiers Dashiell Hammett avec Dorothy Parker, une dame de la bonne société newyorkaise qui écrivait des critiques. (USA)

291

ARTIST / KÜNSTLER / ARTISTE:

290 Glenna Lang
291 Tom Lulevitch
292, 293 Edward Sorel

DESIGNER / GESTALTER / MAQUETTISTE:

290–293 Judy Garlan

ART DIRECTOR / DIRECTEUR ARTISTIQUE:

290–293 Judy Garlan

PUBLISHER / VERLEGER / EDITEUR:

290–293 The Atlantic Monthly

292

293

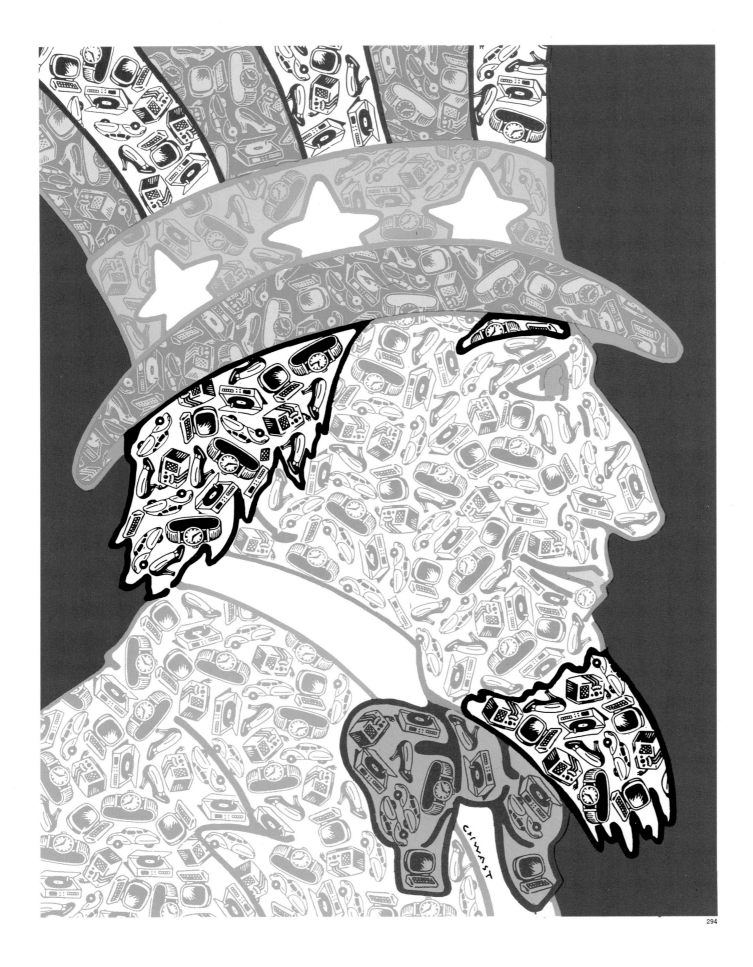

Magazine Illustrations
Zeitschriften-Illustrationen
Illustrations de périodiques

295

296

ARTIST / KÜNSTLER / ARTISTE:

294 Seymour Chwast
295 Edward Sorel
296 Philippe Weisbecker
297 Jean Michel Folon

DESIGNER / GESTALTER:

294–297 Judy Garlan

ART DIRECTOR:

294–297 Judy Garlan

PUBLISHER / VERLEGER / EDITEUR:

294–297 The Atlantic Monthly

294–297 Illustrations from *The Atlantic* magazine. Fig. 294: illustration in actual size for "The Next American Frontier": Fig. 295: for a humorous poem on "Think Tanks" (ideas groups) in green tones; Fig. 296: "When Foreign Aid Fails"; Fig. 297: "What is it about?"—concerning the nuclear defence race. (Watercolour, mainly red and yellow.) (USA)

294–297 Illustrationen aus *The Atlantic*. Die Themen: «Neue Richtung der US-Industriepolitik» (Abb. 294); «Ideen-Gruppen (Doppeldeutigkeit des englischen Wortes Tanks) haben für die Politiker das Denken übernommen» (Abb. 295, Grüntöne); «Falsche Entwicklungshilfe (Abb. 296, mehrfarbig); «Atomarer Rüstungswettlauf» (Abb. 297, Aquarell). (USA)

294–297 Illustrations pour *The Atlantic*. Fig. 294: «Nouvelle orientation de l'industrie des Etats Unis». Fig. 295, tons verts: «Les tanks (les idées-forces) ont remplacé la pensée chez les politiciens». Fig. 296, polychrome: «Une aide au développement inadéquate». Fig. 297, aquarelle: «La course aux armements nucléaires». (USA)

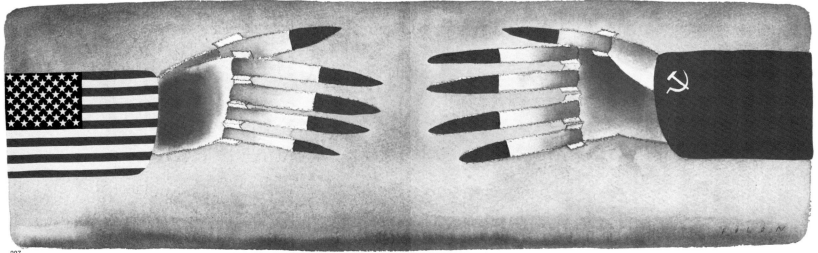

297

298

299

300

301

302

303

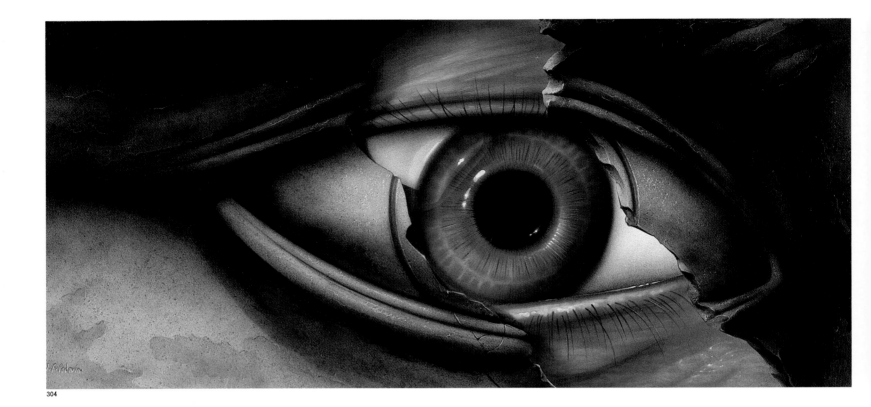

304

ARTIST / KÜNSTLER / ARTISTE:

304, 305 Jean-François Podevin
306–308 Roy Pendleton

DESIGNER / GESTALTER / MAQUETTISTE:

306 Ken Ovryn
307 Jack Slawtag
308 Douglas Norgard

ART DIRECTOR / DIRECTEUR ARTISTIQUE:

304, 305 Hildegard Kron
306 John Eskwith
307 John Lux
308 Douglas Norgard

PUBLISHER / VERLEGER / EDITEUR:

304, 305 Omni Publications International Ltd.
306 Outside Magazine
307 Chicago Tribune
308 David C. Cooke Publishing Co.

304, 305 Illustration and introductory double spread to accompany a story: "The man who always wanted to travel", published in the *Omni* magazine. (USA)
306 Illustration for an article about off-beat ideas, here for a video cassette showing tropical fish—thereby eliminating the need to buy an aquarium, in *Outside* magazine. (USA)
307 Olive-green and white illustration for a Halloween cover ghost story in the *Chicago Tribune*, in which a dead girl reappears at inopportune moments and places. (USA)
308 The theme of this illustration in the youth magazine *Sprint* is a woman coming to grips with her terminal illness. (USA)

304, 305 Illustration und einleitende Doppelseite zu einer Geschichte mit dem Titel «Der Mann, der immer reisen wollte», erschienen in der Zeitschrift *Omni*. (USA)
306 Eine Video-Kassette über tropische Fische als Ersatz für das Aquarium ist Gegenstand dieser mehrfarbigen Illustration für einen Artikel im *Outside*-Magazin. (USA)
307 Illustration in Olivgrün für eine Geschichte in *Chicago Tribune*, in der es um ein totes Mädchen geht, das zu sehr ungelegenen Zeiten unter den Lebenden herumgeistert. (USA)
308 Illustration für das Jugend-Magazin *Sprint*. Hier geht es um eine Frau, die mit einer unheilbaren Krankheit zurechtkommen muss. (USA)

304, 305 Illustration et première double page d'une histoire intitulée: «L'homme qui voulait toujours voyager», publiée dans le magazine *Omni*. (USA)
306 Une cassette vidéo sur les poissons tropicaux à la place d'un aquarium, tel est le thème de cette illustration polychrome pour un article du magazine *Outside*. (USA)
307 Illustration en vert olive pour une histoire du *Chicago Tribune* où il est question d'une jeune fille morte qui revient parmi les vivants à des moments inopportuns. (USA)
308 Illustration pour le magazine de jeunes *Sprint*. On y parle d'une femme qui doit se faire à l'idée d'être atteinte d'une maladie incurable. (USA)

307

305

306

308

309

310

ARTIST / KÜNSTLER / ARTISTE:

309–311 Brad Holland

DESIGNER / GESTALTER / MAQUETTISTE:

309, 310 Bruce Hansen

ART DIRECTOR / DIRECTEUR ARTISTIQUE:

309, 310 Tom Staebler
311 Fred Woodward

PUBLISHER / VERLEGER / EDITEUR:

309, 310 Playboy Enterprises, Inc.
311 Texas Monthly

311

309, 310 Illustration and complete double spread to accompany an article in *Playboy* about an alleged rape which was, several years later, recanted by the young victim. (USA)
311 "How Others See Us." Full-page illustration in the *Texas Monthly*, which relates to the image and myth of Texas as the State of "wild extremes" and of rich Texan oil tycoons, created by John Bainbridge in his book *The Super Americans.* (USA)

309, 310 Illustration und vollständige Doppelseite für einen Beitrag in *Playboy* über eine angebliche Vergewaltigung und den späten Widerruf der Beschuldigungen durch das Opfer. (USA)
311 «Wie andere uns sehen.» Ganzseitige Illustration aus *Texas Monthly* für einen Beitrag über das Buch «Super-Amerikaner» von John Bainbridge und das darin gezeichnete Bild des Texaners, das durch den Ölreichtum geprägt ist. (USA)

309, 310 Illustration et double page complète d'un article de *Playboy* sur un prétendu viol et la rétractation tardive des accusations formulées par la soi-disant victime. (USA)
311 «Comment les autres nous voient.» Illustration du *Texas Monthly* pour un article sur le livre de John Bainbridge, «Super-Américains». Elle représente l'image du Texan enrichi par le pétrole. (USA)

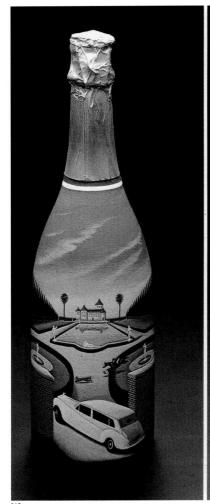

THE JOYS OF SUCCESS

getting there may be half the fun—but being there isn't half bad

compiled by JEAN PENN

OK, SO YOU WORKED late at the office again last night. Or you feel as if your entire life is on hold while you finish your M.B.A. You're tired, you're cranky and you're wondering, Why am I *doing* this?

For many of us, it's never been enough simply to get by. Somewhere in our formative years, we latched onto the concept of success. Whether or not it appealed to us, we usually accepted the fact that all the world respects a success; and besides, it's the successful guy who has the big bank account, the two (or more) vacation homes, the fast cars and who almost always gets the girl. And that's the point of success, right?

Well, maybe. The rewards of success mean different things to different people at different stages of life. So with that in mind, we approached an eclectic group of people who have reached the top of their fields and asked them to tell us what it is they *most enjoy* about their success. Freedom from worry? Live-in help? Early retirement? A spare Porsche to drive when the Mercedes is in the shop?

Their answers, a wonderful mix of materialism and philosophy, may surprise you—as well as make those late nights at the office seem more worth while.

TOM BROKAW, 44 (anchor man, *NBC Nightly News*): Luxury makes me uncomfortable. That's not to say I haven't enjoyed the fruits of success, but I found that once I could afford everything I wanted, my tastes still didn't change that much. I didn't want the ostentatious car or the French villa in the countryside. My tastes remained fundamentally the same. For instance, after the Democratic Convention in San Francisco, *(continued on page 230)*

ILLUSTRATION BY JOHN O'LEARY

312

Magazine Illustrations
Zeitschriften-Illustrationen
Illustrations de périodiques

312 Introductory double spread for a feature in which personalities tell what success means to them and what they most enjoy about it. In *Playboy* magazine. (USA)
313 Full-page reproduction of a picture painted on canvas to illustrate "The Inspectors"—an article in the series "Technology for Peace", appearing in the magazine *Science*. Sombre tones. (USA)
314 "Young Men, Old Money." Illustration in colour for a feature in *Playboy* about the Dartmouth College (New Hampshire) fraternities. (USA)
315 Introductory double spread for a story about an American hotel owner living on a tropical island, where life for him is far from paradisal. (USA)

312 «Die Freuden des Erfolgs.» Einleitende Doppelseite für einen Beitrag über dieses Thema im Magazin *Playboy*. (USA)
313 Ganzseitige Reproduktion eines auf Leinwand gemalten Bildes in gedämpften Farben, als Illustration für eine im Magazin *Science* veröffentlichte Reihe, deren Thema die Überwachung der friedlichen Nutzung der Atomenergie ist. (USA)
314 «Junge Männer, altes Geld.» Mehrfarbige Illustration für einen Beitrag im *Playboy*, in dem es um eine Studenten-Verbindung geht. (USA)
315 Einleitende Doppelseite für eine Geschichte im *Playboy*. Ort des Geschehens ist eine tropische Insel. (USA)

312 «Les joies de la réussite». Double page introduisant un article sur ce thème, paru dans le magazine *Playboy*. (USA)
313 Reproduction pleine page d'une peinture sur toile aux couleurs atténuées illustrant une série consacrée au contrôle de l'utilisation pacifique de l'énergie nucléaire, publiée dans le magazine *Science*. (USA)
314 «Jeunes gens, vieil argent». Illustration polychrome pour un article de *Playboy* où il est question d'une association d'étudiants. (USA)
315 Double page introduisant une histoire dans *Playboy*. L'action se situe dans une île tropicale où il ne fait pas toujours bon vivre. (USA)

313

314

EASY IN THE ISLANDS

tillman owned an exotic hotel in the tropics—and found trouble in paradise

fiction
By BOB SHACOCHIS

THE DAYS WERE SMALL, pointless epics, long wind-ups to punches that always drifted by cartoon fashion, as if each simple task were meaningless unless immersed in more theater and threat than bad opera.
It was only Monday noon and already Tillman had been through the wringer. He had greased the trade commissioner to allow a pallet of Campbell's consommé to come ashore, fired one steel band for their hooliganism and hired another, found a carpenter he was willing to trust to repair the back veranda that was so spongy in spots that Tillman knew it was only a matter of days before a guest's foot burst through the surface into whatever terrors lived below in the tepid darkness, restocked on vitamins from the pharmacy, argued with the crayfish regulatory bureau about quotas. And argued with the inscrutable cook, a fat country woman who wore a wool watch cap and smoked hand-rolled cigars; argued with both maids, muscle-bound Lemonille and the other one, who wouldn't reveal her name; argued with the gardener, who liked to chop everything up; argued with the customs house; argued with the bartender, Jevanee. And although he had not forthrightly won any of these encounters, he had won them enough to forestall the doom that would one day descend on

60

ILLUSTRATION BY KINUKO Y. CRAFT

315

147

316

317

318

ARTIST / KÜNSTLER / ARTISTE:

316 Marshall Arisman
317–319 Anita Kunz

DESIGNER / GESTALTER / MAQUETTISTE:

316 Len Willis
317, 319 Greg Paul
318 Jackie Young

ART DIRECTOR / DIRECTEUR ARTISTIQUE:

316 Tom Staebler
317, 319 Greg Paul
318 Jackie Young

AGENCY / AGENTUR / AGENCE – STUDIO:

318 Ink

PUBLISHER / VERLEGER / EDITEUR:

316 Playboy Enterprises, Inc.
317 Sunshine Magazine
318 The Financial Post
319 New Age Journal

316 Illustration in about actual size for an article: "Pay me now or pay me later", about the investigators of the Child Support Enforcement Unit, published in *Playboy* magazine. (USA)
317 Full-page illustration in the *Sunshine Magazine* about how people in Florida can prepare for a nuclear holocaust. (USA)
318 Illustration in mainly brown and blue tones to accompany an article about Trust companies, in *The Financial Post* magazine. (CAN)
319 The positive aspects of polygamy is the subject of the article to which this illustration relates, from *The New Age Journal.* In brown and blue-grey tones. (USA)

316 Detail einer über die ganze Doppelseite reichenden Illustration für einen Artikel über die Eintreibung von Alimenten, erschienen im Magazin *Playboy.* (USA)
317 Ganzseitige, mehrfarbige Illustration zu einem Beitrag im *Sunshine Magazine:* Wie die Bevölkerung von Florida einer Atomkatastrophe begegnen kann. (USA)
318 Illustration, vorwiegend in Braun- und Blautönen, für einen Artikel über grosse Konzerne, erschienen im Wirtschaftsmagazin *The Financial Post.* (CAN)
319 Die positiven Aspekte der Polygamie sind Gegenstand dieser Illustration aus der Zeitschrift *The New Age Journal;* in Braun- und Blaugrautönen. (USA)

316 Détail d'une illustration couvrant toute une double page, pour un article sur le recouvrement des pensions alimentaires, paru dans le magazine *Playboy.* (USA)
317 Illustration pleine page polychrome pour un article du *Sunshine Magazine:* comment la population peut faire face à une catastrophe nucléaire en Floride. (USA)
318 Illustration d'un article sur les grands konzerns publié par le magazine économique *The Financial Post.* Prédominance de tons bruns et bleus. (CAN)
319 Les aspects positifs de la polygamie, tel est le sujet de cette illustration parue dans la revue *The New Age Journal.* En brun et gris-bleu. (USA)

319

ARTIST / KÜNSTLER / ARTISTE:

320 Mel Odom
321 Gayle Kabaker
322 Ed Paschke

DESIGNER / GESTALTER / MAQUETTISTE:

320 Kerig Pope
321 Karen Gutowsky
322 Len Willis

ART DIRECTOR / DIRECTEUR ARTISTIQUE:

320–322 Tom Staebler

PUBLISHER / VERLEGER / EDITEUR:

320–322 Playboy Enterprises, Inc.

320

320–322 Complete page and double spreads from *Playboy* magazine. Fig. 320 illustrates a story by Gabriel García Márquez about the double life of a governess: "Miss Forbes's Summer of Happiness". Soft pastel tones, background in airbrush technique. Fig. 321 relates to an article entitled "What women talk about when they talk about men"; in strong colours. Fig. 322 is for an article by Ransom Satchell about rape. (USA)

320–322 Vollständige Seite und Doppelseiten aus dem Magazin *Playboy*. Abb. 320 illustriert eine Erzählung von Gabriel García Márquez über das Doppelleben einer Gouvernante: «Miss Forbes' Sommer des Glücks.» Sanfte Pastelltöne, Hintergrund in Spritztechnik. Abb. 321 gehört zu einem Artikel mit dem Titel (und Wortspiel): «Worüber Frauen sprechen, wenn sie über Männer sprechen.» In kräftigen Farben. In Abb. 322 geht es um einen Beitrag von Ransom Satchell: «Ein anderer Aspekt der Vergewaltigung.» (USA)

320–322 Page complète et doubles pages du magazine *Playboy*. La fig. 320 illustre un récit de Gabriel García Márquez évoquant la double vie d'une gouvernante: «L'été du bonheur de Miss Forbes». Tons pastel, fond sprayé. La fig. 321 se rapporte à un article intitulé: «De quoi les femmes parlent quand elles parlent des hommes» (jeu de mots en anglais); couleurs vives. La fig. 322 accompagne un article de Ransom Satchell: «Un autre aspect du viol.» (USA)

Magazine Illustrations
Zeitschriften-Illustrationen
Illustrations de périodiques

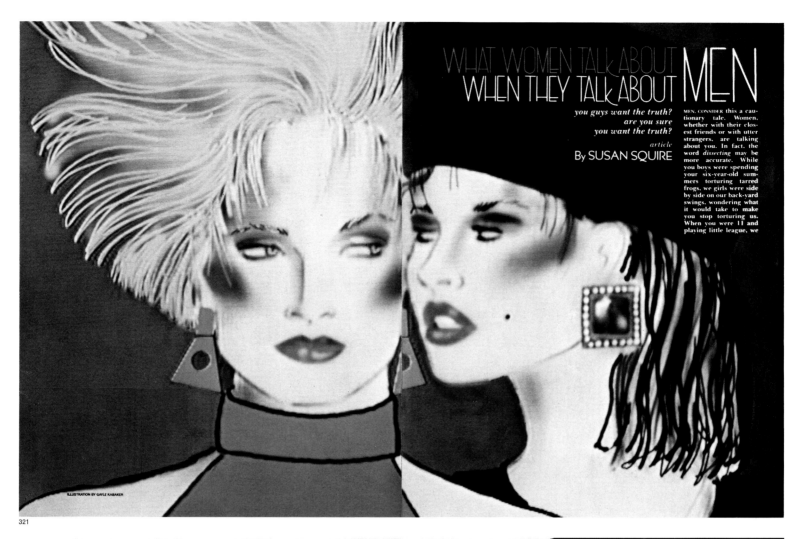

WHAT WOMEN TALK ABOUT WHEN THEY TALK ABOUT MEN

you guys want the truth?
are you sure
you want the truth?

article
By SUSAN SQUIRE

MEN. CONSIDER this a cautionary tale. Women, whether with their closest friends or with utter strangers, are talking about you. In fact, the word *dissecting* may be more accurate. While you boys were spending your six-year-old summers torturing tarred frogs, we girls were side by side on our back-yard swings, wondering what it would take to make you stop torturing us. When you were 11 and playing little league, we

ILLUSTRATION BY GAYLE KABAKER

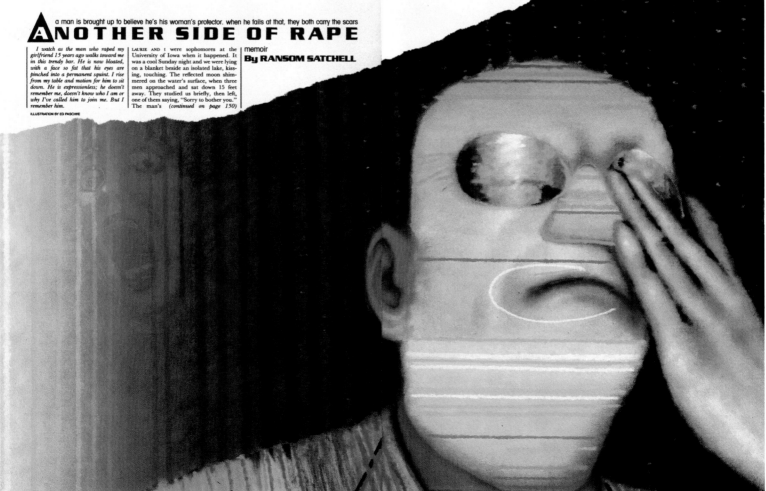

a man is brought up to believe he's his woman's protector. when he fails at that, they both carry the scars

ANOTHER SIDE OF RAPE

I watch as the man who raped my girlfriend 15 years ago walks toward me in this trendy bar. He is now bloated, with a face so fat that his eyes are pinched into a permanent squint. I rise from my table and motion for him to sit down. He is expressionless; he doesn't remember me, doesn't know who I am or why I've called him to join me. But I remember him.

ILLUSTRATION BY ED PASCHKE

LAURIE AND I were sophomores at the University of Iowa when it happened. It was a cool Sunday night and we were lying on a blanket beside an isolated lake, kissing, touching. The reflected moon shimmered on the water's surface, when three men approached and sat down 15 feet away. They studied us briefly, then left, one of them saying, "Sorry to bother you." The man's *(continued on page 150)*

memoir
By RANSOM SATCHELL

323

Bringing It All Back Home

There was a time when it seemed the family was incompatible with women's freedom. Now it seems that women's freedom and family might together create the best of all possible worlds.

Several years ago, my husband left me alone with my mother-in-law when a sudden change in plans brought her to our house during a weekend Vincent had to fly east on business.

We had, or so I thought, almost nothing in common. Rachel's ancestors were French Canadians who immigrated to Maine and worked in the woolen mills. My family comes from a line of Irish toughs and failed aristocrats. How was I to deal with her, a woman I barely knew and whose relation to me was as muddy as a New England spring? How was she to deal with me? For while I knew she was glad her son had married, I also knew she found me strange.

Neither of us had any tradition to help us out. If the roles of mother and daughter are strained and tangled in our society, then the roles of daughter- and mother-in-law are worse: the object solely of Henny Youngman jokes.

That first afternoon, tension and confusion filled the house, and Rachel and I withdrew to separate rooms and the haven of solitary pursuits. But when evening came, we were forced out into the kitchen. Somehow we got through dinner. Afterward, in front of the blazing fireplace, Rachel sat down to do yoga. Because of a longstanding illness, she must stretch her muscles every day to keep herself walking. Watching this tiny woman struggling to touch her hand to her ankle, I was moved out of my own self-concern. I sat down next to her and asked, "Would you teach me how?" We sat on the floor, facing each other. "Put one leg out in front," Rachel said, and we began.

The next morning, we went to Mass together, and I saw, in the happy greeting given to Rachel by the members of my church, the recognition of that elusive and delicate, but extremely compelling, thing we call family.

At home once more, Rachel and I made juice, from grapes freshly picked from the vines of a friend.   continued

By Nora Gallagher

324

Magazine Illustrations
Zeitschriften-Illustrationen
Illustrations de périodiques

ARTIST / KÜNSTLER / ARTISTE:

323 Matt Mahurin
324 Anita Kunz
325 Dave La Fleur
326 Bidjan Assadipour
327 Etienne Delessert

DESIGNER / GESTALTER / MAQUETTISTE:

323 Bruce Hansen
324 Bambi Nicklen
327 Judy Garlan

ART DIRECTOR / DIRECTEUR ARTISTIQUE:

323 Tom Staebler
324 Bambi Nicklen
325 Greg Paul
326 A. Taheri
327 Judy Garlan

PUBLISHER / VERLEGER / EDITEUR:

323 Playboy Enterprises, Inc.
324 San José Mercury News
325 New Age Journal
326 Kayhan Publications Ltd.
327 The Atlantic Monthly

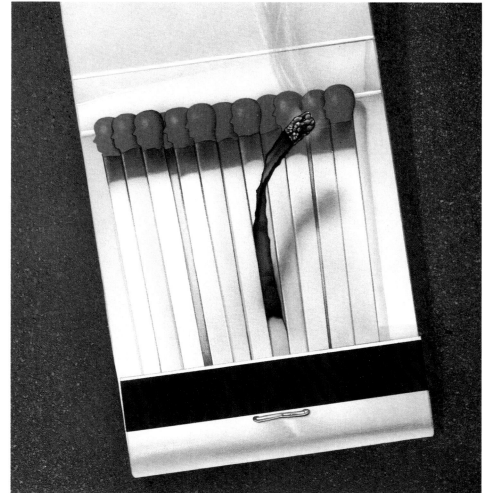

325

326

327

328

ARTIST / KÜNSTLER / ARTISTE:

328 H. G. Magnus
329 François Brosse
330 Peter Sis
331, 332 Hisako Naiki

DESIGNER / GESTALTER / MAQUETTISTE:

329 Eric Fauchère
331, 332 Akira Miwa

ART DIRECTOR / DIRECTEUR ARTISTIQUE:

328 Wolfgang Behnken
329 Eric Fauchère
330 Rhoda Gubernick
331, 332 Akira Miwa

PUBLISHER / VERLEGER / EDITEUR:

328 Gruner & Jahr AG & Co.
329 Hachette
330 The Atlantic Monthly
331, 332 Nagasaki-Do

331

329

330

332

Magazine Illustrations
Zeitschriften-Illustrationen
Illustrations de périodiques

328 Introductory double spread with black-and-white illustration for a series in *Stern* entitled "The Sorcerer's Apprentices". Here, the subject is Robert Oppenheimer and his team of physicists working on the atom bomb at Los Alamos—"The Town of Lost Souls". (GER)
329 Double spread from *Cinq sur Cinq*, with the French "super hero", who bears all the qualities and all the faults of his compatriots. In blue and magenta. (FRA)
330 Black-and-white illustration from a travel article in *The Atlantic* about Berlin: "East Side, West Side". (USA)
331, 332 Illustrations for an "Anthology of Love". (JPN)

328 Einleitende Doppelseite zu einer Serie im *Stern*, hier mit dem «Monstrum», eine ironisch verfremdete Darstellung des ersten Atommeilers. Illustration in Schwarzweiss. (GER)
329 Doppelseite aus *Cinq sur Cinq* mit dem französischen «Superman», der alle Qualitäten und vor allem alle Fehler seiner Landsleute besitzt. In Blau und Magenta. (FRA)
330 Illustration in Schwarzweiss für einen Reisebericht über Berlin in *The Atlantic*. (USA)
331, 332 Illustrationen aus einer japanischen «Anthologie der Liebe». (JPN)

328 Double page introduisant une série d'articles publiée dans *Stern*, intitulée «Les apprentis-sorciers», où il est question de la bombe atomique. Ici, le «monstre», une interprétation pleine d'ironie du premier réacteur nucléaire. En noir et blanc. (GER)
329 Double page de *Cinq sur Cinq* avec le «Superman» français qui a toutes les qualités, mais surtout les défauts de ses compatriotes. En bleu et magenta. (FRA)
330 Illustration en noir et blanc pour un reportage sur Berlin paru dans *The Atlantic*. (USA)
331, 332 Illustrations tirées d'un livre illustré japonais intitulé «Anthologie de l'amour». (JPN)

Magazine Illustrations
Zeitschriften-Illustrationen
Illustrations de périodiques

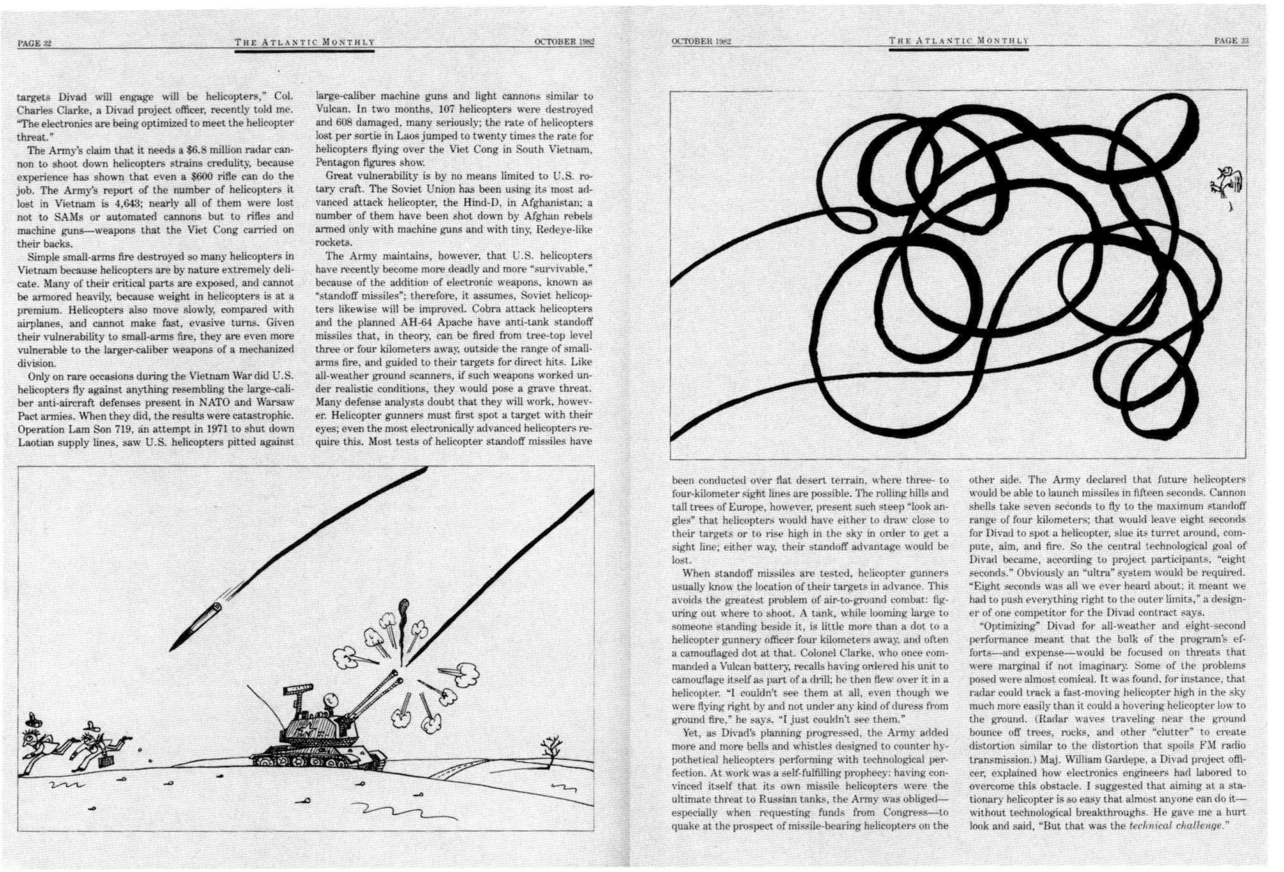

PAGE 32 — THE ATLANTIC MONTHLY — OCTOBER 1982

targets Divad will engage will be helicopters," Col. Charles Clarke, a Divad project officer, recently told me. "The electronics are being optimized to meet the helicopter threat."

The Army's claim that it needs a $6.8 million radar cannon to shoot down helicopters strains credulity, because experience has shown that even a $600 rifle can do the job. The Army's report of the number of helicopters it lost in Vietnam is 4,643; nearly all of them were lost not to SAMs or automated cannons but to rifles and machine guns—weapons that the Viet Cong carried on their backs.

Simple small-arms fire destroyed so many helicopters in Vietnam because helicopters are by nature extremely delicate. Many of their critical parts are exposed, and cannot be armored heavily, because weight in helicopters is at a premium. Helicopters also move slowly, compared with airplanes, and cannot make fast, evasive turns. Given their vulnerability to small-arms fire, they are even more vulnerable to the larger-caliber weapons of a mechanized division.

Only on rare occasions during the Vietnam War did U.S. helicopters fly against anything resembling the large-caliber anti-aircraft defenses present in NATO and Warsaw Pact armies. When they did, the results were catastrophic. Operation Lam Son 719, an attempt in 1971 to shut down Laotian supply lines, saw U.S. helicopters pitted against large-caliber machine guns and light cannons similar to Vulcan. In two months, 107 helicopters were destroyed and 608 damaged, many seriously; the rate of helicopters lost per sortie in Laos jumped to twenty times the rate for helicopters flying over the Viet Cong in South Vietnam, Pentagon figures show.

Great vulnerability is by no means limited to U.S. rotary craft. The Soviet Union has been using its most advanced attack helicopter, the Hind-D, in Afghanistan; a number of them have been shot down by Afghan rebels armed only with machine guns and with tiny, Redeye-like rockets.

The Army maintains, however, that U.S. helicopters have recently become more deadly and more "survivable," because of the addition of electronic weapons, known as "standoff missiles"; therefore, it assumes, Soviet helicopters likewise will be improved. Cobra attack helicopters and the planned AH-64 Apache have anti-tank standoff missiles that, in theory, can be fired from tree-top level three or four kilometers away, outside the range of small-arms fire, and guided to their targets for direct hits. Like all-weather ground scanners, if such weapons worked under realistic conditions, they would pose a grave threat. Many defense analysts doubt that they will work, however. Helicopter gunners must first spot a target with their eyes; even the most electronically advanced helicopters require this. Most tests of helicopter standoff missiles have

OCTOBER 1982 — THE ATLANTIC MONTHLY — PAGE 33

been conducted over flat desert terrain, where three- to four-kilometer sight lines are possible. The rolling hills and tall trees of Europe, however, present such steep "look angles" that helicopters would have either to draw close to their targets or to rise high in the sky in order to get a sight line; either way, their standoff advantage would be lost.

When standoff missiles are tested, helicopter gunners usually know the location of their targets in advance. This avoids the greatest problem of air-to-ground combat: figuring out where to shoot. A tank, while looming large to someone standing beside it, is little more than a dot to a helicopter gunnery officer four kilometers away, and often a camouflaged dot at that. Colonel Clarke, who once commanded a Vulcan battery, recalls having ordered his unit to camouflage itself as part of a drill; he then flew over it in a helicopter. "I couldn't see them at all, even though we were flying right by and not under any kind of duress from ground fire," he says. "I just couldn't see them."

Yet, as Divad's planning progressed, the Army added more and more bells and whistles designed to counter hypothetical helicopters performing with technological perfection. At work was a self-fulfilling prophecy: having convinced itself that its own missile helicopters were the ultimate threat to Russian tanks, the Army was obliged—especially when requesting funds from Congress—to quake at the prospect of missile-bearing helicopters on the other side. The Army declared that future helicopters would be able to launch missiles in fifteen seconds. Cannon shells take seven seconds to fly to the maximum standoff range of four kilometers; that would leave eight seconds for Divad to spot a helicopter, slue its turret around, compute, aim, and fire. So the central technological goal of Divad became, according to project participants, "eight seconds." Obviously an "ultra" system would be required. "Eight seconds was all we ever heard about; it meant we had to push everything right to the outer limits," a designer of one competitor for the Divad contract says.

"Optimizing" Divad for all-weather and eight-second performance meant that the bulk of the program's efforts—and expense—would be focused on threats that were marginal if not imaginary. Some of the problems posed were almost comical. It was found, for instance, that radar could track a fast-moving helicopter high in the sky much more easily than it could a hovering helicopter low to the ground. (Radar waves traveling near the ground bounce off trees, rocks, and other "clutter" to create distortion similar to the distortion that spoils FM radio transmission.) Maj. William Gardepe, a Divad project officer, explained how electronics engineers had labored to overcome this obstacle. I suggested that aiming at a stationary helicopter is so easy that almost anyone can do it—without technological breakthroughs. He gave me a hurt look and said, "But that was the *technical challenge.*"

333

ARTIST / KÜNSTLER / ARTISTE:

333–335 J. C. Suarès
336–338 Tullio Pericoli

DESIGNER / GESTALTER / MAQUETTISTE:

333 J. C. Suarès/Judy Garlan

ART DIRECTOR / DIRECTEUR ARTISTIQUE:

333 Judy Garlan

PUBLISHER / VERLEGER / EDITEUR:

333 The Atlantic Monthly
334, 335 The Nation
336–338 L'Espresso

CULTURA

ANNIVERSARI

MANZONI, CIOÈ L'ITALIA

di NELLO AJELLO

A duecento anni dalla morte del grande scrittore, "I Promessi Sposi" sono sempre più attuali. Questo capolavoro, che cattivi insegnanti spesso ci hanno fatto odiare, è ancora oggi il ritratto del nostro paese. Perché?

Roma. Alessandro Manzoni nacque giusto due secoli fa e il suo romanzo — se ci riferiamo all'edizione definitiva del 1840 — sta per compiere 145 anni. Una lunga carriera nel corso della quale il romanziere lombardo ha somministrato a quasi dieci generazioni di suoi connazionali insegnamenti letterari, suggerimenti storici, avvertimenti morali, moniti religiosi, stimoli critici, consigli linguistici. Ma anche tanta, tanta noia. Misfatto, quest'ultimo, del quale Manzoni non fu responsabile né complice ma, almeno in gran parte, vittima incolpevole.

Il luogo nel quale si è consumata questa ingiustizia è la scuola. Lì, "I Promessi Sposi" sono stati letti per lunghi decenni come il classico del buon senso italiano o, peggio, come un testo di edificazione religiosa. Di rado, a memoria d'uomo, un grande libro è stato sottoposto ad una cosmesi più mefitica. Perfino l'aspetto fisico del suo autore ne ha risentito. Sulla copertina delle edizioni scolastiche spiccava infatti il dagherrotipo di un Manzoni vecchio, un po' ingobbito, il portamento nobile e stanco, i favoriti candidi, sulle labbra un sorriso appena enigmatico e visibilmente amaro: un monumento alla Rispettibilità, un mausoleo dei Buoni Sentimenti. C'è da giurare che pochi quattordicenni, che imparavano «Addio, monti sorgenti dall'acque» oppure «Scendeva dalla soglia di uno di quegli usci», abbiano mai sospettato che, quando descriveva quelle scene Alessandro Manzoni avesse dai trentacinque ai quarantadue anni (in anni più maturi si limitò a limarle e a riscriverle). Aveva cioè l'età in cui i loro padri vanno a sciare, giocano a tennis e tutt'al più accettano di abbandonare il windsurf.

L'abitudine a travestire Manzoni in malinconici panni curiali è ancora in parte diffusa. A un ragazzo cui capita di confessare che il romanzo non gli piace o gli concilia il sonno forse non potrà più capitare ciò che accadde a Paolo Murialdi, oggi noto studioso di mass-media e nel 1934 studente di ginnasio: nel Regio istituto Cristoforo Colombo di Genova dev'esserci ancora un registro di classe dove, nella casella riservata alle note di biasimo, si legge sotto il suo nome un anatema minaccioso scritto dalla professoressa di lettere: «L'alunno ha dichiarato di non amare il Manzoni». Nei successivi quarant'anni, a parità di noia, è molto cresciuta — è vero — la libertà di parola. Ma, insieme, si è moltiplicata quella che André Gide ha definito «la difesa ironica dell'adolescente». Una difesa sfoderata di fronte a numerose calamità, dall'obbligo di assistere alle prediche a quello di ascoltare i racconti del nonno. Anche, talvolta, quelli di nonno Manzoni.

Eppure, gli antidoti non mancherebbero. Il tentativo di dimostrare che «il cantore di Renzo e Lucia» è un romanziere vivo e persino piacevole merita di essere fatto. Nelle scuole di oggi, per altro, sono molti gli insegnanti che si sforzano di estrarre, da quello sterminato repertorio didascalico che è il testo man- >>>

QUESTO SERVIZIO

Che cosa è stato, ed è, per noi Alessandro Manzoni? Una vittima, incolpevole, della noia costruita sul suo romanzo? Un monumento alla rispettabilità, un mausoleo dei Buoni Sentimenti? Persino nella scuola, dove per anni è stata consumata questa ingiustizia ai suoi danni, lo si sta riabilitando. Dimostrare che Manzoni è attuale e che la storia dei "Promessi Sposi", la si può leggere anche oggi nella cronaca dei quotidiani non è difficile, così come riconoscere il suo impegno di scrittore progressista.

A due secoli dalla nascita e a 145 anni dall'edizione definitiva del suo romanzo cerchiamo di rispondere a queste domande, di capire perché, tutto sommato, si possa dire oggi "Manzoni, cioè l'Italia".

Alcuni scrittori rivisitano, poi, una decina dei personaggi più significativi del romanzo, da Renzo e Lucia, a Don Abbondio all'Azzeccagarbugli. Mentre Fruttero e Lucentini indagano su che cosa si nasconde "dietro" questi personaggi, a chi somigliano davvero. Leonardo Sciascia ricostruisce, documenti alla mano, uno dei casi più inquietanti in cui possa imbattersi un manzoniano praticante come lui. Umberto Eco spiega, rileggendo la prima pagina dei "Promessi Sposi", come la grande narrativa dell'Ottocento abbia influenzato il cinema. Edoardo Sanguineti si occupa dell'opera poetica, Tullio De Mauro della lingua. E infine abbiamo voluto sottolineare alcuni aspetti meno noti della vita privata dello scrittore.

I lettori troveranno anche allegata all' "Espresso", in regalo, la "Storia della colonna infame" con introduzione di Leonardo Sciascia.

Disegno di TULLIO PERICOLI

62 · L'ESPRESSO · 24 FEBBRAIO 1985 — L'ESPRESSO · 24 FEBBRAIO 1985 · 63

336

333 Double spread from *The Atlantic* with an article about a high-tech US army anti-aircraft weapon which, claims the author, is useless at hitting targets and once even boomeranged. (USA)
334, 335 Drawings as political commentary in *The Nation.* (USA)
336 Double spreads with polychrome illustrations from *L'Espresso* on the bicentenary of the birth of Italian author Manzoni. (ITA)
337, 338 Full-colour illustrations of Torricelli (inventor of the barometer) and physicist André Ampère (founder of electromagnetism, amp=electric current unit) from a series in *L'Espresso.* (ITA)

333 Doppelseite aus *The Atlantic* mit einem Artikel über ein hochtechnisiertes Abwehrsystem der US-Armee, das nach Ansicht des Autors unbrauchbar ist und sich sogar als Bumerang erwies. (USA)
334, 335 Zeichnungen als politische Satire in *The Nation.* (USA)
336 Doppelseite mit mehrfarbiger Illustration aus *L'Espresso* zum 200sten Geburtstag des italienischen Autors Manzoni. (ITA)
337, 338 Farbige Darstellungen des Evangelisten Torricelli, Erfinder des Barometers, und des Physikers und Mathematikers André Ampère, aus der Rubrik «Geniale Erfinder» in *L'Espresso.* (ITA)

333 Double page pour *The Atlantic:* d'un article sur la haute technicité du système de défense américain qui, selon l'auteur, est inutilisable et qui avait même un effet de boomerang. (USA)
334, 335 Dessins de satire politique pour *The Nation.* (USA)
336 Double page de *L'Espresso* avec illustration polychrome pour le 200e anniversaire de l'écrivain Manzoni. (ITA)
337, 338 Portraits en couleurs de Torricelli, inventeur du baromètre, et André Ampère, physicien et mathématicien, pour la rubrique «Inventeurs géniaux» de *L'Espresso.* (ITA)

334

335

Evangelista Torricelli - il barometro

337

André Ampère - l'elettrodinamica

338

339

340

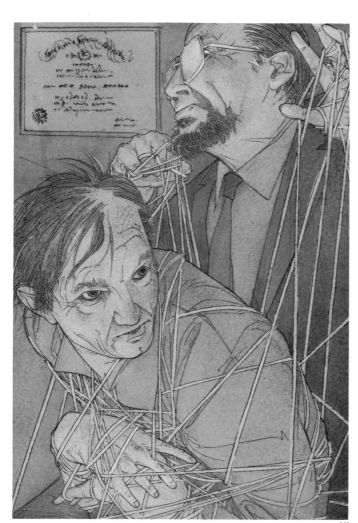

341

342

339 Full-page illustration in coloured pencil as introduction to the "Kernel" section in the magazine *Byte*. (USA)
340 Full-colour illustration for an article in the *Outside* magazine, entitled "Healing Hands", about the efficacy of massage for "knotted muscles". (USA)
341, 342 From the series in *Time* magazine with the title "Behaviour". Fig. 341 refers to some dubious methods of certain therapists; in pastel tones. Fig. 342 (in sepia) concerns the help given to victims of torture. (USA)
343 Cover illustration of the Spanish magazine *Cambio-16*. (SPA)
344 Illustration relating to the increasing violence in rock groups' video clips which are shown on television. For *Video* magazine. (USA)

339 Ganzseitige Farbstiftillustration als Einleitung einer Rubrik mit dem Titel «Kern», in der Fachzeitschrift *Byte*. (USA)
340 Illustration für einen Beitrag im Magazin *Outside* über Massage und ihre heilsame Wirkung auf «verknotete Muskeln». (USA)
341, 342 Aus einer regelmässig im Magazin *Time* unter dem Titel «Verhalten» erscheinenden Serie. Hier zu den Problemen des Verhältnisses Therapeut/Patient (Abb. 341, in Pastelltönen) und der geretteten Opfer von Folterungen (Abb. 342, in Sepia). (USA)
343 Umschlag-Illustration für die spanische Zeitschrift *Cambio-16*. (SPA)
344 Illustration über die zunehmende Gewalttätigkeit in den am Fernsehen gezeigten Video-Clips von Rock-Gruppen. Für *Video*. (USA)

339 Illustration pleine page aux crayons de couleurs introduisant une rubrique du magazine professionnel *Byte* intitulée «Graine». (USA)
340 Illustration d'un article du magazine *Outside* sur l'effet bénéfique des massages en cas de contractions muscula res. (USA)
341, 342 D'une série intitulée «Comportements» paraissant périodiquement dans le magazine *Time*. Ici, les problèmes posés par l'attitude d'un thérapeute envers son patient (fig. 341, tons pastel) et les séquelles des victimes de la torture ayant survécu (fig. 342, sépia). (USA)
343 Illustration pour la couverture du magazine espagnol *Cambio-16*. (SPA)
344 Illustration sur la violence toujours plus grande dans les vidéo-clips des groupes de rock à la télévision. Pour *Video*. (USA)

344

343

ARTIST / KÜNSTLER / ARTISTE:

339 Maciek Albrecht
340 Jean-François Podevin
341 David Johnson
342 Matt Mahurin
343 Roman Gonzalez Teja
344 Andrzej Dudzinski

DESIGNER / GESTALTER / MAQUETTISTE:

339 Roslyn Frick
342 Laurie Olefson

ART DIRECTOR / DIRECTEUR ARTISTIQUE:

339 Roslyn Frick
340 Ken Ovryn/John Eskwith
341, 342 Rudolph Hoglund
343 Ramon Gonzalez Teja
344 Amy Gotlieb

PUBLISHER / VERLEGER / EDITEUR:

339 McGraw-Hill Publishing Co.
340 Outside Magazine
341, 342 Time, Inc.
343 Hobby Press

ARTIST / KÜNSTLER / ARTISTE:

345, 346 Ralph Steadman
347 Odile Quellet
348 Nery Cruz

DESIGNER / GESTALTER:

347 Marie-Josée Chagnon
348 Nery Cruz

ART DIRECTOR:

345, 346 Simon Scott
347 Marie-Josée Chagnon
348 Ed Guthero

PUBLISHER / VERLEGER:

345, 346 Harrap Ltd.
347 André Ducharme
348 Pacific Press

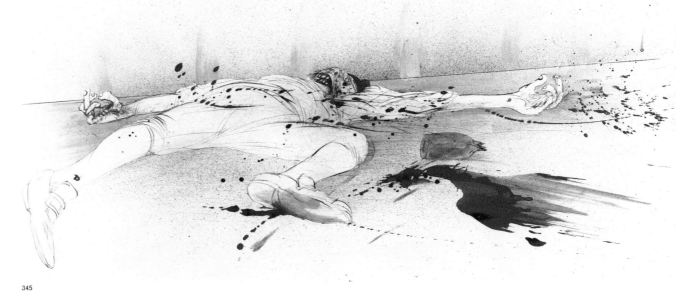

345

346

345, 346 Illustrations by Ralph Steadman from the R. L. Stevenson classic *Treasure Island*, published by Harrap of London. (GBR)
347 Illustration in black and white for an article in the magazine *Montréal* concerning the flagging strength of sportsmen. (CAN)
348 Illustration for an article in the magazine *Signs of the Times*, published by *Pacific Press*. (USA)

345, 346 Illustrationen für eine im Verlag Harrap, London, erschienene Ausgabe von Robert Louis Stevensons *Schatzinsel*. (GBR)
347 Illustration in Schwarzweiss für einen Beitrag in der Zeitschrift *Montréal*, in dem es um das Nachlassen der Kräfte von Sportlern geht. (CAN)
348 Illustration für einen Artikel in der Zeitschrift *Signs of the Times* von *Pacific Press*. (USA)

345, 346 Illustrations tirées d'une édition de *L'île au trésor* de Robert Louis Stevenson, publiée chez Harrap, à Londres. (GBR)
347 Illustration en noir et blanc pour un article sur l'affaiblissement des forces des sportifs, paru dans le magazine *Montréal*. (CAN)
348 Illustration d'un article paru dans le magazine *Signs of the Times*, publié par *Pacific Press*. (USA)

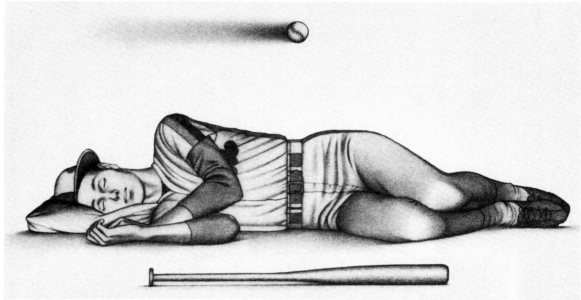

347

348

349

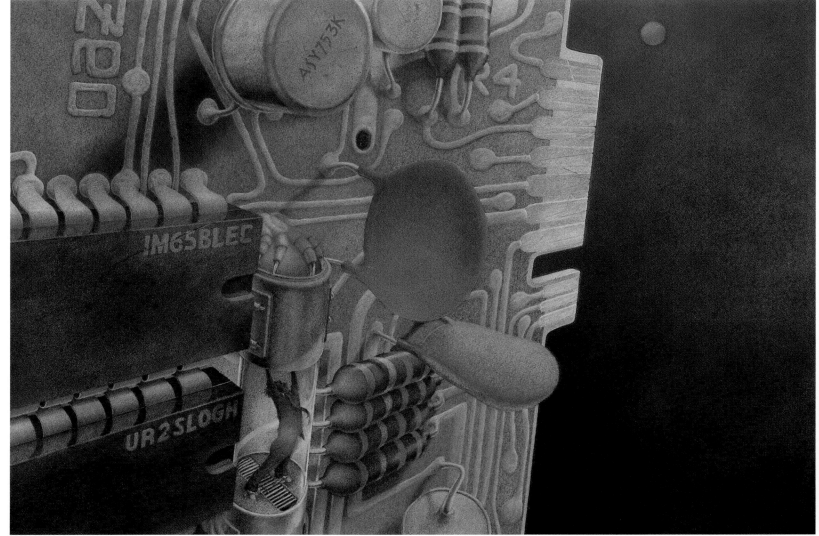

351

ARTIST / KÜNSTLER / ARTISTE:

349, 350 Brian Ajhar
351 James Tughan
352 Heseler & Heseler

DESIGNER / GESTALTER / MAQUETTISTE:

351 James Tughan

ART DIRECTOR / DIRECTEUR ARTISTIQUE:

349, 350 Louis Cruz
351 Steve Manley
352 Manfred Neussl

PUBLISHER / VERLEGER / EDITEUR:

349, 350 Success Magazine
351 Canadian Business Magazine
352 Burda-Verlag

350

352

349, 350 Illustration (watercolour, ink, coloured pencil) and complete double spread from the business magazine *Success!*. The article states that managements have a lot to learn from some aspects in the successful way the Mafia manages its business, as featured in the book *The Godfather* for instance. (USA)
351 For an article in *Canadian Business* about computer technicians suffering from burnout in their professional careers. (CAN)
352 Illustration in mainly sand and soft brown tones, for a story in *Die Freundin* magazine. (GER)

349, 350 Illustration (Aquarell, Tusche, Farbstift) und vollständige Doppelseite aus dem Wirtschaftsmagazin *Success!*. In dem Artikel geht es um ein Buch, das aufdeckt, wie man von der Mafia lernen kann, was Management anbetrifft. (USA)
351 Illustration für einen Artikel in *Canadian Business* über Computer-Techniker, die sich beruflich verbrauchen. (CAN)
352 Illustration in sanften Farben (vorwiegend Sand- und Brauntöne) für einen Roman in der Zeitschrift *Die Freundin* mit dem Titel «Gastfreundschaft». (GER)

349, 350 Illustration (aquarelle, encre, crayon de couleur) et double page complète du magazine économique *Success!*. L'article en question évoque un livre qui révèle comment apprendre de la mafia tout ce qui a trait au management. (USA)
351 «Des lumières qui baissent». Illustration pour un article du *Canadian Business* sur les informaticiens qui s'épuisent au travail. (CAN)
352 Illustration aux couleurs atténuées (prédominance de tons sable et bruns) pour un roman intitulé «Hospitalité» publié dans le magazine allemand *Die Freundin*. (GER)

353

354

ARTIST / KÜNSTLER / ARTISTE:

353 Terry Widener
354 George Stavrinos
355 Lou Beach
356, 357 Gael Burns
358 Hans Hillmann

DESIGNER / GESTALTER / MAQUETTISTE:

354 Theo Kouvatsos
355 Lynn Staley
356, 357 Gael Burns

ART DIRECTOR / DIRECTEUR ARTISTIQUE:

353 David Harris
354 Tom Staebler
355 Lynn Staley
356, 357 Gael Burns
358 Hans-Georg Pospischil

PUBLISHER / VERLEGER / EDITEUR:

353 Dallas Times Herald
354 Playboy Enterprises, Inc.
355 The Boston Globe
356, 357 Time Inc.
358 Frankfurter Allgemeine Zeitung GmbH

353 Full-page polychrome illustration for the Christmas Story—as seen from Joseph's standpoint and told in an updated Texas version', from *Dallas City* magazine. (USA)
354 Illustration in brown and yellow tones for an article on John Mellencamp, in *Playboy*. (USA)
355 "Tall, but wiry"—for an article on orthodontics, in *The Boston Globe Magazine*. (USA)
356, 357 Illustration and complete cover for a special advertising section in the magazine *Fortune* with the title "Office Systems for the Eighties". (USA)
358 Double spread for an article on Boston, in the *Frankfurter Allgemeine Magazin*. (GER)

353 Ganzseitige, mehrfarbige Illustration für eine Weihnachtsgeschichte, in der das Geschehen, in die heutige Zeit verlegt, von Josefs Standpunkt aus erzählt wird. Aus *Dallas City*. (USA)
354 Illustration in Braun- und Gelbtönen für einen Beitrag über John Mellencamp im *Playboy*. (USA)
355 Illustration für einen Beitrag über Kieferorthopädie in *The Boston Globe Magazine*. (USA)
356, 357 «Office» – Illustration und vollständiger Umschlag für eine Sonderbeilage der Zeitschrift *Fortune*, die modernen Büroausstattungen gewidmet ist. (USA)
358 Doppelseite aus einem Artikel über Boston im *Frankfurter Allgemeine Magazin*. (GER)

353 Illustration polychrome pleine page pour une histoire de Noël: l'action, racontée du point de vue de Joseph, est transposée à notre époque. Publiée dans *Dallas City*. (USA)
354 Pour un article sur John Mellencamp dans *Playboy*. Illustration en bruns et jaunes. (USA)
355 Illustration d'un article du *Boston Globe Magazine* sur l'orthodontie. (USA)
356, 357 «Office» – Illustration et couverture complète d'un supplément du magazine *Fortune* consacré aux nouveaux équipements de bureaux. (USA)
358 Double page d'un article sur Boston paru dans le *Frankfurter Allgemeine Magazin*. (GER)

355

356

357

FORTUNE

SPECIAL ADVERTISING SECTION, OCTOBER 14, 1985

OFFICE
SYSTEMS
FOR THE
EIGHTIES:
THE PRODUCTIVITY
CHALLENGE

358

wiedergekämpft im neu erbauten Bunker Hill Pavilion. Noch zitternd vor Aufregung will sich der unermüdliche Postrevolutionär eine Pause gönnen. Es soll nicht sein. Ein Stück Papier wird ihm in die Hand gedrückt, ein Test. Nun muß er ganz und gar Farbe bekennen. „Patriot oder Loyalist" nennt sich das „revolutionäre Quiz". Sein Statement Nummer 6: Die Regierung ist öfter der Feind als der Freund der Freiheit. (Einverstanden: 3 Punkte. Etwas einverstanden: 2 Punkte. Etwas nicht einverstanden: 1 Punkt. Nicht einverstanden: 0 Punkte.) Statement Nummer 12: Eine Gruppe marschierender Männer ist eine Gefahr für den Frieden. (Einverstanden: 0 Punkte. Etwas einverstanden: 1 Punkt. Etwas nicht einverstanden: 2 Punkte. Nicht einverstanden: 3 Punkte.) Gesamtergebnis: 0 bis 7 Punkte – reise lieber ab oder laß dich teeren und federn. 23 bis 29 Punkte – du bist ein guter Patriot. 30 bis 36 Punkte – du darfst die Unabhängigkeitserklärung eigenhändig mitunterzeichnen.

Revolutionäre Vergangenheit zieht sich durch Boston wie ein roter Faden, und das zweifach. Einer amerikanischen Ariadne gleich schickt die Stadt ihre Besucher wohlgesichert in ihr labyrinthisches Zentrum, der von ihr vorbereitete „freedom trail", ein tatsächlich roter Faden aus Farbe oder in den Gehsteig eingelassenen Ziegelsteinen, führt sie meilenweit durch Geschichte und läßt dabei nicht einen historischen sight außer Sicht. Nicht das Holzhaus des Silberschmieds Paul Revere, dessen nächtlichen Ritt nach Lexington und Concord Henry Wadsworth Longfellow so poetisch fälschte und amerikanische

Stadt der Balance: Revolutionäre Geschichte zieht sich wie ein Ariadnefaden durch Boston, die Stadt der antienglischen Teekisten-Party, wo weltberühmte Zentren der High-Technology – hier residieren fünfzig Colleges und Universitäten, Harvard und das MIT – Kapital anlocken

 月刊 染織α

特集●紬織りの秘訣
アーナベラのバティック　小山修三

9
1983
No.30

359

月刊 染織α

特集●ろうけつ染のテクニック
ラダックの曼荼羅　渡辺正子

8
1983
No.29

360

ARTIST / KÜNSTLER / ARTISTE:

359–361 Hirata Yorikazu
362 Mark Hess
363 Guy Billout
364 Brian Ajhar
365 Matt Mahurin
366 Barbara Bellingham (Photo)

DESIGNER / GESTALTER / MAQUETTISTE:

359–361 Hirata Yorikazu

ART DIRECTOR / DIRECTEUR ARTISTIQUE:

359–361 Hirata Yorikazu
362 Rudolph Hoglund
363, 365 Ken Kendrick
364 Randy Dunbar
366 Janetta Lewin

PUBLISHER / VERLEGER / ÉDITEUR:

359–361 Senshoku to Seikatsu-sha
362 Time Inc.
363, 365 The New York Times
364 The Daily News Magazine
366 The Observer Magazine

 月刊 染織α

特集●現代のタペストリー
新連載　型染デザイン入門　増田義範

6
1984
No.39

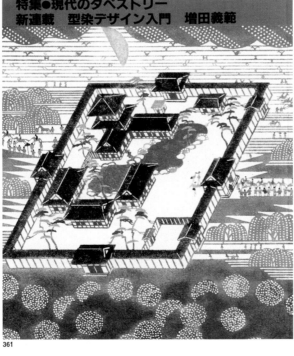

361

362

359–361 Three complete covers of the textile dyeworks magazine *Senshoku Alpha*. Illustrations for the covers of this trade magazine are invariably dyed on Japanese paper. (JPN)
362 Full-colour cover of an issue of *Time* magazine. (USA)
363 Cover of *The New York Times Magazine*, in blue and red tones. (USA)
364 Illustration in watercolour, ink and crayon for the cover of the *Daily News Magazine*, relating to an article in which a famous American personality speaks out on US football. (USA)
365 Cover of *The New York Times Magazine* with the "Iron Curtain". (USA)
366 Cover of the magazine supplement to the Sunday newspaper *Observer*. This issue, in March, is devoted to all aspects of hair, and the pun is on the subtitle "March Hair" (March Hare). (GBR)

359–361 Umschläge einer Fachzeitschrift für die Textilindustrie. (JPN)
362 «Was tötet all die Bäume?» Mehrfarbiger Umschlag einer Ausgabe des Magazins *Time* zum Thema des Waldsterbens. (USA)
363 «Wie man die Frauenbewegung wieder in Bewegung bringt.» Umschlag des *New York Times Magazine* in Blau- und Rottönen. (USA)
364 Illustration (Aquarelltechnik, Tusche, Farbstift) für den Umschlag des *Daily News Magazine*, in dem sich eine in den USA bekannte Persönlichkeit zur Frage «Fussball am Montagabend» äussert. (USA)
365 Umschlag des *New York Times Magazine* mit dem «eisernen Vorhang»: «Was wir wirklich über Russland wissen.» (USA)
366 Umschlag des vom *Observer* herausgegebenen Magazins *Living Extra*. Hier eine Ausgabe, die dem Thema «Haar» gewidmet ist. (GBR)

363

365

364

366

Die grosse Versuchung

367

ARTIST / KÜNSTLER / ARTISTE:

367, 370, 371 Wolf Barth
368 Barták
369 Christoph Gloor
372 Celestino Piatti

ART DIRECTOR / DIRECTEUR ARTISTIQUE:

367–372 Werner Meier

PUBLISHER / VERLEGER / EDITEUR:

367–372 Nebelspalter Verlag

367–372 Examples of covers for the Swiss humorous/satirical weekly magazine *Nebelspalter*. Fig. 367: "The Great Temptation"—pink border, couple in black and white, shop display models clothed in bright colours; Fig. 368: for the theme of the week: "Modern Taboos" (in which we are trapped). Pink and orange-striped wallpaper; Fig. 369 relates to an article about MUBA (Basle Trade Fair); Fig. 370 is for "The Year of Youth"; Fig. 371: "On Hunters and the Hunted"—for an October issue; Fig. 372: "Farewell Winter–Bravo Carnival" (with a pun in the German title: "Winter ade—Fasnacht olé"). (SWI)

367–372 Beispiele von Umschlägen für die humoristisch-satirische, schweizerische Wochenzeitschrift *Nebelspalter*. Abb. 367: «Die grosse Versuchung» – Umrandung in Pink, Paar in schwarzer respektive weisser, Schaufensterpuppen in bunter Kleidung; Abb. 368: Umschlag zum Wochenthema, den modernen Tabus, die uns gefangenhalten. Rosa- und orangegestreifte Tapete; Abb. 369 gehört zu einem Artikel über die MUBA (Basler Mustermesse); Abb. 370: zum «Jahr der Jugend»; Abb. 371: «Von Jägern und Gejagten» – für eine Oktober-Ausgabe; Abb. 372: «Winter ade – Fasnacht olé», in Abwandlung des Ausdrucks «... – scheiden tut weh.» (SWI)

367–372 Exemples de couvertures de l'hebdomadaire satirique suisse *Nebelspalter*. Fig. 367: «La grande tentation» – cadre rose vif, couple en noir et en blanc, mannequins habillés de vêtements colorés. Fig. 368: couverture sur le thème des tabous modernes, dont nous sommes prisonniers; tapisserie à rayures roses et oranges. Fig. 369: l'illustration se rapporte à un article sur la MUBA (Foire Suisse d'echantillons de Bâle). Fig. 370: à propos de «l'année de la jeunesse». Fig. 371: «Des chasseurs et des chassés» – pour un numéro d'octobre. Fig. 372: «Adieu l'hiver – vive le carnaval». (SWI)

368

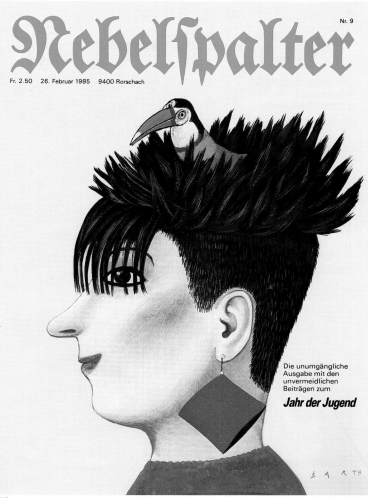

Von Jägern und Gejagten

377

378

Magazine Covers
Zeitschriftenumschläge
Couvertures de périodiques

ARTIST / KÜNSTLER / ARTISTE:

373, 374 Gretchen Dow Simpson
375 Eugene Mihaesco
376 Lonni Sue Johnson
377, 378 Tullio Pericoli

ART DIRECTOR / DIRECTEUR ARTISTIQUE:

373–376 Lee Lorenz
377, 378 Serena Rossetti

PUBLISHER / VERLEGER / EDITEUR:

373–376 The New Yorker
377, 378 L'Espresso

373–376 Examples of covers for *The New Yorker* magazine. Fig. 375 shows a scene which is typical of New York's classier areas—the canopies at which the doormen stand to hail taxis for their patrons. Fig. 376: scenes of New York, with the ubiquitous water-tanks up on the roofs. (USA)
377, 378 Complete cover and illustration for an issue of *L'Espresso*. The subject is the (1985) upcoming political elections in Italy and the Vatican's partisanship with the Democrazia Cristiana. (ITA)

373–376 Beispiele von Umschlägen für die Zeitschrift *The New Yorker*. Abb. 375 zeigt eine Szene, die für New Yorks teure Gegenden typisch ist: Die Baldachine mit den Taxis herbeiwinkenden «Doormen». Abb. 376: New Yorker Strassenbilder mit den typischen Wasserbehältern auf den Dächern. (USA)
377, 378 Vollständiger Umschlag und Illustration für eine Ausgabe von *L'Espresso*. Das Thema sind die (1985) bevorstehenden politischen Wahlen in Italien und die deutliche Parteinahme des Vatikans für die Democrazia Cristiana. (ITA)

373–376 Exemples de couvertures du magazine *The New Yorker*. La fig. 375 représente une scène typique des beaux quartiers newyorkais: les entrées couvertes avec les grooms hélant les taxis. Fig. 376: scènes de New York avec les réservoirs d'eaux sur les toits. (USA)
377, 378 Couverture complète et illustrations pour un numéro de *L'Espresso*. Il a pour thème les élections politiques prochaines (en 1985) en Italie et l'engagement très net du Vatican en faveur de la Democrazia Cristiana. (ITA)

379

ARTIST / KÜNSTLER / ARTISTE:

380 Anita Kunz
381 Mireille Levert
382 Dugald Stermer
383, 384 Steven Guarnaccia
385 Richard McNeel

ART DIRECTOR / DIRECTEUR ARTISTIQUE:

380, 382 Veronique Vienne
381 Hamo Abdallian
383 Gerard Sealy
384 Lynn Staley
385 Ronn Campisi

PUBLISHER / VERLEGER / EDITEUR:

379 Time Inc.
380, 382 San Francisco Examiner
381 James Dawe
383 The Plain Dealer Publishing Co.
384, 385 The Boston Globe

381

Magazine Covers
Zeitschriftenumschläge
Couvertures de périodiques

379 Cover of a special issue of the business magazine *Fortune*. (USA)
380, 382 For *California Living Magazine*, the Sunday supplement of the *San Francisco Sunday Examiner & Chronicle*. Fig. 380 concerns an article about John McCosker, director of the Steinhart Aquarium; Fig. 382 illustrates a cover story about the increase in the number of elderly persons and their care. (USA)
381 Cover of the *Montréal* magazine, referring to an autumn fashion show. (CAN)
383 Cover of an issue of *The Plain Dealer Magazine* on "fitness". (USA)
384, 385 For two issues of the *Boston Globe Magazine*. Fig. 384 contains the winners of the annual *Globe* photo contest, pale green sky; Fig. 385 questions the efficiency of modern dairy farming, blue background. (USA)

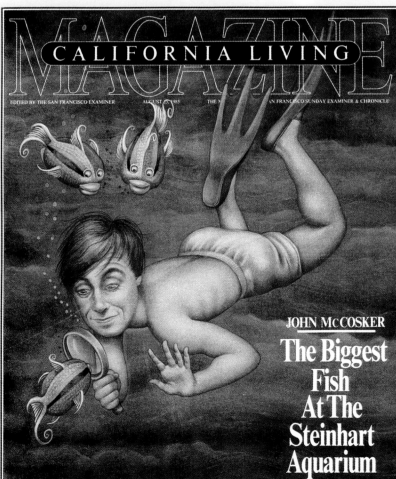

380

382

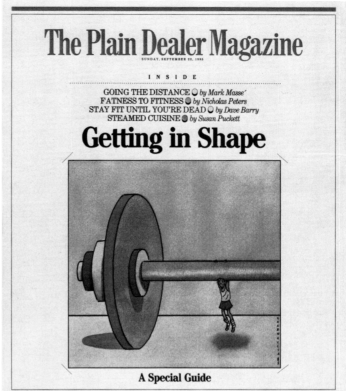

383

384

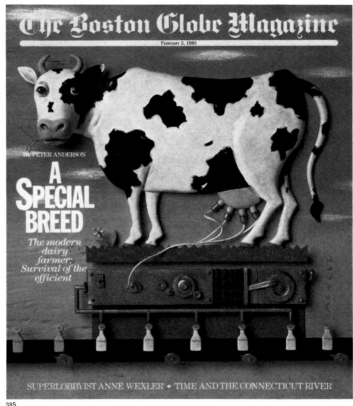

385

379 Umschlag einer Spezialausgabe des Wirtschaftsmagazins *Fortune* über PCs. (USA)
380, 382 Für *California Living Magazine*, die Sonntagsbeilage des *San Francisco Sunday Examiner & Chronicle*. Abb. 380 gehört zu einem Artikel über John McCosker, Direktor des Steinhart-Aquariums; Abb. 382 illustriert die Titelgeschichte über Probleme, mit denen Angehörige pflegebedürftig gewordener alter Menschen konfrontiert sind. (USA)
381 Der Umschlag des Magazins *Montréal* bezieht sich auf eine Herbstmodeschau. (CAN)
383 Umschlag für eine Fitness-Ausgabe des *Plain Dealer Magazine*. Zarte Farben. (USA)
384, 385 Für zwei Ausgaben des *Boston Globe Magazine*. Abb. 384 enthält die Gewinner des jährlich vom *Boston Globe* organisierten Photowettbewerbs (hellgrüner Himmel); Abb. 385 handelt vom Problem moderner Milchwirtschaft (blauer Hintergrund). (USA)

379 Pour un numéro spécial de *Fortune* sur les ordinateurs personnels. (USA)
380, 382 Pour le *California Living Magazine*, supplément dominical du *San Francisco Sunday Examiner & Chronicle*. La fig. 380 se réfère à un article sur John McCosker, directeur de l'Aquarium Steinhart. Fig. 382: illustration sur les problèmes des gens dont les parents doivent être pris en charge. (USA)
381 Une présentation de mode automne en couverture du magazine *Montréal*. (CAN)
383 «Se mettre en forme»: couverture du *Plain Dealer Magazin*. Tons pastel. (USA)
384, 385 Pour deux numéros du *Boston Globe Magazine*. La fig. 384 présente les gagnants du concours annuel de photos organisé par le *Boston Globe* (ciel vert clair); la fig. 385 évoque le problème des laiteries modernes. (USA)

386

3/85
Mai/
Juni

DM 9,—
SFR 9,—
ÖS 75,—
HFL 11,25
LIT. 7000
PTS 575,—

Männer
VOGUE

GELD
DIE AKTIEN,
DIE ES BRINGEN.
DAS HEISSESTE
STEUER-PARADIES

30 SEITEN MODE:
SO LÄSSIG
WIE NOCH NIE

**DER GRÖSSTE
LANDSCHWINDEL
ALLER ZEITEN**

**ERFOLGSFORMEL
GEGEN GLATZEN**

DER QUERSCHLÄGER: FJS

387

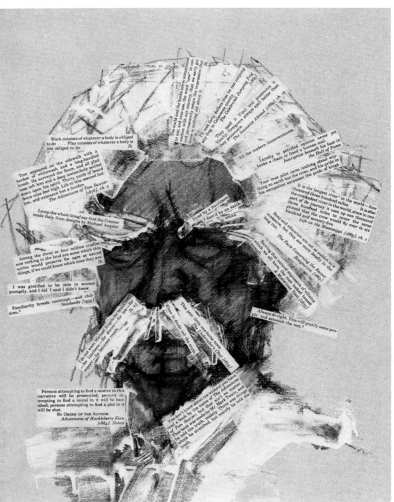

388

NOVEMBER 25, 1985 · $1.95

SOCIALISM
& IRVING HOWE

Anita Desai: India as Fantasyland
WHATEVER HAPPENED TO CESAR CHAVEZ? · WHY ARE WE GIVING NUKES TO CHINA?

THE NEW
REPUBLIC

Front-runner

**The Kennedy
Revival**

by Fred Barnes

389

390

ARTIST / KÜNSTLER / ARTISTE:

386, 387 Philip Burke
388 Mickey Patel
389 Paul Davis
390, 391 Herrmann Degkwitz

DESIGNER / GESTALTER / MAQUETTISTE:

386 Ruth Ansel
388 Mickey Patel
389 Paul Davis
390, 391 Thomas Bonnie/Manfred Igogeit

ART DIRECTOR / DIRECTEUR ARTISTIQUE:

386 Charles Churchward
387 Beda Achermann
388 Nand Katyal
389 Dorothy Wickenden
390, 391 Rainer Wörtmann

AGENCY / AGENTUR / AGENCE – STUDIO:

389 Paul Davis Studio

PUBLISHER / VERLEGER / EDITEUR:

386 Condé Nast Publications, Inc.
387 Condé Nast Verlag GmbH
388 United States Information Service
389 New Republic Magazine
390, 391 Spiegel-Verlag

391

386 Caricature of Henry Kissinger for *Vanity Fair*. (USA)
387 Polychrome cover of an issue of *Männer Vogue* with an article about the Minister President of Bavaria, Franz Josef Strauss. (GER)
388 Snippets from the writings of Mark Twain are placed over his portrait in this collage to complement a feature about his life and work, in *Span*, a magazine issued by the United States Information Service in New Delhi. (IND)
389 Full-colour cover of *The New Republic* magazine. (USA)
390, 391 Illustration and complete cover of *Der Spiegel*. Rough translation of the title: "The High Flyers of Geneva". (GER)

386 Karikatur Henry Kissingers aus *Vanity Fair*. (USA)
387 Mehrfarbiger Umschlag einer Ausgabe der *Männer Vogue* mit einem Artikel über Bayerns Ministerpräsidenten. (GER)
388 Eine Collage mit Ausschnitten aus seinen Büchern vervollständigt hier ein ganzseitiges Porträt von Mark Twain für einen Beitrag über sein Leben, aus dem Magazin *Span*, das vom US Information Service für Indien herausgegeben wird. (IND)
389 Mehrfarbiger Umschlag von *The New Republic*, zu einer Spekulation über eine mögliche Kandidatur Ted Kennedys. (USA)
390, 391 Illustration und Umschlag des *Spiegels*. (GER)

386 Caricature d'Henry Kissinger dans *Vanity Fair*. (USA)
387 Couverture polychrome d'un numéro du *Männer Vogue* contenant un article sur le président du conseil bavarois. (GER)
388 Ce portrait pleine page de l'écrivain américain Mark Twain, un collage de textes découpés dans ses livres, illustre un article sur la vie de l'écrivain paru dans le magazine *Span*, édité en Inde par le US Information Service. (IND)
389 Couverture polychrome pour *The New Republic* qui évoque une possible candidature de Ted Kennedy. (USA)
390, 391 Illustration et couverture du *Spiegel*. (GER)

392 Complete cover of C&D, a magazine for art and architecture. (JPN)
393 Cover of an issue of *Print*, in which the new spirit in Japanese design is dealt with. (USA)
394 The issue of *Typo Mondo*, of which this is the cover, is devoted entirely to calligraphy. The whole publication was created and designed throughout by Jean Larcher. (FRA)
395, 396 Covers of two issues of the medicinal trade magazine *Algos*. (ITA)

392 Vollständiger Umschlag von C&D, einem Magazin für Kunst und Architektur. (JPN)
393 Umschlag einer Ausgabe von *Print*, in der über neues japanisches Design berichtet wird. (USA)
394 Umschlag einer Ausgabe von *Typo Mondo*, die der Kalligraphie gewidmet ist und vollständig von Jean Larcher kreiert und gestaltet wurde. (FRA)
395, 396 Umschläge von zwei Ausgaben der medizinischen Fachzeitschrift *Algos*. (ITA)

392 Couverture complète de C&D, un magazine d'art et d'architecture. (JPN)
393 Couverture de *Print* pour un numéro sur le nouveau design japonais. (USA)
394 Couverture d'un numéro de *Typo Mondo* consacré à la calligraphie: il a été entièrement conçu et réalisé par Jean Larcher. (FRA)
395, 396 Couvertures de deux numéros de la revue médicale *Algos*. (ITA)

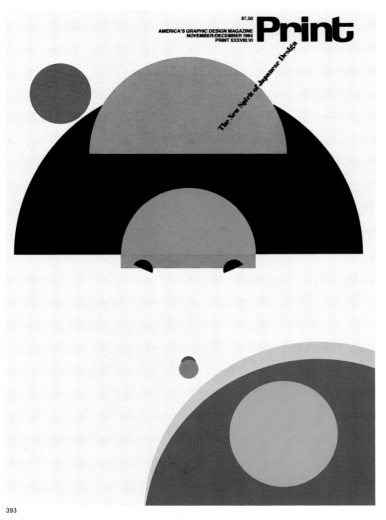

393

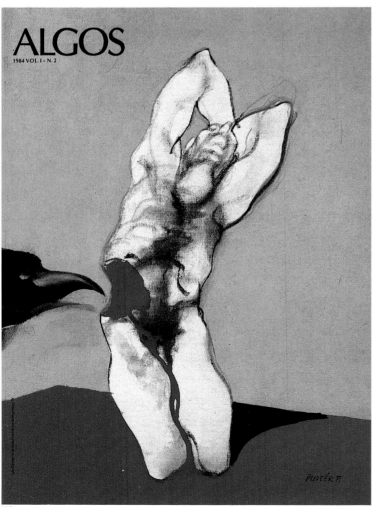

395

396

397

398

Trade Magazines
Fachzeitschriften
Revues professionnelles

397–399 Cover, page and double spread from *Graphic Relief*, a quarterly magazine, each issue of which introduces an illustrator and a photographer. The examples shown in Figs. 397, 398 are by artist Christoph Blumrich; Fig. 399 is for an article about the Helvetica typeface. The H is red. (USA)
400, 401 "Our First Ever"—the title applies to the first "Annual of Typographical Design Issue" published by the quarterly *Graphic Relief* magazine. Fig. 400 is red on white (with small text in black); Fig. 401 is in full colour. The artist featured here (together with a photographer) is Barry Root. (USA)

397–399 Umschlag, Seite und Doppelseite aus *Graphic Relief*, einer Zeitschrift, die jeweils einen Illustrator und einen Photographen vorstellt. Die hier gezeigten Beispiele sind von Christoph Blumrich; in Abb. 399 geht es um einen Beitrag des Herausgebers über die Helvetica (rotes H). (USA)
400, 401 «Our First Ever» (unsere Allererste) – Seite und Doppelseite aus der ersten Ausgabe von *Graphic Relief*, die der Typographie gewidmet ist. Abb. 400 ist rot auf Weiss (kleine Schrift schwarz), Abb. 401 ist mehrfarbig. Der hier zusammen mit einem Photographen vorgestellte Künstler ist Barry Root. (USA)

397–399 Couverture, une page simple et une double page du magazine *Graphic Relief*. Dans chaque numéro, on présente un illustrateur et un photographe: ici, des exemples d'illustrations de Christoph Blumrich. La fig. 399 se rapporte à un article sur l'Helvetica (H en rouge). (USA)
400, 401 «Our First Ever» (Notre tout premier) – Page et double page du premier numéro de *Graphic Relief*, consacré à la typographie. La fig. 400 est en rouge sur fond blanc (petits caractères en noir), la fig. 401 est polychrome. C'est l'artiste Barry Root qui est présenté ici avec un photographe. (USA)

400

ARTIST / KÜNSTLER:

397, 398 Christoph Blumrich
399, 400 David Brier
401 Barry Root

DESIGNER / GESTALTER:

397–401 David Brier

ART DIRECTOR:

397–401 David Brier

AGENCY / AGENTUR / AGENCE:

397–401 D. Brier Design Works

PUBLISHER / VERLEGER:

397–401 D. Brier Design Works

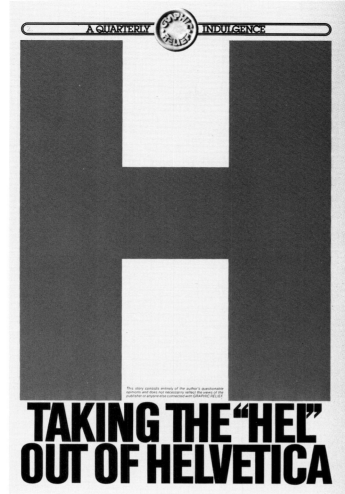

This story consists entirely of the author's questionable opinions and does not necessarily reflect the views of the publisher or anyone else connected with GRAPHIC RELIEF.

TAKING THE "HEL" OUT OF HELVETICA

"It's boring." "It's overused." "You can't do anything with it!" ¶ No, they're not talking about white formica. Here's another clue: "Oh no! Not helvetica again!" ¶ Helvetica — or helios, depending on where you buy type, is the most protean, most maligned and most magnificent sans serif face of all. ¶ "Magnificent!!?!" you say, "It is to laugh." ¶ Before you start laughing, think of this: IT WORKS. Helvetica has every attribute of the perfect face—including aesthetics. ¶ Stop laughing and face it (caution: word at play). Anything which has earned a position of such wide-spread use and abuse over so many years that it has reached the sublime celebrity of being "too ordinary," must have something grand about it. ¶ Like LEGIBILITY. If that's not important to you, you may be the one who ordered "8-point Old English caps" for Adelle's antique ad, and you shouldn't be reading this in the first place. The rest of us appreciate the client's desire to have hir¹ copy read. Some of us even share that desire. ¶ And FLEXIBILITY. You can create eye-catching heads, distinctive sub-heads and miles and miles of body copy as small as ant tracks without sacrificing legibility, all with a symmetry that is undeniable. Look at this page as though you'd never seen helvetica before and you'll marvel at the visual logic of it. ¶ AND TYPESETTERS UNDERSTAND IT! Even cheapo shops manned by secretarial-pool rejects can (and usually do) deliver decently letterspaced jobs. ¶ So the next time a helvetica job comes upon your plate, enjoy it. Savor its polite malleability; smile secretly to yourself as you anticipate the client's cheerful countenance as s/he² praises the wonderful job you've done for hem³. And if that doesn't work you into a frenzy of appreciation, consider this possibility: Tomorow's assignment could be a shoe catalog in Times Roman.

□¹ Of course this is stupid, but I refuse to be accused of "sexist" writing. □² One small step for equality in print, a giant step back for reason. □³ This one exceeds my limit. I'll just take my chances with he and she and his and hers, thank you. And if that's "sexism," well . . . that's too bad.

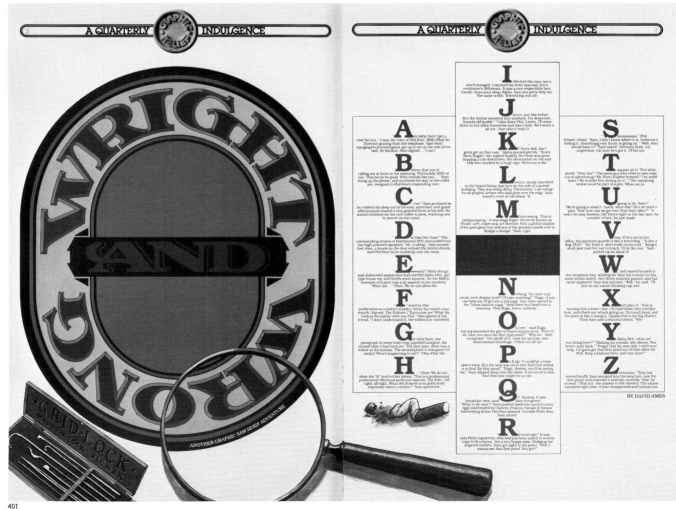

BY DAVID AMES

399

401

402

Trade Magazines
Fachzeitschriften
Revues professionnelles

ARTIST / KÜNSTLER / ARTISTE:

402 Brian Ajhar
403 Cathy Hull
404, 405 H. H. Jung
406 Sue Coe

DESIGNER / GESTALTER / MAQUETTISTE:

404, 405 H. H. Jung

ART DIRECTOR / DIRECTEUR ARTISTIQUE:

402 Margaret Ottosen
403 Malcolm Froumann
404–406 H. H. Jung

PUBLISHER / VERLEGER / EDITEUR:

402 Money Magazine
403 NYU Law
404–406 Good News

402 Illustration (watercolour, ink and crayon) for an article in the magazine *Money*, entitled "Tips on Tipping". Mainly in tones of old rose and green-beige. (USA)
403 Black-and-white illustration in the professional magazine *NYU Law*, for an article debating the point of whether the US multi-national corporations around the world should come under United States jurisdiction. (USA)
404–406 Complete pages (all illustrated in oil on canvas) from *Good News*, a magazine for illustration, photography and text. Fig. 404: Yves Saint Laurent's portrait in a contrast of cold and warm colours; Fig. 405: predominantly in blue tones, with red scarf and yellow sand; Fig. 406 is entitled "Vigilante", in green tones with yellow and red. (GER)

403

404

405

402 Illustration (Wasserfarbe, Tusche und Buntstift) für einen Artikel in der Zeitschrift *Money* mit guten Ratschlägen zum Thema «Trinkgelder». Altrosa und Lindgrün überwiegen. (USA)
403 Schwarzweiss-Illustration in der Fachzeitschrift *NYU Law* zur Frage, ob bei multinationalen US-Firmen amerikanisches Recht rund um die Welt Gültigkeit haben soll. (USA)
404–406 Vollständige Seiten (alle Illustrationen in Öl auf Leinwand) aus *Good News*, einer Zeitschrift für Illustration, Photo und Text. Abb. 404: Yves Saint Laurent (Kontrast von kalten und warmen Farben); Abb. 405: vorwiegend Blautöne, rotes Tuch, gelber Sand; Abb. 406 trägt den Titel «Vigilante» (Bürgerwehr). Grüntöne mit Gelb und Rot. (GER)

402 Illustration (aquarelle, encre et crayon de couleur) pour un article de *Money*, dans lequel on donne de bons conseils à propos des pourboires. Vieux rose et tilleul prédominants. (USA)
403 Illustration en noir et blanc de la revue professionnelle *NYU Law* sur la question de la validité du droit américain pour les US multinationales à l'étranger. (USA)
404–406 Pages complètes (toutes les illustrations sont réalisées à l'huile sur toile) de *Good News*, une revue spécialisée dans l'illustration, la photo et le texte. Fig. 404: Yves Saint Laurent (contraste de couleurs chaudes et froides); fig. 405: prédominance de bleus, étoffe rouge, sable jaune; fig. 406: «Vigilants». Tons verts, jaune et rouge. (GER)

© SUE ■ COE ■ NEW YORK ■ 1985 ■

406

407 Page from an article in *Sport* magazine devoted to the complexity of the knee. Legs in pink, green and beige, bone joints in pale yellow, cartilages in pink. (USA)
408, 409 Cover with black-and-white illustrations on the themes of "frustration" and "isolation" from two issues of the "Bulletins for Swiss Psychologists". (SWI)
410 Full-colour illustration (linocut) in actual size from *Psychology Today*. The article relates to facial expressions and physical responses to emotions (including rise in finger temperature, increase in heartbeat rate and difference in response in the two brain halves). (USA)
411 Etching for the German Medical Association's magazine *Medizin heute* (Medicine Today), entitled "What does the nine of spades mean?" (GER)

407 Dem Knie gewidmete Seite mit mehrfarbiger Illustration aus dem Magazin *Sport*. (USA)
408, 409 Umschläge mit Schwarzweiss-Illustrationen zu verschiedenen Themen für zwei Ausgaben des *Bulletins der Schweizer Psychologen*. (SWI)
410 Mehrfarbige Illustration in Originalgrösse aus *Psychology Today*. Der dazugehörige Beitrag befasst sich mit dem Einfluss des Gesichtsausdrucks (als Folge von Empfindungen oder auch simuliert) auf die Temperatur der Finger und auf den Herzschlag. (USA)
411 Farbradierung für die vom Deutschen Ärzte Verlag herausgegebene Zeitschrift *Medizin heute*: «Was bedeutet Pik Neun?» (GER)

407 Page consacré au genou avec illustration polychrome, pour le magazine *Sport*. (USA)
408, 409 Couvertures de deux numéros du *Bulletin suisse des psychologues* avec des illustrations en noir et blanc sur les thèmes de la frustration et de l'isolement. (SWI)
410 Illustration polychrome grandeur nature tirée de *Psychology Today*. L'article en question porte sur le rapport existant entre l'expression du visage (qu'elle soit le résultat d'une sensation ou qu'elle soit simulée) et des phénomènes physiologiques, tels que la température des doigts ou des palpitations cardiaques. (USA)
411 Eau-forte en couleurs réalisée pour le magazine *Medizin heute*, édité par la société des médecins allemands: «Que signifie le neuf de pique?» (GER)

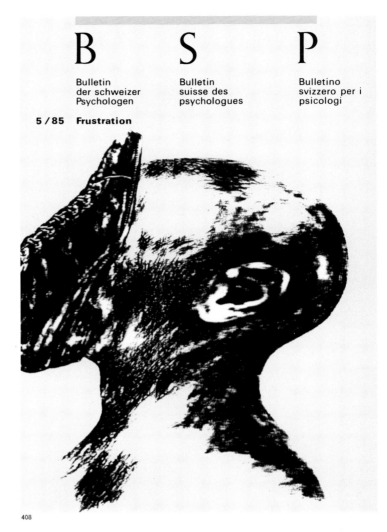

408

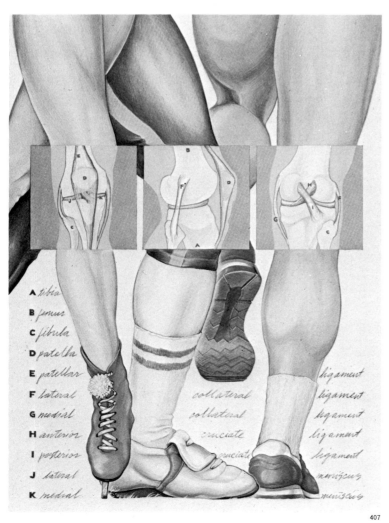

407

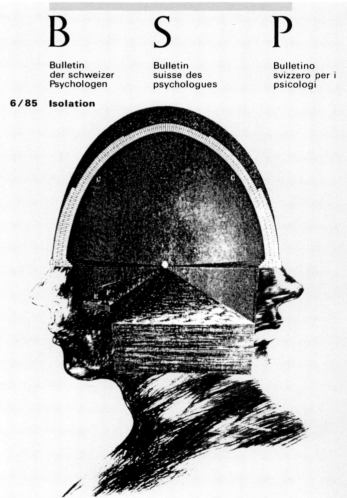

409

ARTIST / KÜNSTLER / ARTISTE:

407 Narda Lebo
408, 409 Lilian Perrin
410 Frances Jetter
411 Eduard Prüssen

ART DIRECTOR / DIRECTEUR ARTISTIQUE:

407 Jeri Hansen
410 Anne K. DuVivier

PUBLISHER / VERLEGER / EDITEUR:

407 Sport Magazine
408, 409 Verband Schweizer Psychologen
410 Ziff-Davis Publishing
411 Deutscher Ärzte Verlag

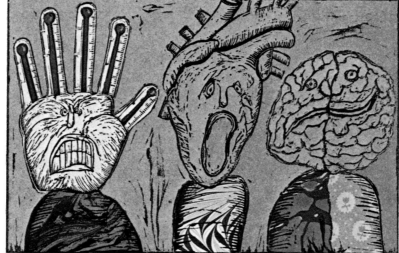

410

Trade Magazines
Fachzeitschriften
Revues professionnelles

411

412

ARTIST / KÜNSTLER / ARTISTE:

412 Jerzy Kolacz
413 Brian Ajhar
414, 415 Eugene Mihaesco
416 John Segal

DESIGNER / GESTALTER / MAQUETTISTE:

416 Margaret Wollenhaupt

ART DIRECTOR / DIRECTEUR ARTISTIQUE:

412 Steve Manley
413 Sharon Bystrek
414, 415 Roslyn Frick

AGENCY / AGENTUR / AGENCE – STUDIO:

412 Reactor Art & Design

PUBLISHER / VERLEGER / EDITEUR:

412 Canadian Business Magazine
413 Business Week Magazine
414, 415 McGraw–Hill Publishing Co.
416 The American Institute of Graphic Arts

Trade Magazines
Fachzeitschriften
Revues professionnelles

412 Full-page illustration in *Canadian Business* magazine for an article about the performance expected from a management executive. (CAN)
413 Illustration (watercolour, ink, crayon) in actual size for an article in *Business Week* entitled "Good Rules for a Fair Divorce". (USA)
414, 415 Illustrations from BYTE magazine relating to stories about computers. (USA)
416 Illustration for a cover of the quarterly publication AIGA *Journal of Graphic Design*. Printed in black and white on bone-white grooved stock. (USA)

412 In *Canadian Business* veröffentlichte Illustration für einen Artikel über die beruflichen Leistungen, die von einem Unternehmensleiter erwartet werden. (CAN)
413 Illustration (Aquarell, Tusche, Farbstift) in Originalgrösse für einen Beitrag in *Business Week:* «Grundregeln für eine faire Scheidung.» (USA)
414, 415 «Computer-Erzählung», «Computer-Stadt», Illustrationen für ein Computer-Magazin. (USA)
416 Illustration für einen Umschlag der Vierteljahrespublikation AIGA *Journal of Graphic Design*. Schwarz auf festem, gerilltem, weisslichem Papier. (USA)

412 Illustration publiée dans le *Canadian Business* pour un article sur les performances professionnelles auxquelles s'attend un chef d'entreprise. (CAN)
413 Illustration grandeur nature (aquarelle, encre de Chine, crayon de couleur) pour un article du *Business Week*: «Les règles fondamentales du divorce à l'amiable.» (USA)
414, 415 «Conte d'ordinateurs» et «Cité d'ordinateurs». Pour une revue d'informatique. (USA)
416 Illustration pour la couverture d'une publication trimestrielle, AIGA *Journal of Graphic Design*. En noir, sur papier vergé blanc. (USA)

413

414

415

416

ARTIST / KÜNSTLER / ARTISTE:

417, 419 Frances Jetter
418 Eugene Mihaesco
420 Geoffrey Moss
421 John Jude Palencar
422 Cameron Wasson

ART DIRECTOR / DIRECTEUR ARTISTIQUE:

417, 418, 421, 422 Tina Adamek
419 Patrick JB Flynn
420 Barrie Stern

PUBLISHER / VERLEGER / EDITEUR:

417, 418, 421, 422 McGraw-Hill Publishing Co.
419 The Progressive
420 Venture Magazine, Inc.

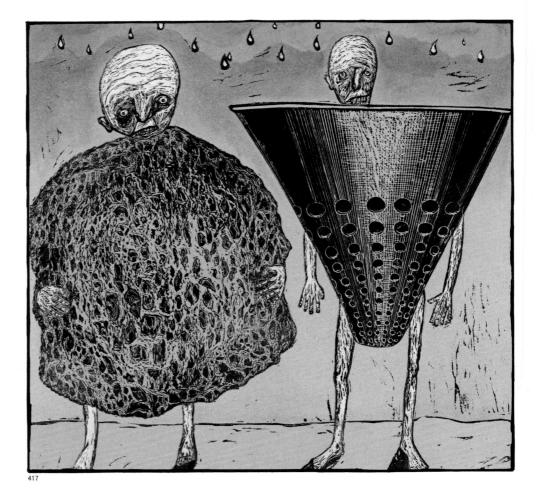

417

420

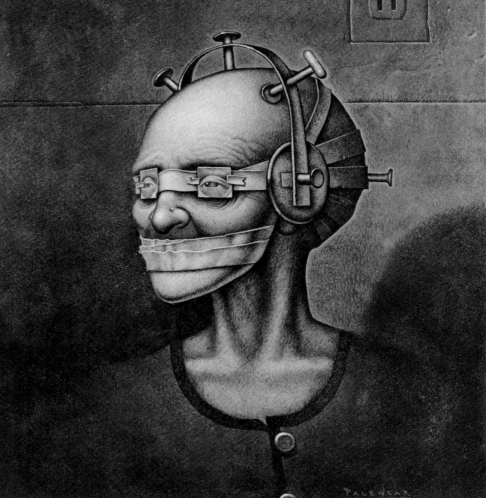

421

418

419

422

417 Illustration for an issue of the medical trade magazine *Postgraduate Medicine*. The accompanying article deals with disease of the prostata. (USA)
418 Black-and-white illustration in actual size for an article in *Postgraduate Medicine* about the effects of the decision to "free" inmates from mental hospitals. (USA)
419 Linocut in black and white for an article about the homeless, in *The Progressive*. (USA)
420 Illustration in black on yellowish paper from the magazine *Venture*. The article concerns a method of losing weight by a surgical balloon implant in the patient's stomach. (USA)
421, 422 Illustrations from *Postgraduate Medicine* for articles about neurologic complaints in the elderly (Fig. 421 in sombre colours) and leg oedema (Fig. 422 in bright colours on a background in grey tones). (USA)

417 Illustration für eine Ausgabe der medizinischen Fachzeitschrift *Postgraduate Medicine*. In dem dazugehörigen Artikel geht es um die Erkrankung der Prostata. (USA)
418 Schwarzweiss-Illustration in Originalgrösse für einen Artikel in *Postgraduate Medicine* über das Scheitern eines Experiments, der Befreiung von Patienten aus Nervenheilstätten. (USA)
419 Linolschnitt in Schwarzweiss für einen Artikel über Obdachlose in *The Progressive*. (USA)
420 Illustration in Schwarz auf gelblichem Papier aus der Zeitschrift *Venture*. Es geht um ein Mittel zum Abnehmen in Form eines Ballons, der in den Magen des Patienten kommt. (USA)
421, 422 Illustrationen aus *Postgraduate Medicine* für Beiträge über neurologische Erkrankungen im Alter (Abb. 421, in düsteren Farben) und Gewebewassersucht an den Beinen (Abb. 422, in heiteren Farben vor Hintergrund in Grautönen). (USA)

417 Illustration d'un numéro de la revue professionnelle *Postgraduate Medicine*. L'article en question porte sur les maladies de la prostate. (USA)
418 Illustration grandeur nature noir et blanc pour un article du *Postgraduate Medicine* sur l'échec d'une expérience, libérer les patients des hôpitaux psychiatriques. (USA)
419 Linogravure illustrant un article sur les sans-logis dans *The Progressive*. (USA)
420 Illustration en noir sur papier jaunâtre du magazine *Venture*. Il est question d'une méthode d'amaigrissement: on introduit un ballon dans l'estomac du patient. (USA)
421, 422 Illustrations du *Postgraduate Medicine* pour des articles sur les maladies neurologiques chez les gens âgés (fig. 421, couleurs sombres) et les œdèmes aux jambes (fig. 422, couleurs vives sur fond grisâtre). (USA)

423

424

425

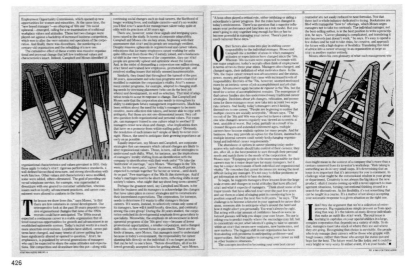

426

423 Cover of a sample preview edition of the bi-monthly magazine *Step-by-Step Graphics*, devized as a continuing education course in the graphics field. Mainly in brown and grey. (USA)
424–426 Colour illustration and complete double spreads form the house organ of AT&T. Figs. 424 and 426: a study of career tendencies; Fig. 425: corporate education; costs and benefits. (USA)
427 From a magazine for *Ericsson*: "Human Factors and Information Technology". (USA)

423 Umschlag einer Probenummer der Zeitschrift *Step-by-Step Graphics*, die als «Weiterbildungskurs» für kreativ Tätige der Graphikbranche konzipiert ist. Überwiegend in Braun und Grau. (USA)
424–426 Farbillustration und vollständige Doppelseiten aus der Hauszeitschrift von AT&T. Abb. 424 und 426 gehören zu einer Studie über unterschiedliche «Karrieretendenzen» der 50er bis 80er Jahre; in Abb. 425 geht es um Konkurrenzfähigkeit durch Weiterbildung des Personals. (USA)
427 Aus einer Zeitschrift von *Ericsson*: «Menschliche Belange und Informationssysteme». (USA)

423 Couverture d'un spécimen de *Step-by-Step Graphics*, un magazine conçu comme «cours de formation complémentaire» pour les créateurs graphiques. Prédominance de brun et gris. (USA)
424–426 Illustration en couleurs et doubles pages complètes du journal d'entreprise d'AT&T: pour une étude de l'évolution des carrières et des avantages de la formation continue. (USA)
427 D'une revue d'*Ericsson*: «Le facteur humain et les systèmes d'information». (USA)

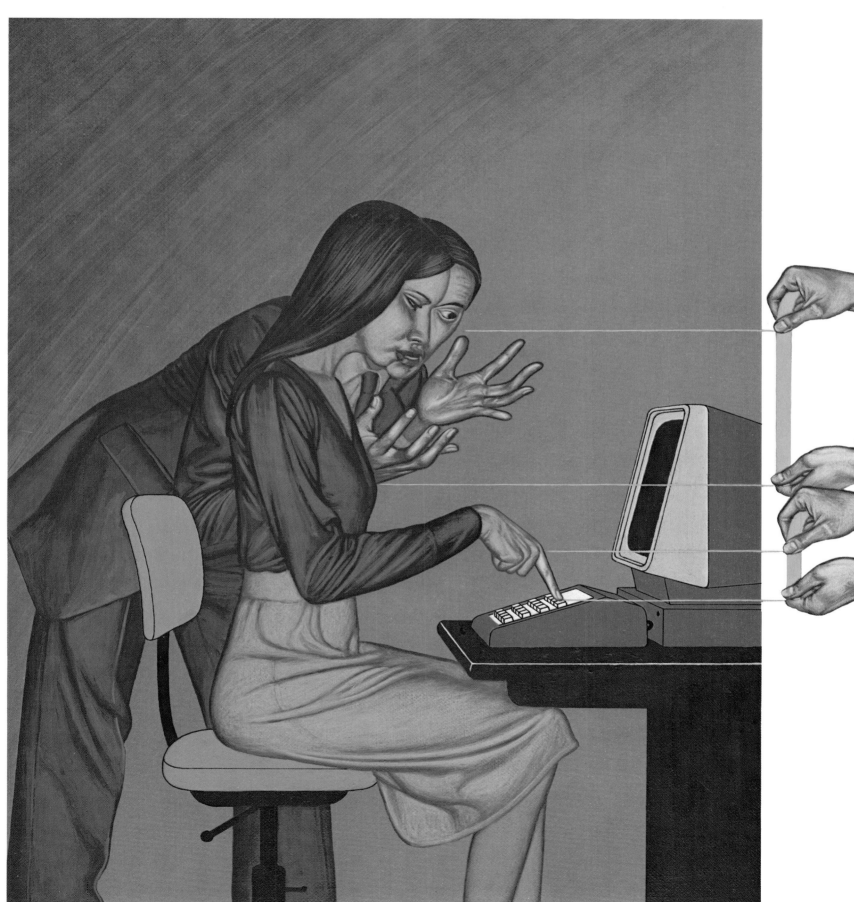

427

428

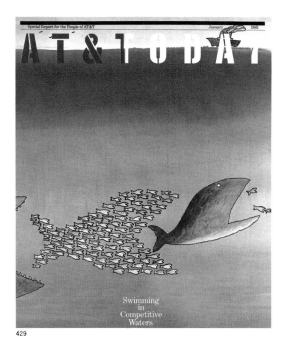

429

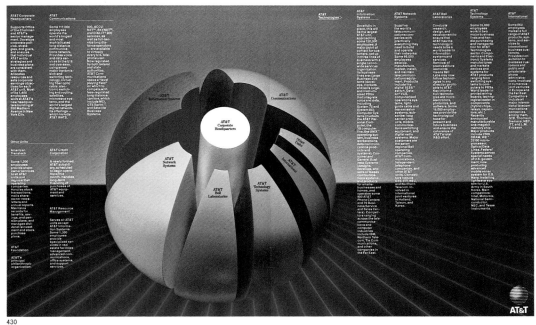

430

House Organs
Hauszeitschriften
Journaux d'entreprise

ARTIST / KÜNSTLER / ARTISTE:

428, 432 Milton Glaser
431 John Alcorn

DESIGNER / GESTALTER / MAQUETTISTE:

428–432 Richard Hess

ART DIRECTOR / DIRECTEUR ARTISTIQUE:

428–432 Richard Hess/Ellie Elsner

AGENCY / AGENTUR / AGENCE – STUDIO:

428–432 Hess & Hess

PUBLISHER / VERLEGER / EDITEUR:

428–432 AT&T

431

432

428–432 Full-page illustration, cover and double spreads from the large-format house organ *AT&T Today*. Figs. 428, 432 relate to an article on cost-cutting, wrongly assumed by some employees that it was a case of "cutting off the nose to spite the face"; The illustration in fig. 429 shows a cover on the subject of market competition; Fig. 430 presents the various divisions of the company; Fig. 431 (in soft brown, yellow and green tones) relates to a one-dollar charge on customers' telephone bills to "build a bridge for the future" of the American telephone system. (USA)

428–432 Seite, Umschlag und Doppelseiten aus der grossformatigen Hauszeitschrift der Telephonegesellschaft AT&T. Abb. 428, 432 gehören zu einem Beitrag über Kosteneinsparungen, die bei einigen Angestellten auf Unverständnis stossen könnten. (Die Illustration bezieht sich auf die Redensart «die Nase abschneiden, nur um das Gesicht zu ärgern»); Abb. 429 zeigt den Umschlag mit einem Kommentar zum Thema Konkurrenz; Abb. 430 stellt die verschiedenen Geschäftsbereiche des Unternehmens dar; die Illustration in Abb. 431 (in sanften Braun-, Gelb- und Grüntönen) bezieht sich auf einen Beschluss, allen Kunden zwecks Finanzierung und Ausbau des bestehenden Netzes monatlich einen Dollar Grundgebühr mehr zu verrechnen. (USA)

428–432 Une page, couverture et doubles pages du journal d'entreprise grand format de la société de téléphone AT&T. Les fig. 428 et 432 se rapportent à un article sur les compressions de frais (illustration du dicton «se couper le nez, juste pour vexer son visage»). La fig. 429 montre la couverture avec un commentaire sur la concurrence. La fig. 430 présente les différentes branches de l'entreprise. L'illustration de la fig. 431 (teintes douces dans les bruns, jaunes et verts) fait allusion à la décision de faire payer un dollar de plus par mois à chaque abonné pour financer le réseau et «édifier un pont pour l'avenir» du système de télécommunications américain. (USA)

433

Annual Reports
Jahresberichte
Rapports annuels

434

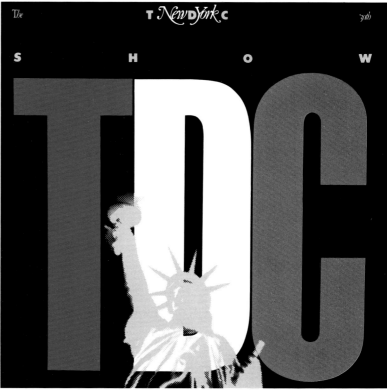

435

ARTIST / KÜNSTLER / ARTISTE:

433 Joyce MacDonald
434 RAG
435 Oswaldo Miranda (Miran)
436 Haruo Hanawa/Masahiro Takeguchi

DESIGNER / GESTALTER / MAQUETTISTE:

433 David Hillman/Sarah Pyne
435 Oswaldo Miranda

ART DIRECTOR / DIRECTEUR ARTISTIQUE:

433 David Hillman
434 Cathy Brennan
435 Oswaldo Miranda

AGENCY / AGENTUR / AGENCE – STUDIO:

433 Pentagram
434 Johnson & Simpson
435 Miran Studio
436 Diamond Ltd.

PUBLISHER / VERLEGER / EDITEUR:

433 Ericsson Information Systems
436 IBM Japan

433 For *Ericsson*, from an article about information technology in developing countries. (USA)
434 Unpublished watercolour in soft gold, pink and green tones, for an article about a new computerized testing procedure called "branching". For an annual report. (USA)
435 For an exhibition organized by the Type Directors Club (New York), held in Brazil. (USA)
436 From a Japanese IBM magazine. The subject is business and political affairs. (JPN)

433 Für *Ericsson*: Illustration aus einem Artikel über Informatik und Entwicklungsländer. (USA)
434 Unveröffentlichtes Aquarell in zarten Farben zu einem neu entwickelten Testsystem, das «Branching» genannt wird. Für einen Jahresbericht des Educational Testing Service. (USA)
435 Für eine Ausstellung des Type Directors Club, New York, die in Brasilien stattfindet. (USA)
436 Aus einer japanischen IBM-Zeitschrift für Leser aus Politik und Wirtschaft. (JPN)

433 Pour *Ericsson*: au sujet de l'informatique dans les pays en voie de développement. (USA)
434 Projet d'aquarelle aux couleurs subtiles pour un nouveau système de test appelé «Branching». Conçu pour un rapport annuel de l'Educational Testing Service. (USA)
435 Pour une exposition au Brésil du Type Directors Club de New York. (USA)
436 D'une revue d'IBM au Japon pour des spécialistes de la politique et de l'économie. (JPN)

436

437

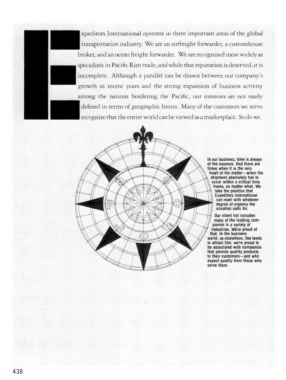

Expeditors International operates in three important areas of the global transportation industry. We are an airfreight forwarder, a customhouse broker, and an ocean freight forwarder. We are recognized most widely as specialists in Pacific Rim trade, and while that reputation is deserved, it is incomplete. Although a parallel can be drawn between our company's growth in recent years and the strong expansion of business activity among the nations bordering the Pacific, our interests are not easily defined in terms of geographic limits. Many of the customers we serve recognize that the entire world can be viewed as a marketplace. So do we.

In our business, time is always of the essence. And there are times when it is the very heart of the matter—when the shipment absolutely has to occur within a critical time frame, no matter what. We take the position that Expeditors International can react with whatever degree of urgency the situation calls for.

Our client list includes many of the leading companies in a variety of industries. We're proud of that. In the business world, as elsewhere, like tends to attract like: we're proud to be associated with companies that provide quality products to their customers—and who expect quality from those who serve them.

438

Quality of service is the reason our company has become a major factor in the industry in such a short time. Our prices are always competitive – but seldom the least expensive. Our computer programs are state of the art, but not really that far ahead of those used by other leading companies. What distinguishes our company from others is our people. They're experienced, mature professionals. Every officer of the company has at least 10 years in the business – and most of them have worked together for most of those years. They're wide- ly traveled, with firsthand knowledge about the places we and our custom-   ers have operations. They have earned reputations as good people   to do business with – – Expeditors International.

There was a time when the airfreight business was highly seasonal—and there still are more-or-less predictable peaks and valleys over the course of a year. But we've found that efficient, high quality service tends to moderate the cycles. The more our clients can rely on us for smooth, orderly, efficient service, the more orderly and manageable (and less expensive) their own inventories become and the smoother the overall cycle.

On every shipment our office at the origin contacts our office at the destination with essential information—the carrier, when the shipment left, when it is expected to arrive, the airway bill and other information. On routine shipments, the procedure allows us to anticipate arrival and prepare for it. When problems occur, we can attack them quickly from both ends, inform our client, and be a step or two down the road toward a solution.

We prefer long term, high quality relationships with our carriers. Such relationships are conducive to clear agreements about how we want things done; the familiarity with each other's methods and procedures leads to efficiency; the size of our total business with a few carriers gives us the visibility we need when it counts. Our policy may cost a little more, but it more than makes up for the difference in reliability and quality of service.

我們是遠東最大的國際空運公司之

439

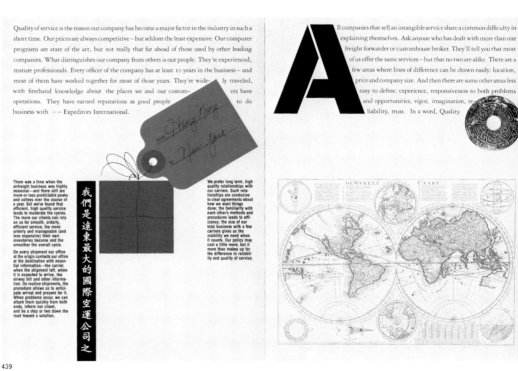

All companies that sell an intangible service share a common difficulty in explaining themselves. Ask anyone who has dealt with more than one freight forwarder or customhouse broker. They'll tell you that most of us offer the same services – but that no two are alike. There are a few areas where lines of difference can be drawn easily: location, price and company size. And then there are some other areas less easy to define: experience, responsiveness to both problems and opportunities, vigor, imagination, re   liability, trust. In a word, Quality.

ARTIST / KÜNSTLER / ARTISTE:

437 Paul Hogarth
438, 439 David Watanabe
441 Judy Pedersen

DESIGNER / GESTALTER / MAQUETTISTE:

437 Paul Anthony
438, 439 John Van Dyke
440 Any Dubois

ART DIRECTOR / DIRECTEUR ARTISTIQUE:

437 Alan Fletcher
438, 439 John Van Dyke
440 Jacques Tribondeau
441 Janice Fudyma/Craig Bernhardt

AGENCY / AGENTUR / AGENCE – STUDIO:

437 Pentagram
438, 439 Van Dyke Company
441 Bernhardt, Fudyma Design

PUBLISHER / VERLEGER / EDITEUR:

440 Esso SAF
441 General Foods Corporation

437 Complete dust jacket showing front and back flaps, for an annual report of Geers Gross Advertising Ltd., an advertising agency with offices in London and New York. (GBR)
438, 439 Page and double spread from an annual report of an international transport firm. (USA)
440 Cover on the subject of mineralogy for the house organ *Pétrole Progrès* issued by the *Esso Exxon* Group. Illustration in black with turquoise (and other) colour accents. (FRA)
441 Cover of the house organ of the coffee company *Maxwell House*, issued by *General Foods*. "Coffee at the sidewalk cafe: a pleasure found round the globe." (USA)

437 Vollständiger Schutzumschlag mit vorder- und rückseitiger Klappe für einen Jahresbericht der Geers Gross Advertising Ltd., einer Werbeagentur mit Büros in London und New York. (GBR)
438, 439 Seite und Doppelseite aus einem Jahresbericht einer internationalen Transportfirma. (USA)
440 Umschlag zum Thema Gestein für die Hauszeitschrift *Pétrole Progrès* der *Exxon*-Gruppe. Illustration in Schwarz mit dezenten Farbakzenten. (FRA)
441 Umschlag für die Hauszeitschrift der Kaffee-Unternehmung *Maxwell House* von *General Foods*: «Kaffee im Strassen-Café, ein Vergnügen, das man überall in der Welt finden kann.» (USA)

437 Jaquette (y compris les deux rabats) d'un rapport annuel de Geers Gross Advertising Ltd., une agence de publicité qui a des bureaux à Londres et à New York. (GBR)
438, 439 Page et double page d'un rapport annuel d'une maison de transports internationaux. (USA)
440 Couverture sur le thème des cristaux, roches et minéraux pour *Pétrole Progrès*, la revue du Groupe *Exxon*. Illustration en noir, rehaussée de quelques accents colorés. (FRA)
441 Couverture de la revue d'entreprise des cafés *Maxwell House* de *General Foods*: «Du café à la terrasse d'un café, un plaisir qu'on trouve dans le monde entier.» (USA)

440

441

195

442

IPD Boulder's
business future is
a very positive
story. Each of the
site's businesses
is pursuing rapidly
expanding areas
with tremendous
business oppor-
tunities. This spe-
cial "Directions"
publication is in-
tended to provide
you with an over-
view of these busi-
ness oppor-
tunities.
–A. A. Magdall, IPD
vice president,
systems printing
and copiers

Directions
A Special Report

IBM

Information Products Division
Boulder, Colorado
May 1985
George L. Corsilia,
Site General Manager
Prepared and published by IBM
Information Products Division,
Communications Department,
Boulder, Colorado 80301-9191.
Design: Pam Wolf, Tom Bluhm,
IBM Boulder Design Center.
Editor: Dwayne Cox.
Contributing Writer: Donna Joy
Newman.
Photography: Rodger Ewy.

444

Annual Reports
Jahresberichte
Rapports annuels

442 Front cover of the 1985 annual report of *Mobil,* showing the clear lines of the roof of their new "Pegasus 21" filling stations. (USA)
443 Cover of an annual report (part one of two parts) of the Manufacturers Hanover Corporation, which has a magazine-like format. In blue and green tones symbolizing change. (USA)
444–448 Cover and double spreads from two issues of IBM's house organ. Figs. 444–446 are from an issue about the firm in Boulder, Figs. 447, 448: from the issue on "People". (USA)

445

447

446

448

442 Umschlagvorderseite des Jahresberichtes 1985 für *Mobil*, hier die klaren Linien der Überdachungen der neuen «Pegasus 21» Tankstellen. (USA)
443 Umschlag für einen Jahresbericht der Manufacturers Hanover Corp., der wie ein Magazin gestaltet ist. Die Illustration in Blau- und Grüntönen symbolisiert Veränderungen. (USA)
444–448 Umschlag und Doppelseiten aus zwei Ausgaben der Hauszeitschrift von IBM. Abb. 444–446 gehören zu einer Nummer über die Fabrik in Boulder, Abb. 447, 448 zur Ausgabe «Menschen». (USA)

442 Les lignes nettes de l'auvent des nouvelles stations-service «Pegasus 21» ornent la page de couverture du rapport annuel 1985 de *Mobil*. (USA)
443 Couverture d'un rapport annuel de Manufacturers Hanover Corp., conçu comme un magazine. L'illustration dans des tons verts et bleus symbolise les changements. (USA)
444–448 Couverture et doubles pages de deux exemplaires du journal d'IBM. Fig. 444–446: d'un numéro sur l'usine de Boulder. Fig. 447, 448: d'un numéro intitulé «les gens». (USA)

449

451

452

ARTIST / KÜNSTLER / ARTISTE:

449, 452 Folon
450 R. O. Blechman/Richard Hess
451, 453 Marshall Arisman

DESIGNER / GESTALTER / MAQUETTISTE:

449, 450, 452 Richard Hess
451, 453 Tom Sizemore

ART DIRECTOR / DIRECTEUR ARTISTIQUE:

449, 450, 452 Richard Hess/Ellie Elsner
451, 453 Wayne Burkart

AGENCY / AGENTUR / AGENCE – STUDIO:

449, 450, 452 Hess & Hess
451, 453 Deere & Co./In House

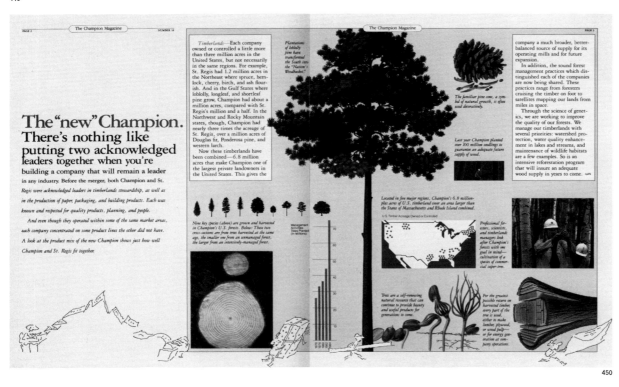

450

449, 452 Illustration and complete double spread from an annual report of the paper manufacturers *Champion*, here about the history, growth and importance of newspapers. (USA)
450 Double spread with full-colour illustrations relating to the forest, from No. 14 of *Champion's* house organ (published after the merger with papermakers *St. Regis*). (USA)
451, 453 Complete double spread and illustration in actual size for an article on automation entitled "Future Fright", from the *JD Journal*, the house organ of *John Deere*. (USA)

449, 452 Illustration und vollständige Doppelseite aus einem Jahresbericht des Papierherstellers *Champion*, hier über Geschichte und Bedeutung der Zeitung. (USA)
450 Doppelseite mit Farbillustrationen zum Thema «Wald» aus Nr. 14 der Hauszeitschrift von *Champion*, herausgegeben nach der Fusionierung mit dem Papierfabrikanten *St. Regis*. (USA)
451, 453 Vollständige Doppelseite und Illustration in Originalgrösse für einen Beitrag mit dem Titel «Zukunftsangst». Aus dem *JD Journal*, der Hauszeitschrift von *John Deere*. (USA)

449, 452 Illustration et double page complète d'un rapport annuel du fabricant de papiers *Champion*; ici, l'histoire et le développement des journaux. (USA)
450 Sur le thème de la forêt, double page complète illustrée en couleurs du nº 14 de la revue d'entreprise de *Champion*, publié après le fusionnement avec *St. Regis*. (USA)
451, 453 Double page complète et illustration grandeur nature d'un article intitulé «Peur de l'avenir». Pour *JD Journal*, la revue d'entreprise de *John Deere*. (USA)

**Annual Reports
Jahresberichte
Rapports annuels**

Annual Reports
Jahresberichte
Rapports annuels

454 Complete cover, the illustration of which, as shown here, continues over the inside covers, for an annual report of the Grand Union Co. food producers. The illustration also served as an in-store poster.(USA)
455 Illustration in actual size from the annual report of New England Telephone, a company in the telecommunications field. (USA)
456, 457 Full-page illustrations from a company brochure of *Saint Gobain*, construction and public-works contractors (here—canalization and industrial installations). Fig. 456 in blue, yellow and brown, Fig. 457 in brown and blue-grey. (FRA)

454 Vollständiger Umschlag mit der über die Innenseiten hinausreichenden Illustration für einen Jahresbericht des Lebensmittelkonzerns *Grand Union*. Die Illustration wurde auch für ein Laden-Plakat verwendet. (USA)
455 Illustration in Originalgrösse aus dem Jahresbericht der New England Telephone, eines Unternehmens der Telekommunikations-Branche. (USA)
456, 457 Ganzseitige Illustrationen aus einer Firmenbroschüre des Konzerns *Saint-Gobain*, hier mit Bezug auf die Konstruktions- und Bauarbeiten, auch in öffentlichen Bereichen wie der Wasserversorgung und Kanalisation. Abb. 456 in Blau, Gelb und Braun, Abb. 457 in Braun und Blaugrau. (FRA)

454 Couverture complète d'un rapport annuel du groupe *Grand Union*, géant de l'alimentation. L'illustration s'étend aux pages intérieures. Elle a aussi été réalisée sous forme d'affiche intérieure. (USA)
455 Illustration grandeur nature pour le rapport annuel de l'entreprise de télécommunications New England Telephone. (USA)
456, 457 Illustrations pleine page d'une brochure d'entreprise du groupe *Saint-Gobain*: elles se rapportent aux activités de construction et de travaux publics, notamment en matière de distribution d'eau et de pose de canalisations. Fig. 456 en bleu, jaune et marron; fig. 457 en marron et gris-bleu. (FRA)

ARTIST / KÜNSTLER / ARTISTE:

454 Teresa Fasolino
455 Fred Otnes
456, 457 Christian Broutin

DESIGNER / GESTALTER / MAQUETTISTE:

454 David Freedman

ART DIRECTOR / DIRECTEUR ARTISTIQUE:

454 Milton Glaser
455 John Olson
456, 457 Georges Lacroix

AGENCY / AGENTUR / AGENCE – STUDIO:

454 Milton Glaser, Inc.
455 Harold Cabot & Co.

454

455

THE GRAND UNION COMPANY
00 BROADWAY
LINWOOD PARK, NEW JERSEY 07407
(01) 794-2000

GRAND
UNION
1984 ANNUAL REPORT

456

457

458

458–460 Double spreads from the "Signal Companies Inc. Annual Report for Young People 1984". The report, printed in bright colours, tells a humorous rhyming story called "Flowers for Mogof" to impress on youngsters the principle of not overspending and it also explains, in simplified language, the national deficit. Fig. 458 shows the company's balance sheet over two years. (USA)
461 Double spread fold-out with pop-up items showing samples from the range of products the Michael Peters Group has completed. Theme of this annual report is "Growth in Industry". (GBR)
462, 463 Title pages of information "newspapers" which are regularly issued by *Ciba-Geigy*. Shown here: "Paediatric perspectives" and "From the language of pain". (SWI)

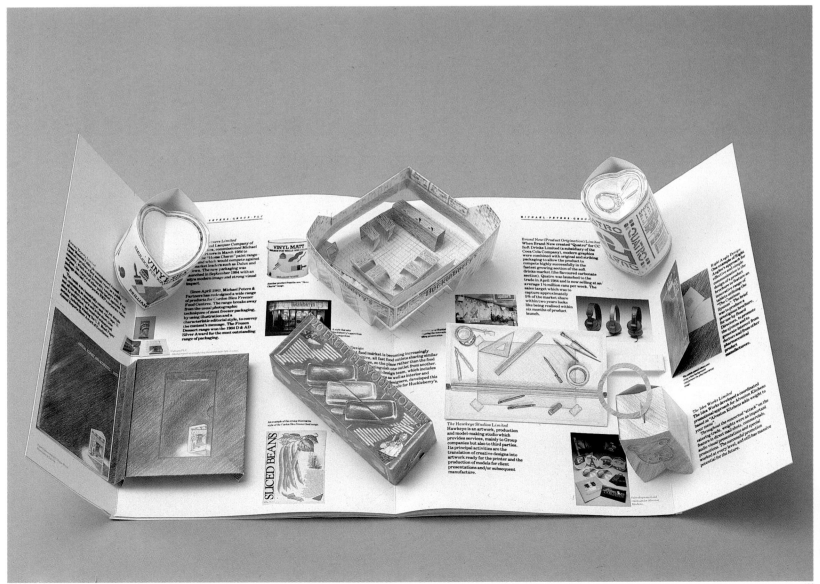

461

459

460

458–460 Doppelseiten aus dem «Jahresbericht für junge Leute» des diversifizierten Unternehmens *Signal*, welches u.a. Teile für Maschinen und Apparate herstellt. Der ganz in Farbe gedruckte Bericht handelt vom nationalen Defizit durch Ausgabenüberschuss, dargestellt (in gereimten Versen) mittels der fiktiven Geschichte «Blumen für Mogof» (Abb. 459 und 460). In Abb. 458 wird zwischen den erzielten Firmenersparnissen in den Jahren 1983 und 1984 verglichen. (USA)
461 Doppelseite mit Pop-up-Gegenständen aus dem Jahresbericht 1984 der Michael Peters Group, London, einer Beratungsfirma für Packungen, Firmendarstellungen und Ladeneinrichtungen. (GBR)
462, 463 Frontseiten einer regelmässig erscheinenden Informationsschrift von *Ciba-Geigy*. (SWI)

458–460 Doubles pages du «Rapport annuel pour les jeunes» de la maison *Signal* qui produit, entre autres, des pièces détachées pour machines et appareils. Ce rapport, tout en couleurs, traite du déficit national causé par l'excédent de dépenses: le sujet est présenté sous la forme d'une histoire fictive (écrite en vers), «Des fleurs pour Mogof» (fig. 459, 460). La fig. 458 permet de comparer les économies réalisées par la firme en 1983 et 1984. (USA)
461 Double page à éléments mobiles du rapport 1984 du Michael Peters Group, Londres, un bureau de consultation pour emballages, installations de magasins et image d'entreprise. (GBR)
462, 463 Premières pages du bulletin d'informations périodique de *Ciba-Geigy*. (SWI)

462

463

464

464 Cover of a richly-illustrated (by Kurt Löb) paperback edition of Gogol's *Petersburg Tales*. In predominantly grey and brown tones. (NLD)
465 Paperback cover for a "post-holocaust" science fiction story. (GBR)
466 *Puppets—The Third World of Ardeshir Mohassess*. Cover in black and white with red background, for a book with drawings by this Iranian artist. (USA)
467 Cover of a children's book from a series about "Troubled Countries". Here—Poland. (USA)

464 Umschlag für eine von Kurt Löb reich illustrierte Taschenbuchausgabe von Gogols *Petersburger Erzählungen*. Überwiegend in Grau- und Brauntönen. (NLD)
465 Taschenbuchumschlag in zarten Farben. Es handelt sich um einen Zukunftsroman. (GBR)
466 «Marionetten – Die Dritte Welt von Ardeshir Mohassess.» Umschlag, schwarzweiss mit rotem Hintergrund, für ein Buch mit Zeichnungen dieses iranischen Künstlers. (USA)
467 Umschlag für ein Kinderbuch aus einer Reihe über Länder in der Krise, hier Polen. (USA)

464 Couverture d'une édition de poche des *Récits de Pétersbourg* de Gogol, abondamment illustrée par Kurt Löb. Prédominance de tons gris et bruns. (NLD)
465 Couverture dans des tons doux pour un roman d'anticipation édité en poche. (GBR)
466 «Marionnettes – Le Tiers Monde d'Ardeshir Mohassess.» Couverture (en noir et blanc sur fond rouge) d'un livre présentant des dessins de cet artiste iranien. (USA)
467 Couverture d'un livre d'enfants d'une série sur les pays en crise: la Pologne. (USA)

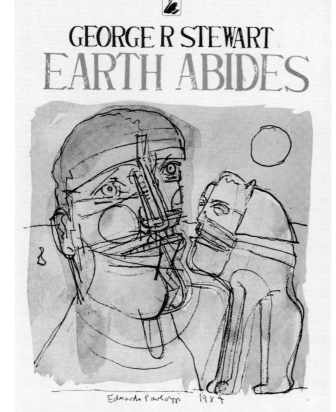

465

466

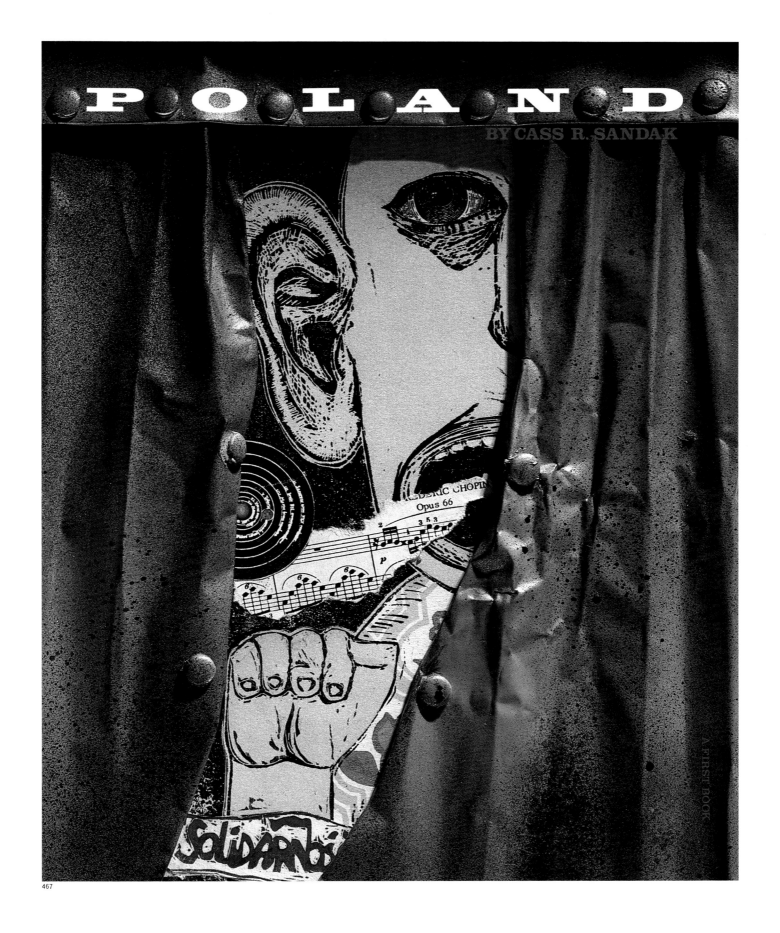

P·O·L·A·N·D

BY CASS R. SANDAK

A FIRST BOOK

467

Book Covers
Buchumschläge
Couvertures de livres

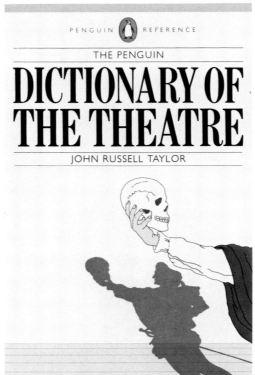

468

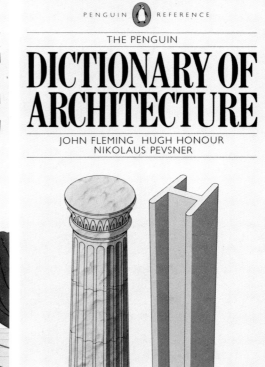

469

470

471

472

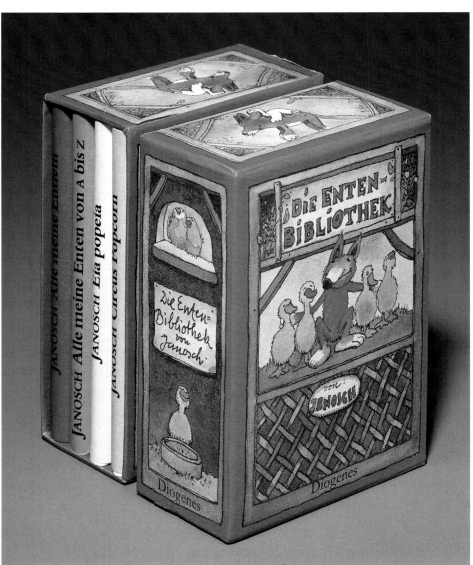

Mighty Mizzling Mouse
and the Red Cabbage House
FRISO HENSTRA

473

474

468, 469 Examples of full-colour covers from a *Penguin* series of various specialized dictionaries. (GBR)
470 Dust jacket for a book containing portraits by Paul Davis; here—Pat Kennedy as a punk and Che Guevara. (USA)
471 Cover, in blue and brown tones, of a children's book entitled "Jeremy—Afraid of Nothing". (SWI)
472, 473 Illustration in actual size and complete dust cover of a picture book about the adventures of a mouse. (USA)
474 Two views of a miniature case containing "The Duck Library"—four books for children by Janosch. Shown in about actual size; published by *Diogenes*. (SWI)

468, 469 Beispiele der mehrfarbigen Umschläge für eine *Penguin*-Reihe von verschiedenen Fachwörterbüchern. (GBR)
470 Schutzumschlag für ein Buch mit Paul Davis' Porträts, hier Pat Kennedy als Punk und Che Guevara. (USA)
471 Umschlag in Blau- und Brauntönen für ein Kinderbuch mit dem Titel «Jeremie – Angst vor nichts». (SWI)
472, 473 Illustration in Originalgrösse und vollständiger Umschlag für ein Bilderbuch über ein Mäusehaus. (USA)
474 Zwei Ansichten einer Miniaturkassette mit vier Bänden (hier ungefähr in Originalgrösse zu sehen) von Janosch für Kinder, erschienen im *Diogenes* Verlag. (SWI)

468, 469 Exemples de couvertures polychromes d'une série de dictionnaires spécialisés publiés par *Penguin*. (GBR)
470 Jaquette d'un livre ornée de portraits de Paul Davis; ici, Pat Kennedy en punk et Che Guevara. (USA)
471 Couverture d'un livre pour enfants des éditions *Nord Sud*. Tons bleus et bruns. (SWI)
472, 473 Illustration grandeur nature et jaquette complète d'un livre sur une maison de souris. (USA)
474 Présenté sous deux angles différents, un coffret miniature contenant quatre volumes de Janosch (presque grandeur nature) pour les enfants, édité par *Diogenes*. (SWI)

476

Book Covers
Buchumschläge
Couvertures de livres

475 Frontispiece of the catalogue for the exhibition "100 Years of Art in Germany" on the occasion of the "International Days" held in Ingelheim-on-the-Rhine. (GER)
476 Complete catalogue cover for an exhibition of ceramics by Miró/Artigas in the New York gallery Matisse. (USA)
477, 478 Illustration and complete cover of a book about packaging from the *Print Casebooks* series. (USA)
479 Dust jacket for a book by American psycho-analyst M. Scott Peck. In black and red on cream background. (ITA)
480 Cover (in colour) of a paperback novel by Remco Campert. (NLD)

475 Frontispiz des Katalogs für eine Ausstellung deutscher Malerei, anlässlich der internationalen Tage in Ingelheim. (GER)
476 Vollständiger Katalogumschlag für eine Ausstellung der Keramiken von Miró/Artigas in der New Yorker Galerie Matisse. (USA)
477, 478 Illustration und vollständiger Umschlag für ein Buch über Verpackungen aus der Reihe *Print Casebooks*. (USA)
479 Umschlag für ein Buch des amerikanischen Psychoanalytikers M. Scott Peck. In Schwarz und Rot auf cremefarbenem Grund. (ITA)
480 Mehrfarbiger Umschlag für einen als Taschenbuch erschienenen Roman des holländischen Autors Remco Campert. (NLD)

475 Frontispice du catalogue d'une exposition de peinture allemande, lors des Journées internationales d'Ingelheim. (GER)
476 Couverture complète du catalogue d'une exposition de céramiques Miró/Artigas à la galerie Matisse à New York. (USA)
477, 478 Illustration et couverture complète d'un livre sur les emballages de la série *Print Casebooks*. (USA)
479 Couverture d'un livre du psychanalyste américain M. Scott Peck. En noir et rouge sur fond crème. (ITA)
480 Couverture polychrome d'un roman de l'auteur hollandais Remco Campert, paru en livre de poche. (NLD)

477

478

479

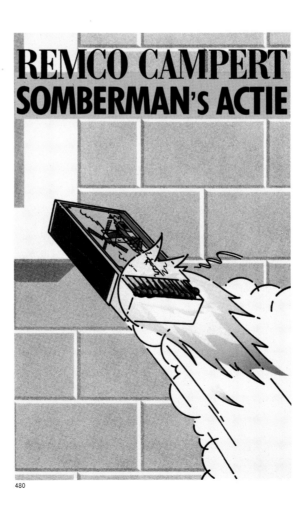
480

ARTIST / KÜNSTLER / ARTISTE:

476 Miró
477, 478 Judy Pedersen
480 Ronald Slabbers

DESIGNER / GESTALTER:

475 Horst Riehl
476 Miró
477, 478 Andrew Kner
479 Lidia Ferrara
480 Ronald Slabbers

ART DIRECTOR:

475 François Lachenal/
     Patricia Rochard
477, 478 Andrew Kner
479 Lidia Ferrara
480 Gerrit Jan Deunk

AGENCY / AGENTUR / AGENCE:

479 Lidia Ferrara

PUBLISHER / VERLEGER / EDITEUR:

475 Boehringer Ingelheim
476 Pierre Matisse Gallery
477, 478 RC Publications
479 CDE, Gruppo Mondadori
480 CPNB

迷って来た鳥の話。

中野真琴著

THOMAS MORUS **Utopia**

MIT BILDERN VON
MICHAEL MATHIAS PRECHTL

BÜCHERGILDE
GUTENBERG

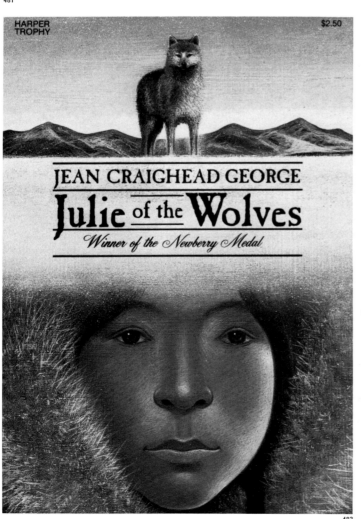

HARPER TROPHY

$2.50

JEAN CRAIGHEAD GEORGE
Julie of the **Wolves**
Winner of the Newberry Medal

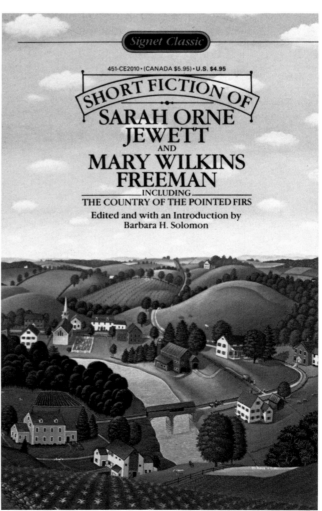

Signet Classic

451-CE2010 • (CANADA $5.95) • U.S. $4.95

SHORT FICTION OF
**SARAH ORNE
JEWETT**
AND
**MARY WILKINS
FREEMAN**
INCLUDING
THE COUNTRY OF THE POINTED FIRS
Edited and with an Introduction by
Barbara H. Solomon

ARTIST / KÜNSTLER / ARTISTE:

481 Yasue Kitima
482 Michael Mathias Prechtl
483 Wendell Minor
484 Mark Hess
485 Stasys Eidrigevičius

DESIGNER / GESTALTER / MAQUETTISTE:

481 Kazumi Nakamura
483 Wendell Minor

ART DIRECTOR / DIRECTEUR ARTISTIQUE:

481 Kazumi Nakamura
483 Al Cetta
484 Susan Bisett

AGENCY / AGENTUR / AGENCE – STUDIO:

481 Try Angle Co. Ltd.
483 Wendell Minor Design

PUBLISHER / VERLEGER / EDITEUR:

481 Toshu Publications
482 Büchergilde Gutenberg
483 Harper Trophy
484 Signet Books
485 ARKA

481 Dust jacket for a book published in Japan by *Tosho* publishers. (JPN)
482 Dust jacket for the book "Utopia" by Thomas Morus, with illustrations by Michael Mathias Prechtl. Wolf in brown-grey with white, sheep in light brown with white. (GER)
483 Cover of a paperback. Mainly in brown, grey and pink tones. (USA)
484 Cover of a paperback collection of short stories. Green and brown tones, blue sky. (USA)
485 Illustration in actual size for the cover of a children's book published by *Arka*. (POL)

481 Schutzumschlag für ein im japanischen *Tosho*-Verlag erschienenes Buch. (JPN)
482 Schutzumschlag für ein von der Büchergilde Gutenberg herausgegebenes Buch mit Bildern von Michael Mathias Prechtl. Wolf in Braungrau mit Weiss, Schaf in Hellbraun mit Weiss. (GER)
483 Umschlag für ein Taschenbuch. Vorwiegend in Braun-, Grau- und Rosatönen. (USA)
484 Umschlag für ein Taschenbuch mit Kurzgeschichten. Grün- und Brauntöne, blauer Himmel. (USA)
485 Illustration in Originalgrösse für den Umschlag eines Kinderbuchs des *Arka*-Verlags. (POL)

481 Jaquette d'un livre paru chez l'éditeur japonais *Tosho*. (JPN)
482 Jaquette d'un ouvrage édité par la Guilde du Livre Gutenberg et illustré par Michael Mathias Prechtl. Loup gris-brun et blanc, agneau brun clair et blanc. (GER)
483 Couverture d'un livre de poche. Tons bruns, gris et roses prédominants. (USA)
484 Couverture d'un recueil de nouvelles édité en poche. Bruns et verts, ciel bleu. (USA)
485 Illustration grandeur nature de la couverture d'un livre d'enfants édité par *Arka*. (POL)

Book Covers
Buchumschläge
Couvertures de livres

485

486

$7.95 394.72948.X

"A masterpiece...the best Kafka biography yet...Brilliantly written, thoroughly researched, richly imagined."—Jim Miller, Newsweek

487

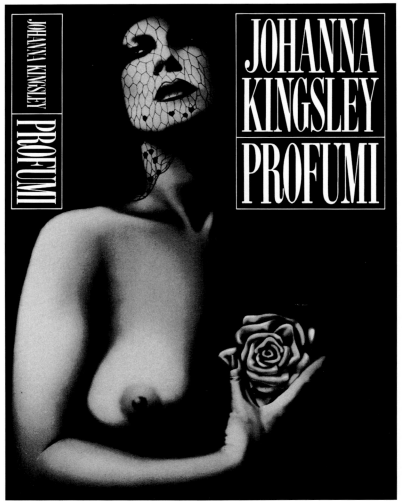

488

489

ARTIST / KÜNSTLER / ARTISTE:

486 Mel Odom
487 Anthony Russo
488 Giovanni Battista Ronco
489 James Marsh
490 Fred Marcellino

DESIGNER / GESTALTER / MAQUETTISTE:

486 Louise Fili
487 Carin Goldberg
488 Lidia Ferrara
489 James Marsh
490 Fred Marcellino

ART DIRECTOR / DIRECTEUR ARTISTIQUE:

486, 490 Louise Fili
488 Lidia Ferrara
489 Stephen Abis

AGENCY / AGENTUR / AGENCE – STUDIO:

488 Lidia Ferrara

PUBLISHER / VERLEGER / EDITEUR:

486, 490 Pantheon Books
489 Vintage Books
488 CDE, Gruppo Mondadori
489 Grafton Books

490

486 Dust jacket in full colour for a collection of gripping short stories by mystery writer Ruth Rendell. (USA)
487 For a biography of Franz Kafka. Black, white, sepia, with text on a yellow background. (USA)
488 Dust cover for a novel about the fictitious Jolaunay family, perfume producers. Yellow rose, black background, white lettering. (ITA)
489 Cover for Keith Waterhouse's latest novel; a paperback edition, one of a series of humorous books. Red devil, auburn hair, blue ground, black-and-white text. (GBR)
490 Dust cover for a novel in which the heroine creates sensational stories—and finds that one comes true. (USA)

486 Mehrfarbiger Schutzumschlag für eine Sammlung fesselnder Kurzgeschichten. (USA)
487 Für eine Franz-Kafka-Biographie. Schwarz, Weiss, Sepia, gelber Schrifthintergrund. (USA)
488 Schutzumschlag für einen Roman über die fiktive Familie Jolaunay, Parfümhersteller. Gelbe Rose, schwarzer Hintergrund, weisse Schrift. (ITA)
489 Umschlag für ein Taschenbuch aus einer humoristischen Reihe. Rotes Teufelchen, rötliche Haare, hellblauer Hintergrund, schwarze und weisse Schrift. (GBR)
490 Schutzumschlag für den Roman über eine Erfinderin phantastischer Geschichten. (USA)

486 Jaquette polychrome conçue pour un recueil de nouvelles captivantes. (USA)
487 Pour une biographie de Franz Kafka. En noir, blanc, sépia, fond du texte jaune. (USA)
488 Jaquette d'un roman mettant en scène les Jolaunay, une famille fictive de fabricants de parfums. Rose jaune, fond noir, texte blanc. (ITA)
489 Couverture d'un livre de poche d'une série humoristique. Petit diable rouge, cheveux rougeâtres, fond bleu clair, texte noir et blanc. (GBR)
490 Jaquette d'un roman sur une femme qui invente des histoires fantastiques. (USA)

Book Covers
Buchumschläge
Couvertures de livres

JOHN CLANCY'S
FAVORITE RECIPES
A Personal Cookbook
BY JOHN CLANCY

491

ARTIST / KÜNSTLER / ARTISTE:

491 Wendell Minor
492 Lonni Sue Johnson
493 Roger Taylor
494 Adam Korpak
495 Shiro Nishiguchi

DESIGNER / GESTALTER / MAQUETTISTE:

491 Wendell Minor
492 Neil Stuart
493 Mervyn Kurlansky / Minaz Nanji
494 Adam Korpak
495 Kenichi Yanagawa

ART DIRECTOR / DIRECTEUR ARTISTIQUE:

491 Harry Ford
492 Neil Stuart
493 Mervyn Kurlansky
494 Adam Korpak
495 Seiki Okuda

AGENCY / AGENTUR / AGENCE – STUDIO:

491 Wendell Minor Design
493 Pentagram
494 Adam Korpak

PUBLISHER / VERLEGER / EDITEUR:

491 Atheneum
492 Viking Penguin
493 Faber & Faber
494 Uusi Kirjakerho
495 Graphic-sha Publishing Co., Ltd.

491 Detail of the cover of a book with the favourite cookery recipes of John Clancy. (USA)
492 Brightly coloured jacket of a novel set in New York in 1895 and which combines the comic and serious, real and illusory. (USA)
493 Dust jacket in black and white with a 3-dimensional effect for an omnibus edition comprising three novels by P. D. James. (GBR)
494 Cover, mainly yellow and brown tones, of a thriller in which a man kills his daughter's murderer. (FIN)
495 Dust jacket of a volume containing an anthology of the works of 230 Japanese illustrators. Red and white harlequin on a grey and black background, gold-coloured lettering. (JPN)

491 Detail des Umschlags für ein Buch mit Kochrezepten des Amerikaners John Clancy. (USA)
492 Farbenfroher Umschlag für einen Roman, dessen Handlung im New York der Jahrhundertwende spielt. (USA)
493 Schutzumschlag mit dreidimensionalem Effekt für einen bei *Faber & Faber* erschienenen Sammelband mit drei Romanen. (GBR)
494 Umschlag, vorwiegend in Gelb- und Brauntönen, für einen Kriminalroman: ein Mann tötet den Mörder seiner Tochter. (FIN)
495 Schutzumschlag für einen Band, in dem 230 japanische Illustratoren vorgestellt werden. Rot-weisser Harlekin vor grauschwarzem Hintergrund, Schrift goldfarben. (JPN)

491 Détail de la couverture d'un livre de recettes de cuisine de l'américain John Clancy. (USA)
492 Couverture de couleurs vives pour un roman dont l'action se déroule dans le New York de 1895. (USA)
493 Jaquette avec effet tridimensionnel pour un volume rassemblant trois romans, édité par *Faber & Faber*. (GBR)
494 Couverture d'un roman policier: Un homme tue le meurtrier de sa fille. Prédominance de jaunes et de bruns. (FIN)
495 Jaquette d'un livre dans lequel sont répertoriés 230 illustrateurs japonais édité par Graphi-sha Publishing Co. Arlequin rouge et blanc sur fond gris-noir, lettres couleur or. (JPN)

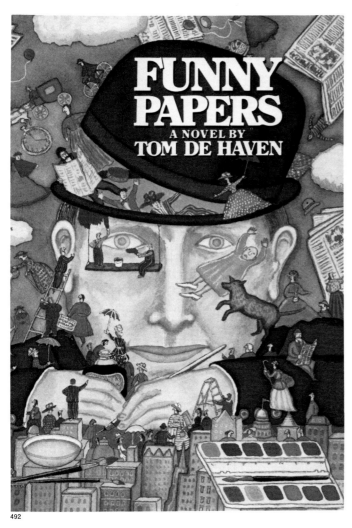

492

493

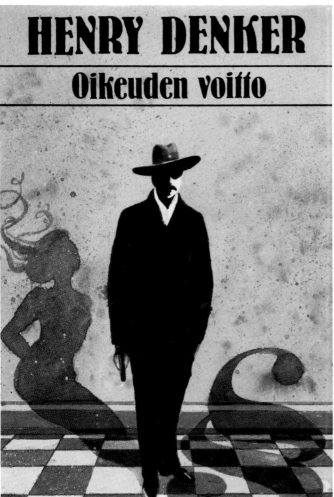

494

495

4

Trademarks

Letterheads

Calendars

Packaging

Record Covers

Schutzmarken

Briefköpfe

Kalender

Packungen

Schallplattenhüllen

Marques et emblèmes

En-têtes

Calendriers

Emballages

Pochettes de disques

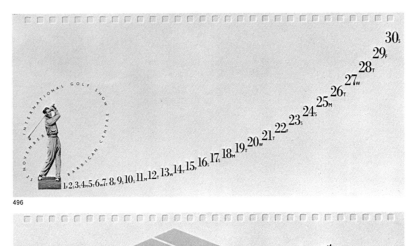

496

497

Calendars / Kalender

499

ARTIST / KÜNSTLER / ARTISTE:

496, 497 Christine Fenn/Ron Mercer
498 Randall Enos
499, 500 Yoshio Hayakawa

DESIGNER / GESTALTER:

496, 497 Cameron Carruthers/
Paul Reeves/Mike Parry
499, 500 Muneaki Andoh/Ryo Miyaishi

ART DIRECTOR:

496, 497 Michael Denny
498 Patrick Flynn
499, 500 Muneaki Andoh

AGENCY / AGENTUR / AGENCE:

496, 497 Roundel Design Group
499, 500 Dentsu Corp.

498

500

496, 497 Sheets from a small spiral-bound calendar for Roundel Design, integrating important sporting dates. Here, a golf show and Wimbledon tennis championship, with both dates marked in dark green, otherwise black, pale green on white ground. (GBR)
498 Illustration from a calendar entitled "Hidden History of the United States" published annually by *The Progressive* magazine, here enforcing the law during prohibition. (USA)
499, 500 Complete sheet and illustration from a calendar for *Central Finance*, with paintings by Yoshio Hayakawa. (JPN)

496, 497 Blätter aus einem kleinen, spiralgehefteten Kalender von Roundel Design, in dem wichtige Sportanlässe vermerkt sind: Hier eine Golfveranstaltung und die Wimbledon-Tennismeisterschaft. Beide Daten in Dunkelgrün, das übrige schwarz und hellgrün. (GBR)
498 Illustration aus einem Kalender mit dem Titel «Die verborgene Geschichte der Vereinigten Staaten», der jährlich von der Zeitschrift *The Progressive* herausgegeben wird. (USA)
499, 500 Vollständiges Blatt und Illustration aus einem Wandkalender für *Central Finance* mit Bildern von Yoshio Hayakawa. (JPN)

496, 497 Feuillets d'un petit calendrier Roundel Design à reliure spirale indiquant les grands événements sportifs, ici un tournoi de golf et les championnats de tennis de Wimbledon. Les deux dates vert foncé, le reste noir et vert clair. (GBR)
498 Illustration d'un calendrier intitulé «Histoire secrète des Etats-Unis» publié chaque année par la revue *The Progressive*. (USA)
499, 500 Feuillet complet et illustration qui y figure. Le calendrier mural en question, illustré par Yoshio Hayakawa, a été réalisé pour *Central Finance*. (JPN)

501

502

501, 502 "Marilyn and Her Pearly Whites." Illustration and complete June sheet from a *Pushpin* calendar in celebration of the 50's. (USA)
503 The slow and careful maturing of Bordeaux wine is depicted in this illustration from a wine diary for *Grants of St. James's*. (GBR)
504 March sheet from a *Daimler-Benz* calendar portraying events which happened between March 1906–1913. Full colour illustration, text printed in white on a clear film overlay. (GER)

501, 502 «Marilyn und ihre Perlweissen.» Illustration und vollständiges Juni-Blatt aus einem *Pushpin*-Kalender, der den 50er Jahren gewidmet ist. (USA)
503 Das langsame und sorgfältige Reifen des Bordeaux-Weins ist Gegenstand dieser Illustration aus einem Wein-Kalender für *Grants of St. James's*. (GBR)
504 Märzblatt aus einem *Daimler-Benz*-Kalender mit mehrfarbiger Darstellung (und Aufführung in weisser Schrift auf durchsichtiger Folie) von Ereignissen zwischen März 1906–1913. (GER)

501, 502 «Marilyn et ses dents blanches comme neige.» Illustration et feuillet de juin complet d'un calendrier *Pushpin* consacré aux années 50. (USA)
503 Illustration figurant dans un calendrier des vins de *Grants of St. James's*. On y présente le long vieillissement des vins de Bordeaux et les soins experts qui leur sont prodigués. (GBR)
504 Feuillet de mars d'un calendrier *Daimler-Benz*. On y représente en polychromie les grandes dates entre mars 1906 et 1913. Texte blanc sur feuillet transparent. (GER)

Calendars
Kalender
Calendries

ARTIST / KÜNSTLER / ARTISTE:

501, 502 Christoph Blumrich
503 Ken Laidlaw
504 Dietrich Ebert

DESIGNER / GESTALTER / MAQUETTISTE:

501, 502 Gail Stampar/Seymour Chwast

ART DIRECTOR / DIRECTEUR ARTISTIQUE:

501, 502 Seymour Chwast
503 Roger Pring
504 H. Lah

AGENCY / AGENTUR / AGENCE – STUDIO:

501, 502 The Pushpin Group
503 Roger Pring & Associates
504 Schellenberg

503

504

221

505

506

505, 506 Examples from a wall calendar for the printers *Rohden*. All illustrated sheets are in duplicate, the under one is shown smooth, the top, as here, folded, with calendarium. (GER)
507–509 Sheets for July, June and December, from a calendar presenting the signs of the Zodiac; black and transparent film overlay on coloured paper (Figs. 508, 509 silver). (HUN)
510–512 Illustrations and complete sheet from the graphic calendar for the Toyo Ink Company. Shown here are two illustrations by Ikko Tanaka, to whom the calendar is dedicated. (JPN)

505, 506 Beispiele aus einem Wandkalender für die Druckerei *Rohden*. Alle Illustrationen sind in zwei Versionen, einmal glatt und einmal – wie hier – gefaltet, mit dem Kalendarium. (GER)
507–509 Die Blätter für Juli, Juni und Dezember aus einem Kalender mit Darstellungen der Sternzeichen, ausgespart auf schwarzer Folie über farbigem Papier (Abb. 508, 509 silber). (HUN)
510–512 Illustrationen und vollständiges Blatt aus einem Graphik-Kalender für *Toyo Ink*, Hersteller von Tuschen. Hier zwei Arbeiten von Ikko Tanaka, dem der Kalender gewidmet ist. (JPN)

505, 506 Exemples tirés d'un calendrier mural de l'imprimerie *Rohden*. Toutes les illustrations apparaissent deux fois, dont l'une, comme ici, pliée avec le calendrier. (GER)
507–509 Feuillets de juillet, juin et décembre d'un calendrier représentant les signes du zodiaque; feuillet transparent et noir sur un fond de papier couleur (fig. 508, 509 argent). (HUN)
510–512 Illustrations et feuillet complet d'un calendrier d'art graphique dédié à Ikko Tanaka par *Toyo Ink*, fabricant d'encres et d'encres de Chine: deux créations de Tanaka. (JPN)

Calendars
Kalender
Calendries

507

508

509

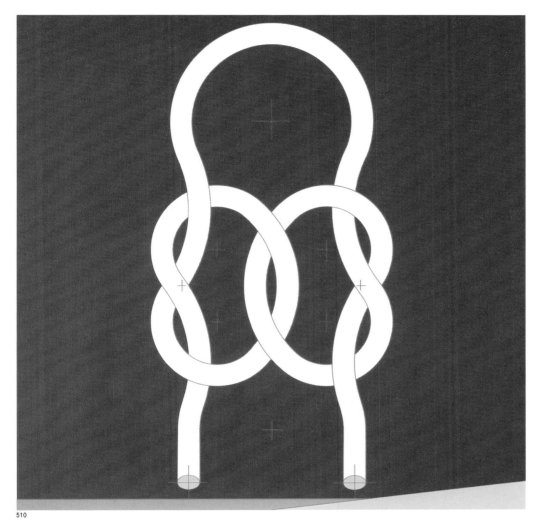

510

512

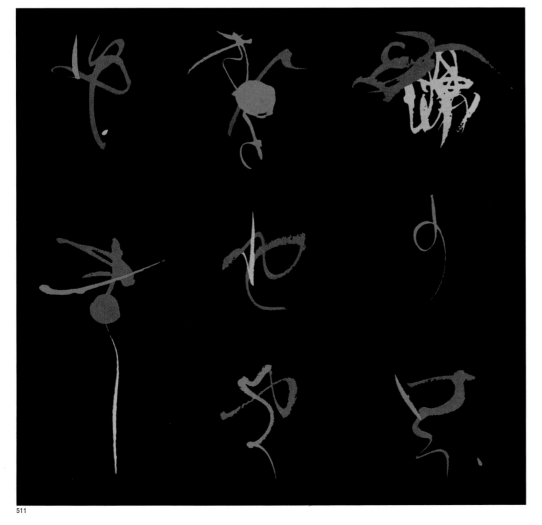

511

ARTIST / KÜNSTLER / ARTISTE:

505, 506 Harald Schlüter
507–509 Crescencia Zelenák
510–512 Ikko Tanaka

DESIGNER / GESTALTER / MAQUETTISTE:

505, 506 Harald Schlüter
510–512 Katsuhiro Kinoshita

ART DIRECTOR / DIRECTEUR ARTISTIQUE:

505, 506 Harald Schlüter
510–512 Ikko Tanaka

AGENCY / AGENTUR / AGENCE – STUDIO:

505, 506 Harald Schlüter Werbeagentur GmbH
510–512 Ikko Tanaka Design Studio

513

515

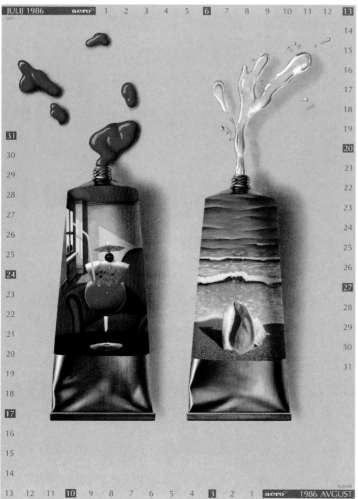

514

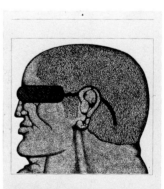

518

ARTIST / KÜNSTLER / ARTISTE:

513, 514 Radovan Jenko/Zvone Kosovelj/
        Dušan Arzenšek (Photo)
515 Michael David Brown
516, 517 Tullio Pericoli
518–520 Herbert Carl Traue

DESIGNER / GESTALTER / MAQUETTISTE:

513, 514 Radovan Jenko
515 Michael David Brown/Cary Hatch
518–520 Herbert Carl Traue

ART DIRECTOR / DIRECTEUR ARTISTIQUE:

513, 514 Radovan Jenko
515 Michael David Brown
518–520 Herbert Carl Traue

AGENCY / AGENTUR / AGENCE – STUDIO:

513, 514 Aero Design Studio
515 MDB Communications, Inc.
518–520 Studio H. C. Traue

513, 514 The March/April and July/August sheets from a calendar for *Aero Chemical*. (YUG)
515 Cover of a hospital calendar to mark its fifteenth anniversary. (USA)
516, 517 Double spread and cover of a pocket diary in which scientists are portrayed, one per month. Shown here are Marie and Pierre Curie. (ITA)
518–520 Complete sheet for the month of June, and the illustration from it—Procrustes (who produced conformity by violent methods) and a further illustration entitled "Culture Adviser" from a calendar with "Heads out of the head" of H. C. Traue. Black and white. (GER)

513, 514 Das März/April- und das Juli/August-Blatt aus einem Kalender für *Aero-Chemical*. (YUG)
515 Deckblatt eines Wandkalenders zum fünfzehnjährigen Bestehen eines Krankenhauses. (USA)
516, 517 Doppelseite und Umschlag einer von der Zeitschrift *Genius* verschickten kleinen Taschen-Agenda, in der Wissenschaftler gezeigt werden; hier Marie und Pierre Curie. (ITA)
518–520 Vollständige Ansicht des Monats Juni, die dazugehörige Darstellung des Prokrustes (als Symbol für selbstauferlegte Zwänge) und eine weitere Illustration mit dem Titel «Kulturreferent», aus einem Wandkalender mit «Köpfen aus dem Kopf» von H. C. Traue. In Schwarzweiss. (GER)

513, 514 Les feuillets de mars/avril et juillet/août d'un calendrier *Aero-Chemical*. (YUG)
515 Couverture d'un calendrier mural pour le 15e anniversaire d'un centre hospitalier. (USA)
516, 517 Double page et couverture d'un petit agenda de poche distribué par le magazine *Genius*, avec des portraits de savants. On voit ici Pierre et Marie Curie. (ITA)
518–520 Feuillet de juin complet, illustration qui y figure – Procruste symbolise les contraintes que l'on s'impose soi-même – et illustration intitulée «conseiller culturel», pour le calendrier mural de H. C. Traue. Noir et blanc. (GER)

Marie e Pierre Curie - la radioattività

516

517

Calendars
Kalender
Calendries

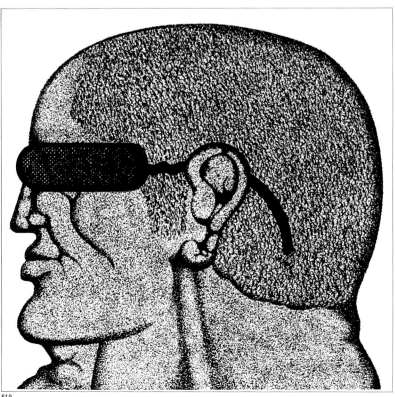

519

520

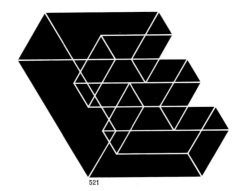

521

522

523

525

524

526

226

521 Logo for the *Ealing Electro-Optics*. (GBR)
522 Logotype for a new cosmetic range by *Shiseido*. (JPN)
523 Logo for Mercedez Commercial Printing in Manila. (PHI)
524 Logo for *SugarCreek;* the "S" is combined with a water element for the name of this exhibition house on an estate. (USA)
525 The Texas Federal/Bright Bank adapts the symbol for the "lone star State" for its logo. (USA)
526 Logo for the paper producers Milliken Mills. (USA)
527 Logotype for Roots, a men's fashion shop in Summit, New Jersey. (USA)
528 Symbol for the International Poster Triennial in Toyama. (JPN)
529 For the *Myer* Emporium—one of the largest Australian firms (department stores, discount stores, restaurants). (AUS)
530 Logo for the industrial packaging firm *Van Leer*. The design's simplicity enables its application in crude processes. (USA)
531 Symbol for the photo-lithographers Emmegi in Rome. (ITA)
532 "Quotes"—name and logo for a new chain of shoe stores. (USA)
533–535 Three symbols for Caremark, Inc. Fig. 534 symbolizes home health care, Fig. 535 symbolizes the pharmacy. (USA)

521 Für die *Ealing Electro-Optics* konzipiertes Signet. (GBR)
522 Schriftzug einer neuen Kosmetiklinie von *Shiseido*. (JPN)
523 Signet der Druckerei Mercedez Commercial in Manila. (PHI)
524 Signet für *SugarCreek*. Der Designer verband ein Symbol für Wasser (Creek = Bach) mit dem Anfangsbuchstaben «S». (USA)
525 Symbol für die Texas Federal/Bright Bank. (USA)
526 Signet für die Papierfabrik Milliken Mills. (USA)
527 Für Roots, ein Herrengeschäft in Summit, New Jersey. (USA)
528 Symbol für eine alle drei Jahre stattfindende Plakatausstellung in Toyama, Japan. (JPN)
529 Für *Myer*, eine der grössten australischen Firmen (mit Warenhäusern, Restaurants etc.) gestaltetes Signet. (AUS)
530 Signet der Packungsfirma *Van Leer*. Die einfachen Formen ermöglichen auch eine Verwendung als Prägestempel. (USA)
531 Von der Lithofirma Emmegi in Rom verwendetes Symbol (ITA)
532 «Quotes» (Anführungszeichen): Name und Logo einer neuen Schuhgeschäftskette. (USA)
533–535 Drei Symbole für Caremark, Inc. Abb. 534 symbolisiert die häuslichen Belange, Abb. 535 die pharmazeutischen. (USA)

521 Emblème créé pour *Ealing Electro-Optics*. (GBR)
522 Pour une nouvelle gamme de cosmétiques *Shiseido*. (JPN)
523 Emblème de l'imprimerie Mercedez Commercial, Manille. (PHI)
524 Emblème de *SugarCreek*. Le graphiste a combiné le symbole de l'eau (creek = ruisseau) avec l'initiale «S». (USA)
525 Symbole créé pour la Texas Federal/Bright Bank. (USA)
526 Emblème de la fabrique de papier Milliken Mills. (USA)
527 Pour les confections masculines Roots à Summit (N. J.). (USA)
528 Emblème d'une exposition d'affiches organisée sous forme de triennale dans la ville japonaise de Toyama. (JPN)
529 Emblème créé pour *Myer*, l'un des groupes australiens les plus importants (grands magasins, restaurants, etc.). (AUS)
530 Emblème de la firme d'emballages *Van Leer*. Le contour simple en facilite l'emploi dans l'étampage. (USA)
531 Emblème de l'atelier de photolitho romain Emmegi. (ITA)
532 «Quotes» (guillemets): nom et logo d'une nouvelle chaîne de magasins de chaussures. (USA)
533–535 Trois emblèmes pour Caremark, Inc. La fig. 534 symbolise les produits ménagers, la fig. 535 les pharmaceutiques. (USA)

527

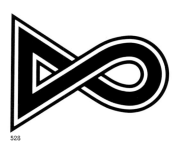

528

529

530

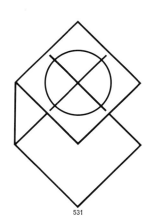

531

532

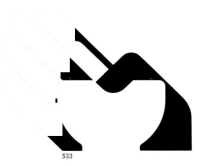

533

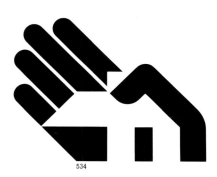

534

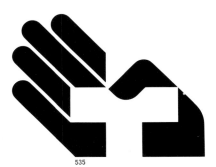

535

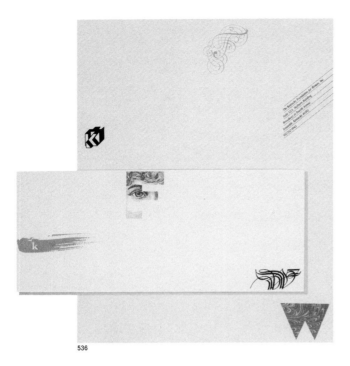

536

537

536 Stationery for the Kentucky Foundation for Women, KFW. (USA)
537 Letterhead and envelope for the firm HBR, with blue, yellow and red. (AUS)
538 Logotype for an Italian fashion store for men. (ITA)
539 Symbol for "Dante's", an American restaurant. (USA)
540 Logo for a team of architects calling themselves "3 B". (USA)
541 For the Design Alliance, a firm of interior designers. (USA)
542 Symbol for an import/export company. (USA)
543 Symbol for the Institute of Coronary Diseases, in Rome. (ITA)
544 Stationery for Suresh Cordo, an Indian photographer. (IND)
545 Red title on this stationery for a record-album company. (USA)
546 Letterhead for a fashion designer in Milan. (ITA)
547 For Sherry Pollack, whose initials are the same as "salt and pepper". (USA)
548, 549 Detail and complete letterhead for a *Nestlé* sponsored public service campaign to help find missing children. (USA)
550 For the Don Weller Institute for the Cure of Design. (USA)

536 Briefpapier und Couvert für die Kentucky Foundation for Women KFW. (USA)
537 Briefpapier mit Umschlag der Firma HBR. Mit Blau, Gelb und Rot. (AUS)
538 Schriftzug eines italienischen Modegeschäfts für Herren. (ITA)
539 Symbol für «Dante's», ein amerikanisches Restaurant. (USA)
540 Signet für ein Architektenteam, das sich «3 B» nennt. (USA)
541 Von der Design Alliance (Innenarchitekten) verwendetes Signet. (USA)
542 Signet einer Import- und Exportfirma. (USA)
543 Symbol des römischen Instituts für Herzkranke. (ITA)
544 Briefpapier für Suresh Cordo, einen indischen Photographen. (IND)
545 Für eine Schallplattenfirma konzipiertes Briefpapier. Rote Schrift. (USA)
546 Briefkopf einer Mode-Designerin in Mailand. (ITA)
547 Für Sherry Pollack (Anfangsbuchstaben von Salz und Pfeffer). (USA)
548, 549 Detail und Briefkopf für ein von *Nestlé* finanziertes Hilfsprogramm, das u. a. die Suche nach vermissten Kindern unterstützen soll. (USA)
550 Für das Don Weller Institut for the Cure of Design. (USA)

536 Papier à lettres et enveloppe de la Kentucky Foundation for Women. (USA)
537 Papier à lettres, enveloppe de la société HBR. Bleu, jaune, rouge. (AUS)
538 Logo d'un magasin de modes masculines en Italie. (ITA)
539 Emblème pour un restaurant américain, le «Dante's». (USA)
540 Emblème d'un bureau d'architecture baptisé «3 B». (USA)
541 Emblème des architectes-décorateurs de la Design Alliance. (USA)
542 Emblème d'une maison d'import-export. (USA)
543 Emblème de l'Institut romain de cardiologie. (ITA)
544 Papier à lettres du photographe indien Suresh Cordo. (IND)
545 Papier à lettres d'un producteur de disques. Texte en rouge. (USA)
546 En-tête d'une designer de mode milanaise. (ITA)
547 Pour Sherry Pollack (mêmes initiales que le sel et le poivre). (USA)
548, 549 Détail et en-tête complet d'un programme d'aide financé par *Nestlé* et assistant entre autres les parents d'enfants disparus. (USA)
550 Pour le Don Weller Institute for the Cure of Design. (USA)

538

539

540

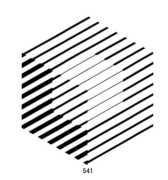

541

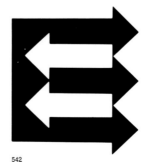

542

543

Trademarks / Letterheads
Schutzmarken / Briefköpfe
Marques et emblèmes / En-têtes

COLUMBIA ALBUMS

SURESH CORDO · PHOTOGRAPHER
MAILING ADDRESS: 44/46 KARANI BUILDING, 4TH FLOOR, RAJA RAM MOHAN ROY ROAD, BOMBAY 400 004

544

545

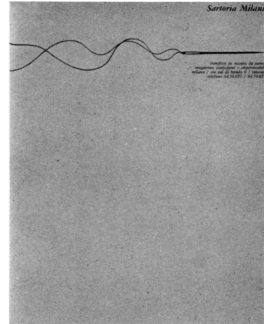

Sartoria Milani

546

Sherry Pollack
200 West 79 Street
New York, NY 10024
(212) 877-3409

547

STREET
SMARTS

A Videotape
Lending Library Program

The Weller Institute
for the Cure of Design, Inc.

Home Office

1906 Aerie Drive
P O Box 726
Park City, Utah 84060-0720

(801) 649-9859

Sponsored by: Nestlé Foods Corporation and Supermarket Communications Systems, Inc.

548

549

550

551

ARTIST / KÜNSTLER / ARTISTE:

551 Hans Reisinger
554 Mark Jones/Ray Hondo
555 Georgia Deaver

DESIGNER / GESTALTER / MAQUETTISTE:

551 Rob van den Berg
552 Lori Murphy
553 Robbie de Villiers
554 Primo Angeli
555 Cal Anderson

ART DIRECTOR / DIRECTEUR ARTISTIQUE:

551 Rob van den Berg
552 David Gauger
553 Robbie de Villiers
554 Hal Riney/Jerry Andelin
555 Cal Anderson

AGENCY / AGENTUR / AGENCE – STUDIO:

551 Millford-Van den Berg Design bv.
552 Gauger & Silva, Inc.
553 Janice Ashby Design Studios
554 Primo Angeli Graphics
555 Georgia Deaver Calligraphy

551 Front and back view of a bottle for white rum, marketed under the *Roncador* label. (NLD)
552 Bottle livery for three different seasoning sauces of Japanese origin marketed in the United States. (USA)
553 Livery for a bottle of liqueur brandy. Text, wire and seal of merit in gold colour, pale blue ribbon. (SAF)
554 Bottle styling and carrier pack for *Weinhard's* beer. (USA)
555 Bottle livery for a Californian champagne. Label and neckband printed in red and black, gold-foil collar. (USA)

551 Vorder- und Rückansicht einer Flasche für weissen Rum der Marke *Roncador.* (NLD)
552 Flaschenausstattung für drei verschiedene Gewürzsaucen japanischen Ursprungs. (USA)
553 Ausstattung für eine Flasche Branntwein. Beschriftung, Draht und Gütesiegel goldfarben, Band hellblau. (SAF)
554 Flaschengestaltung und Tragkarton für *Weinhard*-Bier. (USA)
555 Ausstattung für eine Flasche kalifornischen Champagners. Rot- und schwarzbedruckte Etiketten und Goldfolie. (USA)

551 Recto et verso d'une bouteille de rhum blanc importé de la marque *Roncador.* (NLD)
552 Etude de bouteille pour trois différentes sauces épicées d'origine japonaise. (USA)
553 Etude de bouteille pour une eau-de-vie. Texte, fil métallique et label or, bande bleu clair. (SAF)
554 Bouteille de carton de transport pour la bière *Weinhard.* (USA)
555 Etude de bouteille pour un champagne de Californie. Etiquettes imprimées en rouge et en noir et habillage or. (USA)

552

553

554

555

556

557

558

556 Bottle livery with measure cap for a special alcoholic/coffee mixed drink. (SAF)
557 Styling for a bottle of wine sent as a Christmas gift by *Smith & Milton.* (GBR)
558 Label in actual size for a bottle of French red wine. (CAN)
559 Bottle styling for a semi-sweet, sparkling rosé wine. (SAF)
560 Livery for a bottle of lightly sparkling white wine. (SAF)
561 Stackable bottles for various alcoholic drinks marketed by MAG. (JPN)
562 Cigarette pack in gold-toned blind-embossed foil; with brown band and text. (JPN)

556 Flaschenausstattung mit Messbecher für ein alkoholisches Kaffee-Mixgetränk. (SAF)
557 Ausstattung einer Flasche Wein, als Weihnachtsgeschenk von *Smith & Milton.* (GBR)
558 Etikett in Originalgrösse für eine Flasche französischen Rotweins. (CAN)
559 Flaschengestaltung für halbtrockenen, moussierenden Rosé (Kalte Ente). (SAF)
560 Ausstattung für eine Flasche leicht moussierenden, leichten Weissweins. (SAF)
561 Stapelbare Flaschen für verschiedene alkoholische Getränke der Marke MAG. (JPN)
562 Zigarettenpackung aus blindgeprägter Goldfolie, Schrift und Band braun. (JPN)

556 Bouteille pour un café alcoolisé avec gobelet-doseur en guise de bouchon. (SAF)
557 Conception d'une bouteille de vin, un cadeau de Noël de *Smith & Milton.* (GBR)
558 Etiquette grandeur nature pour un vin rouge français. (CAN)
559 Etude de bouteille pour un rosé mousseux demi-sec (Canard froid). (SAF)
560 Bouteille pour un vin blanc léger moussant légèrement. (SAF)
561 Bouteilles empilables pour diverses boissons alcooliques de la marque MAG. (JPN)
562 Paquet de cigarettes *Hi-Lite* habillé d'or gaufré à sec. Texte et bande en brun. (JPN)

559

561

ARTIST / KÜNSTLER / ARTISTE:

556 Gary Silberman (Photo)
557 Jeremy Haines
558 Heather Cooper
559 Tobie Beele
560 David Thorpe

DESIGNER / GESTALTER / MAQUETTISTE:

556 Janice Ashby
557 Jeremy Haines/Brett Hasserty
558 Heather Cooper
559 Tobie Beele
560 Robbie de Villiers
561 Shigeru Akizuki/
     Masakichi Awashima
562 Shigeru Akizuki

ART DIRECTOR:

556 Janice Ashby
557 Howard Milton
558 Heather Cooper
559, 560 Robbie de Villiers
561, 562 Shigeru Akizuki

AGENCY / AGENTUR / AGENCE – STUDIO:

556, 559, 560 Janice Ashby
     Design Studios
557 Smith & Milton
558 Heather Cooper Illustration & Design

560

562

Packaging
Packungen
Emballages

Packaging
Packungen
Emballages

ARTIST / KÜNSTLER / ARTISTE:

563 David Thorpe
565 Hans Reisinger
567 Claire Armstrong
568 Brian Grimwood

DESIGNER / GESTALTER / MAQUETTISTE:

563 Elsabe Gelderblom
564 Robbie de Villiers
565 Rob van den Berg
566 Gerhard Kern
567 Claire Armstrong
568 Howard Milton

ART DIRECTOR / DIRECTEUR ARTISTIQUE:

563, 564 Robbie de Villiers
565 Rob van den Berg
566 Rudi Weiskam
567 Jane Seager
568 Howard Milton

AGENCY / AGENTUR / AGENCE – STUDIO:

563, 564 Janice Ashby Design Studios
565 Millford-Van den Berg Design bv.
566 Institut für Packungsgestaltung
567 SMS Design Ltd.
568 Smith & Milton

563

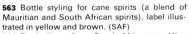

565

563 Bottle styling for cane spirits (a blend of Mauritian and South African spirits), label illustrated in yellow and brown. (SAF)
564 Bottle livery for a South African sparkling wine. Gold foil and pale blue (handwriting) and gold printed on a dark label. (SAF)
565 Packaging for a cat dry-food product. The cats (l. to r.) are: ginger, black and tabby, on a yellow and green background. (NLD)
566 Cooling sleeve made of polystyrene and bottle with coordinated labelling for *Angelburger* spirits. (GER)
567 Partly-printed transparent bags for two sorts of muesli by *Allinson*. The graphics reflect the wholesome quality while the product is still prominent at point of purchase. (GBR)
568 Examples from a range of packaging. Here, tins containing sauces for French cuisine. (GBR)

563 Flaschenausstattung für einen aus Melasse gebrannten Schnaps (Mischung aus Südafrika und Mauritius). Illustration des Etiketts in Gelb und Braun. (SAF)
564 Flaschengestaltung für südafrikanischen Sekt. Goldfolie sowie goldfarben- und (Handschrift) hellblaubedrucktes Etikett. (SAF)
565 Packung für eine Katzen-Trockenfuttermischung. Eine schwarze, eine braun- und eine rotgetigerte Katze; Grund gelb-grün. (NLD)
566 Kühlmantel und Flasche mit übereinstimmendem Etikett für einen Aquavit. (GER)
567 Teilweise bedruckte Klarsichtpackung für zwei Sorten Müesli von *Allinson*. (GBR)
568 Beispiele aus einer Reihe von Dosen mit Saucen für die französische Küche. (GBR)

563 Etude de bouteille pour une eau-de-vie à base de mélasse sud-africaine et mauricienne. Illustration en jaune et en brun. (SAF)
564 Etude de bouteille pour un champagne sud-africain. Feuille or, étiquette or et (pour le texte manuscrit) bleu clair. (SAF)
565 Emballage pour un aliment sec complet pour chats. Chats noir, brun tigré, rouge tigré sur fond vert et jaune. (NLD)
566 Gaine de refroidissement et bouteille pour une eau-de-vie. Etiquettes concordantes. (GER)
567 Emballage transparent (impression partielle) pour deux birchers *Allinson*. (GBR)
568 Echantillons d'une gamme de boîtes de sauces pour la cuisine française. (GBR)

564

566

567

568

569

ARTIST / KÜNSTLER / ARTISTE:

570 Mitei Fujiwara
572 Shigeru Akizuki
574 Shozo Kakutani

DESIGNER / GESTALTER / MAQUETTISTE:

569, 570 Masahiro Oishi
571 Yusaku Kamekura
572 Shigeru Akizuki/Yoshio Hara
573 Kenji Maezawa
574 Shozo Kakutani

ART DIRECTOR / DIRECTEUR ARTISTIQUE:

569 Shingo Oka
570 Masahiro Oishi
571 Yusaku Kamekura
572 Shigeru Akizuki
573 Kenji Maezawa
574 Shozo Kakutani

AGENCY / AGENTUR / AGENCE – STUDIO:

569 Heiwa Shigyo Co. Ltd.
570 Japan Ad-Art Inc.

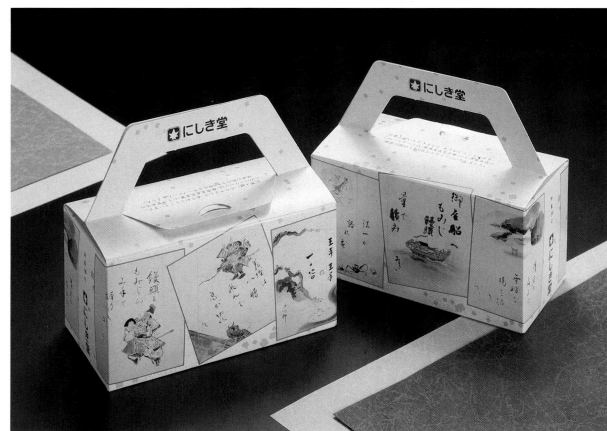

570

569 Gift packaging for traditional Japanese foods; shown is a single pack and a carton folder containing two packs of the product. (JPN)
570 Folding cartons with integrated handles for Japanese cake. White, printed in colour. (JPN)
571 Carrier bags and small bags for a shop. Green, blue and black, on white and grey. (JPN)
572 Packaging concept for the *Seibu* store for various Japanese specialities. (JPN)
573 Carton, shown open and closed, with metal containers, for soft Azuki-bean jelly. In shades of violet and black, on white. (JPN)
574 Carrier bag with cord handles for marine products. Blue shading to black; with grey and red. (JPN)

569 Geschenkverpackung für traditionelle japanische Esswaren, hier eine einzelne und zwei mit einem Kartonwickler zusammengehaltene Schachteln. (JPN)
570 Faltkartons mit integriertem Traggriff für Kuchen. Weisser Karton, mehrfarbig bedruckt. (JPN)
571 Tragtaschen und Tüten für einen Laden. Grün, blau und schwarz auf Weiss und Grau. (JPN)
572 Ausstattungskonzept des Kaufhauses *Seibu* für verschiedene japanische Spezialitäten. (JPN)
573 Karton, hier geschlossen und geöffnet, mit Metalldöschen für Gelee aus Bohnen, eine japanische Spezialität. Violett-Töne und Schwarz auf Weiss. (JPN)
574 Tragtasche mit Kordel für Bootsartikel. Blautöne, Grau und Rot auf Weiss. (JPN)

569 Emballage-cadeau pour des comestibles japonais traditionnels: carton et deux boîtes réunies par un rabat en carton. (JPN)
570 Cartons à pâtisserie à poignées intégrées. Carton blanc, impression polychrome. (JPN)
571 Cabas et sacs en papier pour un magasin. Vert, bleu, noir sur blanc et gris. (JPN)
572 Emballage des grands magasins *Seibu* étudié pour diverses spécialités japonaises. (JPN)
573 Carton montré ouvert et fermé, et petites boîtes métalliques pour la gelée de haricots, spécialité typiquement japonaise. Divers violets et du noir sur fond blanc. (JPN)
574 Cabas à cordelette de transport pour articles de bateau. Bleus, gris, rouge sur blanc. (JPN)

Packaging
Packungen
Emballages

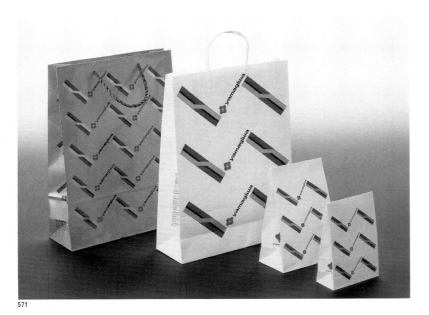

571

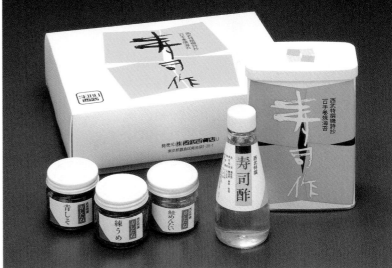

573

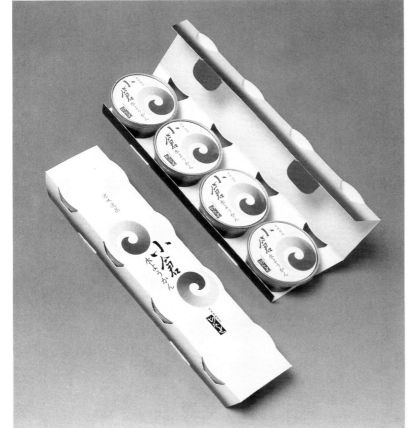

572

574

ARTIST/KÜNSTLER/ARTISTE:

575 Charles Spencer Anderson
576 Angela Staples
577 Hans Reisinger

DESIGNER/GESTALTER/MAQUETTISTE:

575 Charles Spencer Anderson
576 Pamela Virgilio/Carol Rhodes
577 Rob van den Berg
578 Chuck Schmidt
579 Ursmila Kerkar/Dhun Cordo
580, 581 Helmut Schmid
582 Raymond Lee

ART DIRECTOR:

576 Robert P. Gersin
577 Rob van den Berg
578 Kathleen Campbell
579 Ursmila Kerkar/Dhun Cordo
580, 581 Helmut Schmid
582 Raymond Lee/Peter Baker

AGENCY/AGENTUR/AGENCE:

575 The Duffy Design Group
576 Robert P. Gersin Associates Inc.
577 Millford-Van den Berg Design bv.
578 Tom Campbell Design Associates, Inc.
579 Graphitecture
580, 581 JMS
582 Raymond Lee & Associates

575 Label as an example from a range of jars containing spaghetti sauces. (USA)
576 Livery for one of a series of jars with woven raffia covers, here for mixed spice. (USA)
577 Design for containers for various kinds of fruit curd. (BEL)
578 Can design in silver-grey tones for a nutritive quencher for athletes. (USA)
579 Range of packaging and place sets for "The Tiffin Box"—an Indian fast-food restaurant. (IND)
580, 581 Cellophane packaging for sliced bread, and folding cartons for fresh wares from the bakers and confectioners *Kobe Belle*, on which the new logotype is applied. (JPN)
582 Lunchbox-type cartons inscribed "Bach's Lunch" for articles to whet the musical appetite. (CAN)

575 Etikett für eine Flasche mit klassischer italienischer Tomaten-Basilikum-Sauce. (USA)
576 Behälter mit bastüberzogenem Deckel aus einer Serie mit verschiedenen Gewürzen. (USA)
577 Ausstattung von Behältern für verschiedene Sorten Fruchtquark. (BEL)
578 Dosenausstattung, in silbrigen Grautönen, für ein Aufbaupräparat für Sportler. (USA)
579 Verpackungsreihe und Tisch-Sets für ein indisches Schnellimbiss-Restaurant. (IND)
580, 581 Zellophanverpackung für Schnittbrot und Faltschachteln für Frischgebäck der Bäckerei und Konditorei *Kobe Belle*. Ein neuer Schriftzug dient als Gestaltungselement. (JPN)
582 Tragkarton für Artikel, die den musikalischen Appetit befriedigen sollen. (CAN)

575

577

576

578

Packaging
Packungen
Emballages

579

580

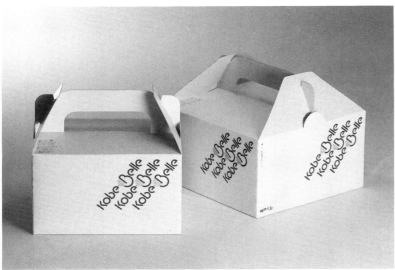

581

582

575 Etiquette pour une bouteille de sauce tomate italienne classique au basilic, type «Napoli». (USA)
576 Boîte à épices type dans une série aux couvercles recouverts de raphia. (USA)
577 Conditionnement de diverses variétés de séré aux fruits. (BEL)
578 Présentation en tons gris argent d'un produit fortifiant pour sportifs. (USA)
579 Gamme d'emballages et sets de table pour un snack indien. (IND)
580, 581 Emballage de pain en tranches sous cellophane et cartons pliants pour les gâteaux frais de la boulangerie-pâtisserie *Kobe Belle,* ornés d'un nouveau logo décoratif. (JPN)
582 Carton genre pique-nique pour des articles de musique «appétissants». (CAN)

583

583 An illustrated collage of famous sights of London (in mainly brown and green tones) for the lid of a box containing the game "Scotland Yard". (USA)
584 Packaging in three sizes for shoes marketed under the *Hot* label. (BRA)
585 Packaging design for computer software for an accounting system. (USA)
586 Bottle styling and packaging for a unit of six bottles of *Trader* beer. (SAF)
587 Examples from a series of gift packs for glass and stoneware bowls for *BodaNova*. (SWE)

583 Illustration aux tons bruns et verts prédominants pour le dessus d'une boîte contenant un jeu de «Scotland Yard». (USA)
584 Emballages carton pour trois pointures de chaussures *Hot* (=chaud). (BRA)
585 Etude d'emballage pour un logiciel de comptabilité. (USA)
586 Etude de bouteille et six-pack pour la bière *Trader*. (SAF)
587 Echantillons de cartons-cadeaux pour les plats de verre et de grès de la marque *BodaNova*. (SWE)

583 Illustration, vorwiegend in Braun- und Grüntönen, für den Deckel einer Schachtel, die ein Spiel mit der Bezeichnung «Scotland Yard» enthält. (USA)
584 Kartonverpackung in drei Grössen für Schuhe der Marke *Hot* (heiss). (BRA)
585 Packungsgestaltung für Computer-Software, die für die Buchhaltung bestimmt ist. (USA)
586 Flaschenausstattung und Verpackung einer Einheit von sechs Flaschen *Trader*-Bier. (SAF)
587 Beispiele aus einer Serie Geschenkkartons für Glas- und Steinzeugschalen von *BodaNova*. (SWE)

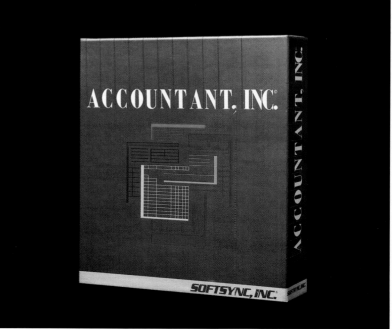

584   585

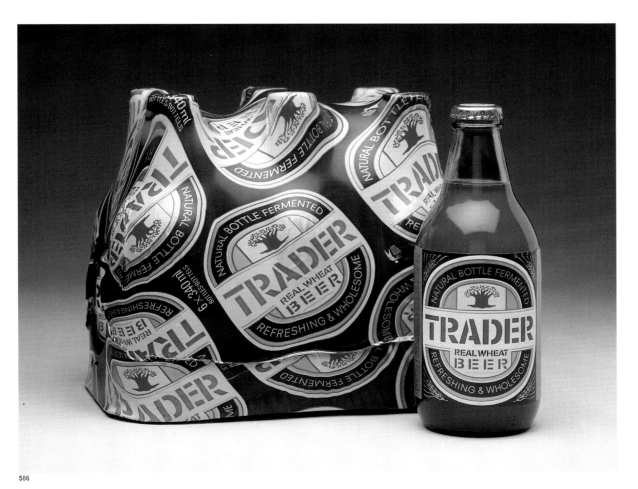

586

Packaging
Packungen
Emballages

ARTIST / KÜNSTLER / ARTISTE:

583 Józef Sumichrast
587 Dan Jonsson

DESIGNER / GESTALTER / MAQUETTISTE:

584 Rogério Martins/Sérgio Liuzzi
585 Mariko Iida
586 Robbie de Villiers
587 Dan Jonsson

ART DIRECTOR / DIRECTEUR ARTISTIQUE:

583 James Bremer
584 Rogério Martins/Sérgio Liuzzi
585 Mariko Iida/Kazuhide Yamazaki
586 Robbie de Villiers
587 Lars Börje Carlsson

AGENCY / AGENTUR / AGENCE – STUDIO:

583 Milton Bradley
584 Cantão Projeto Gráfico
585 Mariko Iida Design
586 Janice Ashby Design Studios
587 Carlsson & Broman

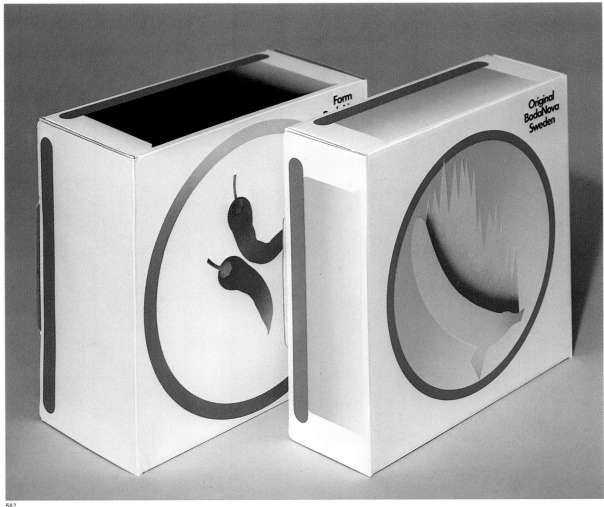

587

588

589

ARTIST / KÜNSTLER / ARTISTE:

589 Nicholas Bouyoukas
591 Christoph Radl/Nathalie DuPasquier
592 Jack Anderson/John Fortune

DESIGNER / GESTALTER / MAQUETTISTE:

588 Howard Milton
589 Nicholas Bouyoukas
590, 593 Liza Feraldis
591 Ettore Sottsass/Christoph Radl/
      Nathalie DuPasquier
592 Jack Anderson/Cheri Huber

ART DIRECTOR / DIRECTEUR ARTISTIQUE:

588 Howard Milton
589 Patty Lowry/Betty Chow
590, 593 Agni Katzourakis
591 John C Jay
592 Jack Anderson

AGENCY / AGENTUR / AGENCE – STUDIO:

588 Smith & Milton
589 Conran's Design Group
590, 593 A & M Katzourakis
591 Sottsass Associati
592 Hornall Anderson Design Works

588 Bottle styling for *Hobec* beer, shown with and without the lid. (GBR)
589 "Good design at good prices" is the promotional theme of *Conran's* for which this carrier bag is designed. The back, front and end views are shown. (USA)
590, 593 Linen bag, printing in red and black, and plastic carrier bag in white and red on black ground, for the shop of the Museum of Cycladic and Ancient Greek Art. (GRE)
591 Carrier bag for *Bloomingdale's* to publicize a "This is Italy" promotion in the store. (USA)
592 Shoe-box, shown here in a stacking group, with one opened, for *Diadora* tennis shoes. (USA)

588 Etude de bouteille, avec et sans système de fermeture, pour la bière *Hobec*. (GBR)
589 Cabas étudié pour la maison d'ameublement *Conran's*, présenté sur toutes ses faces. La devise: «un design intéressant à des prix intéressants». (USA)
590, 593 Cabas des grands magasins *Bloomingdale's* servant à la promotion d'articles italiens. (USA)
591 Cabas des grands magasins *Bloomingdale's* servant à la promotion d'articles italiens. (USA)
592 Cartons à chaussures pour les tennis *Diadora*, montrés empilés et ouvert. (USA)

588 Flaschengestaltung für Bier der Marke *Hobec*, hier Flaschen mit und ohne Verschluss. (GBR)
589 Für das Möbel- und Einrichtungshaus *Conran's* gestaltete Tragtasche (hier von allen Seiten gezeigt) unter dem Motto «Gutes Design zu guten Preisen». (USA)
590, 593 Leinentasche, schwarz- und rotbedruckt, und Plastiktragtasche, weiss und rot auf schwarzem Grund, für den Laden des Museums für kykladische und alte griechische Kunst. (GRE)
591 Tragtasche für das Kaufhaus *Bloomingdale's* als Werbung für italienische Waren. (USA)
592 Karton, hier als Stapeleinheit und geöffnet gezeigt, für *Diadora*-Tennisschuhe. (USA)

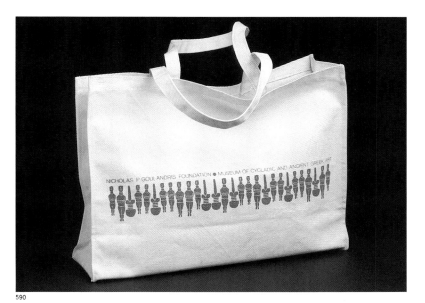

590

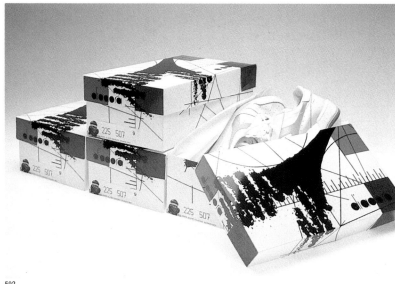

592

591

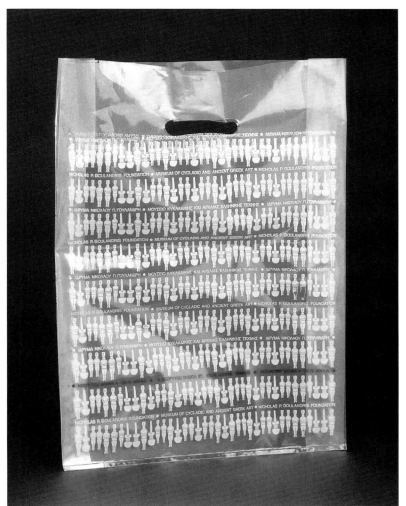

593

ARTIST / KÜNSTLER / ARTISTE:

594, 595 Kinuko Craft
597 Jean Michel Folon

DESIGNER / GESTALTER / MAQUETTISTE:

594, 595 Peter Harrison/Susan Hochbaum
596 Oscar Ribes
597 Alice Hecht

ART DIRECTOR / DIRECTEUR ARTISTIQUE:

594, 595 Peter Harrison
596 Oscar Ribes
597 Larry Long

AGENCY / AGENTUR / AGENCE – STUDIO:

594, 595 Pentagram
596 Création Ribes
597 Weymouth Design

594, 595 Examples of the packaging design for hair products by *Clairol*. (USA)
596 Package styling for a sample mailed to doctors by way of introducing this new medicament. Shown is a closed and opened pyramid element containing four tablets, and the carton which houses four of these elements. (SWI)
597 Polystyrene protective packaging, cartons and glassware for various products marketed by *Corning Medical & Scientific*. (USA)

594, 595 Beispiele der Verpackungsgestaltung für Haarpflegeprodukte von *Clairol*. (USA)
596 Packungsgestaltung für eine Ärzte-Mustersendung anlässlich der Einführung eines neuen Medikamentes. Hier ein geschlossenes und ein geöffnetes Kartonelement mit vier Tabletten und die Schachtel, die vier dieser Elemente aufnimmt. (SWI)
597 Polystyren-Schutzpackung, Faltschachteln und Töpfe für verschiedene Produkte des Pharma-Herstellers *Corning Medical & Scientific*. (USA)

594, 595 Conditionnements créés pour les produits *Clairol* pour les soins des cheveux. (USA)
596 Conditionnement d'échantillon médical pour le lancement d'un nouveau médicament. Elément carton accueillant quatre comprimés. Quatre de ces éléments trouvent place dans la boîte servant à l'expédition. (SWI)
597 Emballages de protection en polystyrène, cartons pliants et bocaux pour divers produits du groupe pharmaceutique *Corning Medical & Scientific*. (USA)

594

595

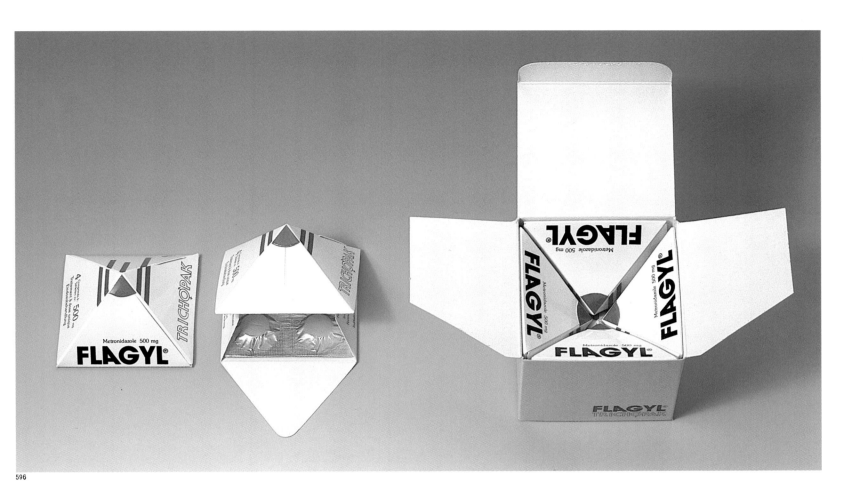

596

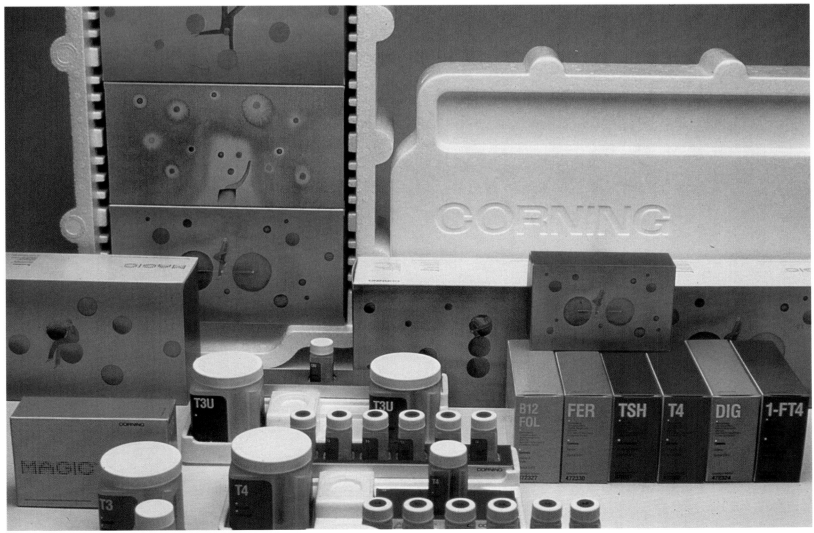

597

598

599

600

601

602

Paper/Papier: Papierfabrik Biberist-Biber GS SK3, blade coated, pure white, 130 gm² and
Biber Offset SK3, pure white, machine-finished, 140 gm² /
Biber-GS SK3, hochweiss, satiniert, 130 gm² und
Biber-Offset SK3, hochweiss, maschinenglatt, 140 gm²

Printed by/ gedruckt von: BDV Basler Druck- und Verlagsanstalt AG,
Zweigstelle BDV Printmedien, Liestal
(colour pages/ Farbseiten + dust jacket/ Schutzumschlag)
Merkur Druck AG, Langenthal (black and white/ schwarzweiss)

Typesetting/ Lichtsatz: Sauerländer AG, Aarau
(Univers, MONOTYPE-Lasercomp)

Binding/ Einband: Buchbinderei Schumacher AG, Bern/ Schmitten

Glossy lamination/ Glanzfoliierung: Durolit AG, Pfäffikon SZ